BULLER: A SCAPEGOAT?

BULLER:
A SCAPEGOAT?

A Life of
General Sir Redvers Buller 1839–1908

by

Geoffrey Powell

LEO COOPER
LONDON

First published in Great Britain in 1994 by
LEO COOPER
190 Shaftesbury Avenue London WC2H 8JL

an imprint of
Pen & Sword Books Ltd
47 Church Street, Barnsley, South Yorkshire S70 2AS

A CIP catalogue record for this book is available
from the British Library

ISBN 0 85052 279 X

Typeset by CentraCet Limited, Cambridge
Printed by Redwood Books
Trowbridge, Wilts.

CONTENTS

MAPS

INTRODUCTION

Thomas Pakenham's monumental *The Great Boer War* did much to stimulate
me to write this book. After reading what will surely remain the definitive
history of that unfortunate conflict, it became clear that Redvers Buller was
a person even more intriguing than I had previously supposed. Maligned for
near on a century as the epitome of Victorian military ineptness, Pakenham
revealed that behind a caricatured façade lay an able and thoughtful soldier,
one who had, as a French observer of the War judged, been given its
toughest job; moreover, he evolved the tactics needed to overcome Boer
defences based upon fortified entrenchments and the recently introduced
quick-firing weapons using smokeless missiles[1]. Remembered as a battlefield
soldier, he was to be held in respect and affection by the Royal Army Service
Corps and its successor, the Royal Corps of Transport, as an able and
imaginative administrator who, in founding their Corps, first placed the
supply and transport services of the Army upon a sound footing. As Sir John
Fortescue, the British Army's first comprehensive historian, recorded
between the two World Wars:

> I have weighed my words carefully before I say that Redvers Buller,
> who made the Army Service Corps, wrought not less towards the
> winning of the late War than Herbert, Lord Kitchener, himself.[2]

Soon after reading Thomas Pakenham's fine book, I came upon Professor
Robin Higham's *A Guide to the Sources of British Military History* in which it
was claimed of Buller that 'this enigmatic man needs further assessment'.[3]
As I found out more about him, I decided that Buller was not so much
enigmatic as a mass of contradictions, an individual who revealed widely
varied facets of his characters to colleagues and to subordinates, to his
soldiers and to his enemies, to artistic friends and to fellow squires, to
cabinet ministers and to reporters.

Four previous biographers had tilled the ground before me. Writing soon after Buller's death, Major Lewis Butler, who knew him slightly and was a member and historian of his Regiment, in a brief book tells us much about his subject's early service. This was followed by Walter Jerrold's popular *Sir Redvers Buller, VC*, published just before the First World War. At the time of his death, however, his widow had asked Fortescue, who knew him well, to write his official biography; this he declined, pointing out that it was 'still too early to tell the whole truth' about one he described as 'the greatest man I ever met'[4]. Nevertheless, he promised to do so later. But the War intervened and by the time it was over, Fortescue's ailing health and work on another lengthy project obliged him to abandon the idea.[5]

In Fortescue's place, Buller's daughter asked Colonel C. H. Melville to undertake the task and his two volumes appeared in 1923. With many of Buller's contemporaries still alive, it was still too early to tell 'the whole truth'; furthermore and in accordance with the wishes of his subject's wife and daughter, Melville was determined that the book would not contain any controversial matter which might lead to correspondence in the press.[6] But to leave such gaps so worried him that he wrote explanatory notes to each volume in which he expanded upon some of these controversial subjects. These notes lay hidden in his family's possession until recently and have helped me to elucidate several points upon which, as Melville wrote:

. . . 'though I was morally certain, actual proof was, and is, impossible to obtain. These I have drawn attention to in these notes, as well as certain opinions of my own, which would certainly have led to unnecessary controversy'.[7]

The fourth book I referred to is *Buller's Campaign* by the distinguished historian Julian Symons and published three decades ago. It deals only with Buller's relief of Ladysmith and is discussed later. In addition, Sir Edmund Gosse, poet and man of letters, contributed an essay in 1900 for *The North American Review*, possibly over eulogistic but informative about an eminent member of the artistic community's attitude towards Buller.

The amount of archival source material available to me was to prove daunting. Some of it had already appeared in printed form, especially in the *Letters of Queen Victoria* and in various biographical works about Lord Wolseley, Lord Roberts, General Sir Ian Hamilton, Lord Milner, Mr Campbell-Bannerman and others. Whenever possible I have checked the published material against the original papers, but unless the differences have been important I have usually used the published extract. However, access to the papers of the 5th Marquess of Lansdowne proved difficult to obtain; consequently quotations are in all cases from secondary sources.

Despite the large quantities of Buller's own papers either in the family's possession, at the Devon Record Office or in the Public Record Office, many of the letters quoted by Melville, especially those written to his wife, have sadly proved elusive. It seems certain that they have either been destroyed or lost.

I must pay a special tribute to Mrs Rosemary Parker, Redver Buller's great-niece and the present owner of the family papers and of Downes, the Buller family home, for the encouragement and help she has given me over a period of almost four years, not least for lending for a considerable period large quantities of valuable documents, including the notebooks of both Buller's daughter and sister, Henrietta. Mrs Parker and her husband, Major Peter Parker, were also kind enough to entertain me at Downes. Needless to say she imposed no restrictions on what I have written; I asked her to read in draft only that part which covers family matters.

Thomas Pakenham's *The Boer War* gave me what I hope was a proper understanding of its background and progress. The author also provided much encouragement and devoted a great deal of his valuable time to discussing my project and answering my questions.

I acknowledge the gracious permission of Her Majesty the Queen for allowing me to use material from the Royal Archives, and I warmly thank Lady de Bellaigue, the Registrar, for her help and advice when I was working at Windsor.

My thanks are also due again to Mrs Parker, and to the Bodleian Library, the Devon Record Office, the Gloucestershire Record Office, the Trustees of the Liddell Hart Centre for Military Archives, the National Army Museum, the Public Record Office and the Royal Corps of Transport Museum for allowing me to quote from manuscript material in their possession. I must also acknowledge the usual unstinting help I received from their librarians and archivists, and also from those of Queen's University, Kingston, Ontario, the Department of National Education of South Africa, the London Library, the Royal Albert Memorial Museum and Art Gallery, Exeter, the Royal Commission on Historical Manuscripts, the Royal Greenjacket Museum, the Royal Military Academy Sandhurst, the Royal United Services Institute for Defence Studies, the Sherwood Foresters Museum, the Staff College Camberley, and, last but in no way least, the librarian of my small local branch of the Gloucestershire Library, Mrs Pat Thompson.

Others who helped and sometimes advised me in a number of different ways were Margaret Lady Heathcote-Amory, Miss Buller of Downes, Mrs Heather Fawcett, Major-General Peter Foster, Lieutenant-Colonel W. A. Lyons (who was also kind enough to present me with a copy of Walter Jerrold's book), Mrs Rosemary Luckraft, Mr Alan G. Melville, my son Colonel John Powell, Mr Brian Robson, Lieutenant-Colonel I. H. McCausland, Dr Edward M. Spiers, Mr John Terraine, Mr James R.

Thomas, Mr A. R. Trotter, Mr H. Vigors and Lieutenant-Colonel Mike Young. As ever, my publisher, Leo Cooper, provided a broad shoulder upon which to lean and, once again, it was a pleasure to have Tom Hartman as my editor. Neil Hyslop most ably drew the maps.

Mike Young was good enough to read and comment upon that part of the book dealing with supplies and transport, as did Mr Brian Robson for the Suakin campaign. Peter Foster generously read and provided sage advice upon the entire typescript. As with all my books, my wife Felicity went through every word at least twice before providing me with her usual kind, stimulating but trenchant advice. For errors that remain, only I am responsible.

The author and publishers are most grateful to those who have kindly lent illustrations used in this book. Their names appear after the appropriate captions.

1

AN AWKWARD YOUNGSTER

In the waiting room of St David's Station, Exeter, the wife of Mr James Wentworth Buller of Downes in Devon lay dying. It was 12 December, 1855. On her way back to Crediton after a Christmas shopping expedition, she had been struck by a lung haemorrhage on the station platform. Alongside her were her two elder sons who had met her at the station, James returning from Oxford for the vacation and Redvers, the younger, from Eton. Both had witnessed the shattering event.[1]

Too ill to be moved, a bed was hastily improvised for Mrs Charlotte Buller in the waiting room, and there she lingered for three days before she died, fanned painstakingly and continuously for hours on end by the sixteen-year-old Redvers.

This young Redvers was a complicated character, a mass of contradictions. Large and burly, he was shy with it like most of his family, but his shyness was not always apparent. Born on 7 December, 1839, his schooling had begun at the age of seven in a not untypical Victorian preparatory school. Already the boy was prone to argue about anything, a habit he never lost. Reprimanded for ringing door bells and running away, a master enquired of him, 'Is this an institution for gentlemen or not?' 'That depends,' began young Buller, a reply that brought him an immediate thrashing, remembered as being unmerciful even by the standards of the day. His headmaster was to recollect that, although extremely clever, he was reluctant to work; Buller afterwards claimed that he could learn anything by reading it over once, but he defied anybody to do so when a master was walking around the room flicking his victims with a driving-whip. He never forgot or forgave the treatment he received there.

From this private school Redvers moved on to Harrow, as did most of his family, but left after a short stay for some unrecorded reason. Eton, however, was prepared to have him, and there he was remembered as a sturdy individual, in no way especially distinguished either at games or work – perhaps because his health in boyhood was always poor. Nevertheless Eton left him with an enduring love for the classics. He fagged for a boy who later became one of the College's most distinguished headmasters, the Rev. Edmond Warre, D.D., who described him as having a will of of own, not always identical with that of his seniors.

Country-bred, Redvers picked up at home skills invaluable in later life. Eminently practical, during the holidays he garnered from the estate workers a sound grounding in carpentry, smithy work, forestry and animal husbandry, crafts that later often surprised his soldiers. He also became an apt and bold horseman. His manual dexterity had become clear from an early age: a delightful little pencil sketch at Downes shows a short train of little trucks carrying three of his siblings, the whole built largely from packing cases by the nine-year-old Redvers. A small pony pulls it all, and he drives the contraption.

The Bullers were a large and self-contained family of seven boys and four girls. Their mother was an unusual woman for her time. Shy like the man she married, and gentle with it, she was the daughter of Lord Henry Howard and niece of the 12th Duke of Norfolk. Her married life was centred almost completely around her family, perhaps by inclination, perhaps because the disease that in the end killed her left her little strength or desire for the social round.

The outcome was that she spent far more time with her children than was the custom for one of her position; what remained was devoted to a continual round of genuine good works among the families of the estate workers and the poor in nearby Crediton. She kept a paid agent to help administer her charity, established and maintained one school completely at her own expense and helped support others. The *Western Times*, in lamenting her death in words that sound sincere, described her also as 'a fair specimen [the adjective is clearly used in its appreciative sense] of what the aristocracy should be – would that we could add of what the aristocracy really are'.[2]

She was a cultivated, well-read woman, a delightful companion, amusing and affectionate, and a fine mimic. Her daughter, Henrietta, recollected how she would teach her brood nursery rhymes, accompanying them on the piano, and how she found ways to make the Bible interesting. As they grew up, she taught them all tolerance of others, very necessary in her family: she, like her husband, was an Evangelist and deeply religious, but there were, of course, many Roman Catholics among her Howard cousins. The faith of her husband and herself was a simple one, devoid of the religiosity common at the time, one which the young Redvers was to retain all his life but which he rarely discussed. To dogma he attached little importance.

His mother's death left Redvers with a void which showed in an increased tenderness towards his younger brothers and sisters. As if to ease his own loneliness, immediately after her death he took charge of the youngest, the two-year-old Audley, bathing and dressing him in the neat-handed way he managed all manual tasks – and this in a Victorian nursery run by a bevy of nursemaids and under-nursemaids.

Four weeks after her mother died, Redvers's eldest sister Julia, writing to her aunt the day after her twenty-third birthday, remarked that 'Redvers returned to Eton last Thursday. I miss him so much, for he is in some ways more thoughtful and companionable to me than any of them'. Then, in May, tragedy struck once more. Julia, to whom Redvers was much attached, herself died. The Bullers were a sickly family, fevers and tuberculosis their scourge, probably because of the shocking state of both the Downes drainage and its water supply. Four years earlier the second sister, Adela, a cripple since birth, had also died. Henrietta (or Hen), Redvers's life-long confidante, was always ailing. Another brother did not pass his teens and James, the eldest, Redvers's closest friend, who had always suffered from ill-health did not reach forty.

Redvers's relationship with his father was rather less happy. James Wentworth Buller outlived his wife by ten years. He was a man of great quality, in all ways a thoroughly worthy individual. Born just before the turn of the century, he had inherited the Downes estate from his father in 1827. Mr Buller was a distinguished scholar, a model landlord, generous in his charities, liberal in his outlook, and, like his wife, understanding towards other religious faiths. No sportsman, he also was devoted to literature and the arts. A local obituary commented that 'he regarded the labour of a poor man as his only fortune, and for which he ought to be fairly remunerated'. This very outspoken journalist remarked also upon Mr Buller's fair dealing with the tradesmen, contrasting this with how so many members of the aristocracy 'put on the screw' and deprived shopkeepers of their fair profit.[3] Typical of his fellows, Mr Buller was a magistrate, commanded his local Yeomanry Regiment, and was chairman of every possible local body from the Turnpike Trust to the Crediton Union.

Between them, Mr Buller's father and grandfather, members of a staunchly Whig family, had represented Exeter in Parliament for near on four decades. In due course James Wentworth took over the family seat but lost it in 1835 because of the unpopularity of his views on the Corn Laws with the local Devon farmers. Twenty-two years later he was persuaded to stand again for the Northern Division of Devon. A reliable worker on the back benches and committees, he rarely spoke in the House, probably because of his shyness. He avoided office, and was said to have declined a peerage, as his father had done before him, declaring that 'Mr Buller of Downes was a finer title than any that could be conferred upon him.'[4] Ambition was no part of the family make-up.

Popular though he was locally, Mr Buller was a reserved and undemonstrative person. Although he enjoyed the company of his children, there was a lack of warmth in his make-up, something that the young Redvers sought, affectionate as he was by nature and desolate at the loss of his mother and Julia. His sister Hen was to write of Redvers 'thoroughly appreciating his father', a form of words clearly chosen with some care. Because his father 'had always a blank cheque as it were in early youth and very simple studious habits', it had been hard for him to comprehend 'the great needs of different habits of modern days'[5], a comment with a not unfamiliar ring. When his father asked him to spend Eton exeats at his London rooms, he failed to send him the journey money: the result was that his son ceased to accept his invitations. Too proud to ask for money, then or later, even when, as a subaltern, he was to be brought to near ruin by a servant bolting with £40 of mess funds he was holding.

In an otherwise generous man, such parsimony was in no way necessary. The Buller estates at Downes and in Cornwall amounted to 5,089 acres with an annual value of £14,137[6], solid wealth for the day and quite enough to support a peerage. Country gentlemen of ancient family, over the years the Bullers had intermarried with some of the greatest families of the land. Their origins lay in Somerset, but in the 16th century a younger son wed a Cornwall heiress and set up there a cadet branch of the family; after another two hundred years, a further satisfactory union brought the Bullers to Downes.

The Cornwall heiress was a Courtenay, the family of the Earls of Devon, who traced their descent to a John de Redvers, a companion of William the Conqueror. Seemingly because of its fine historical ring – it does not appear to have been used previously – James and Charlotte gave this name to their second son. The young Redvers Henry Buller was said to have thoroughly disliked his unusual first name, not surprisingly so. When young he was 'Buck' to the family, but he preferred Henry and had his luggage so marked when he first entered the army. When it was confused with that of a distant cousin, Henry Buller, he gave up the struggle and let things be.

Since Stuart days, it had been rare indeed for a member of the nobility or upper gentry to follow any calling other than the services, the bar or the church – the reason, some say, for the country's eventual industrial decline. Few Bullers of Downes entered the army, but this Redvers decided upon, the choice his[7]. With his brother James due to inherit everything, to such a youngster an outdoor and adventurous life was rather more attractive than either the pulpit or the court-room. What is more, the Crimean War had ended only two years before and the Great Indian Mutiny was in its final stages. The army was very much in the public eye.

The Bullers were, in fact, a little in advance of their time. Another brother, Ernest, became a gunner, but had his career cut short in India by a lion. Chewed twenty-seven times, by some miracle he survived, entered trade and founded a successful china works in Staffordshire. The young Audley also went his own way to become a doctor, an event welcomed by the press who wrote about him that, 'the more men of good breeding and agreeable manners who take to it [medicine] the better for the public.'[8]

From Eton Redvers moved to Flemings, the Tunbridge Wells crammer who prepared the often ill-taught schoolboys for the Sandhurst entrance examination. Flemings was, so Redvers said, 'a sink of iniquity'[9]; after the Eton of the 1850s, it must have indeed been awful to merit the words. However, in the end he entered the Army not through Sandhurst, but by purchase. The former would have cost his parents no more than £100 for his keep there; the expense of purchase is set out in a letter from the Horse Guards dated 10 May, 1858:

I am directed by His Royal Highness the General Commanding in Chief to acquaint you, that, on your lodging the Sum of £450 in the hands of Messrs. McGrigor, His Royal Highness will submit your Name to Her Majesty for the purchase of an Ensigncy in the 60th Foot.[10]

Thirteen days later he received his commission, and on 14 July, at the early age of eighteen, he joined for duty at the Rifle Depot, Winchester.

Why his commission was bought is not known. Perhaps he failed the Sandhurst entrance examination. Perhaps he changed his mind. There was certainly much to be said, then and later, for avoiding the discomforts of Sandhurst's rudimentary military training; to join a regiment direct and pick up the elements of soldiering on the job was a rather more attractive option, not least in the time saved.

Redvers almost failed to become a soldier. Just before being commissioned, he badly cut his leg working in the Downes woods. So severe was the injury that the local doctor insisted that the limb should be amputated so as to save his life. However, the boy objected – sufficiently forcefully to save it, saying that he would rather die with two legs than live with one. Although the injury was to hamper his running and so debar him from games, it in no way curtailed his ability at field sports[11].

The 60th Rifles, later the 2nd Battalion the Royal Green Jackets (The King's Royal Rifle Corps) were high in the pecking order which even today marks the British Army. Raised in 1755 as the Royal American Regiment of Foot for service against the French in Canada, over the years they underwent a variety of changes of name, but were usually known by their number, the '60th', a regiment of four battalions of green-clad riflemen, when Buller joined, as opposed to the single battalion of most of the scarlet-coated line regiments.

Buller was remembered in his regiment for displaying marked independence of mind; respected rather than popular among his fellows, he was reluctant to ingratiate himself with either subalterns or seniors. He would argue about anything anywhere, logically but often in an irritatingly contradictory way. It was a habit that gave rise to his early nickname of 'Judge', bestowed because of his repeated use of the dictum of an ancestor, Judge Buller, that 'The greater the truth the greater the libel'.[12]

His stay at Winchester was short. In January, 1859, he sailed to join the 2nd Battalion in India. The Suez Canal was not to open for another ten years, but the long passage around the Cape of Good Hope was avoided by disembarking passengers at Alexandria, taking them overland to Suez, and then shipping them on to Calcutta. There a 500-mile journey by bullock-train, in charge of a convoy of women and children, took him to Benares, his unit station. It was a salutary experience for a sheltered nineteen-year-old.[13]

Flying columns were still engaged in extirpating the last surviving pockets of mutineers. Whether Buller had his first experience of active service in such work is not known. All that is recorded about him during this, his only time in India, are memories of the massive self-control he would exercise over his temper – which could be dangerous when roused – and his determination, exemplified in his taming of an especially vicious horse, one that had already killed two of its Indian syces. Then, after just a year, his battalion took ship for Hong Kong, acquired only eighteen years before.

The British occupation of Hong Kong was one of the by-products of Western pressure to expand trade with China. Wary of overtures to open normal diplomatic relations and contemptuous of all things stemming from the barbarian Europeans, the Manchu Emperors either ignored or rejected every approach. But the rapid growth of the opium trade provoked them into armed conflict. As gin had corrupted the British during the 18th century, so did opium the Chinese, and for long they had been endeavouring to prohibit its illicit import from India. The first of the so-called Opium Wars ended in 1842 with the ceding of Hong Kong, the opening up of five other Chinese ports to foreign trade and agreement to accept British and French representatives at the Imperial Court. Further hostilities in 1856 culminated three years later in the repulse, at a cost of four ships and 430 men, of a British naval force carrying envoys to Peking.

This clash took place at the heavily defended Taku forts which covered the mouth of the Pei-ho River, 160 miles below the Chinese capital, and to exact retribution there now assembled an Anglo-French expeditionary force of which the 60th Rifles formed part. The allies landed near the forts on 1 August, 1860, and, after a series of preliminary clashes, assaulted and captured them three weeks later. Although the Tartar horsemen, the more formidable part of the Manchu forces, fought gallantly and quite ably, the

6

way to Peking was now open, and on 13 October the city was entered after further fighting. As a punishment for the mistreatment and murder of British and French envoys engaged in trying to negotiate terms, Lord Elgin, the British plenipotentiary, gave orders for the burning of the Summer Palace of the Emperors, 200 glorious buildings set in eighty acres of superb parkland. The French soldiers, ably assisted by their British allies, had already looted and vandalised its priceless contents.

It had been an effective but rather inglorious little war, one in which the young Buller had seen some fighting; although he was unwounded, a horse managed to kick his front teeth in, an accident that left him with a slight but permanent speech impediment. Other details of his activities are sparse, except that much of his time was spent quarrelling with his company commander, an officer remembered for having been one of the biggest fools in the regiment, if not the army, a failing that even then Buller did not suffer gladly. The men of his company were, however, said to have been devoted to the youngster.[14]

Buller was among the many people left with serious doubts about the justice of the war, so much so that for many years he refused to wear the China Medal, a stand that must have aggravated both his seniors and his peers. The destruction of the Summer Palace aroused widespread criticism, both at home and abroad, and, for a decent young man, many aspects of the campaign were nauseating. The Chinese members of the Coolie Corps, recruited at Hong Kong for transport work, and the Indian sepoys, fresh from their punitive post-Mutiny counter-atrocities, between them set an example for rape and plunder. Flogging, forbidden in the French army, did something to help control the British troops, but officers looted as well as their soldiers.

Despite his strong feelings, Buller did acquire a small share of the spoil as presents for his sisters – splendid shawls, chess men and fine old enamel ornaments from the Empress's dressing table[15]. Perhaps they were loot; perhaps he bought them at the official auction of treasures.

An officer who contributed much towards the success of the campaign, one that had been marked by the excellence of its administrative arrangements, was the second senior staff officer to the force, the ambitious twenty-seven-year-old Brevet Lieutenant-Colonel Garnet Wolseley. In Burma, the Crimea and the Indian Mutiny, Wolseley had shown bravery, leadership, intense application and high intelligence, qualities which had brought him near uniquely rapid promotion, achieved without purchase. Lacking money and influence, he had based his career upon the precept that any young officer who wished to distinguish himself in his profession should seek to get himself killed. A missing eye and a permanent limp testified to its conscientous application.

It is not recorded whether Buller and Wolseley knew each other in China.

But they could well have done, as for some reason the young ensign was plucked from the obscurity of his regiment to accompany Lord Elgin on his ceremonial entry into the captured Peking[16].

In September, 1861, Buller's unit at last left China, sailing for England by way of the Cape of Good Hope, a four-month journey. Now a lieutenant, he was posted to the 4th Battalion in Canada. Still 'a raw and self-willed young man, with perhaps no great interest in his profession' as his regimental biographer wrote, 'in Canada he was to be transformed into a trained and professional soldier.'[17]

Fearless of authority, he was as argumentative as ever, taking the unpopular side out of devilment, contradicting his opponent so as to test the basis of an assertion, but happy to be contradicted himself. Tactlessly outspoken, a smile could take the sting out of a criticism. At the same time he was known for his great good nature. But that temper, seemingly equable and usually under complete control, could at times be savage: on one occasion he smashed a chair through a glass door of the ante-room to discourage an officer from another regiment whom he disliked from watching a game of billiards.

Girls were said to have idolized him despite – or perhaps because of – his bluntness of speech. His attraction was due to more than his stature, good looks and generous nature. He also had sensitivity, an appreciation of colour and style: it was said that he always knew what was right for a room and could render accurately the details of a lady's dress.

The change in Buller's attitude towards his profession came about through his outstanding commanding officer, Colonel R.B. Hawley, who brought back to the 60th the then neglected methods of that famous Peninsular War light infantryman, Sir John Moore. Hawley's training was based upon the development of individuality both in his riflemen and his officers. Self-reliance and initiative were encouraged; responsibility he delegated. Drill took its proper place as an instrument and not the be all and end all of training; his soldiers were properly fed and treated as human beings.

As always, leave was there for the asking; fish and game were still plentiful in the lakes and forests. In summer, but more often in winter, parties of three or so would go out after bear, elk and caribou with an Indian guide, backpacking or canoeing their kit and provisions and sleeping in shelters or snowholes. Buller's grounding in the arts of a backwoodsman, first schooled at Downes, was perfected in the forests of Western Canada. It was all excellent military training, something commonplace a century later, but singular in the 1860s.

His interests were wide, extending to the installation of a carpenter's bench in his room. In Canada he began also to study English literature, and 'the more he read it the more he liked it'. Style and harmony were his delight. It was the start of a lifelong addiction, sometimes an embarrassment: his sisters would hide a tempting book if he were visiting them for fear he would pick it up and become lost in it.[18]

For some six years Buller enjoyed what the army had to offer, but promotion was slow, depending as it did upon a combination of seniority and purchase. (The outstandingly able Hawley himself spent thirteen years commanding the 4th Battalion.) Boredom set in. His sole break from routine soldiering was a year in charge of the 'Look Outs', a duty involving a monthly 1,500-mile trip by rail, road and water around fifteen border posts manned by trustworthy men, their purpose to prevent soldiers deserting to seek their fortune in the United States. His relief in 1868 was a Lieutenant William Butler of the 69th Foot, of whom more later, who wrote of Buller, – possibly with a touch of hindsight – as being:

> the best type of regimental officer to be found. Young, active, daring, as keen for service as he was ready to take the fullest advantage of it, he stood even then in the front rank of those young and ardent spirits who might be described as the ruck of Army life which is waiting to get through.[19]

Nevertheless the Army seemed to have little for Buller, but when his seniors learned that he was contemplating sending in his papers, Hawley wrote to Mr Buller that he and others saw his son's departure as a great loss for the army, a career for which he was eminently fitted. Then came the break-through. The adjutant went on long leave and Hawley offered Buller the chance of acting in his place.

Buller's first reaction was to protest that he knew nothing about soldiering. His colonel countered by pointing out that he would teach him. And so he did. From Hawley he learned how to train and administer a regiment.

The two men, despite their disparity in age and rank, were already fast friends. An anecdote says something about their relationship. Canoeing together some time before, Hawley had pointed out that they were approaching dangerous rapids, but the over-confident subaltern refused to admit that there was any risk in continuing. However, when the current strengthened and the danger became undeniable, the younger man suggested pulling for the shore, only for his colonel to refuse on the grounds that he had come so far for Buller's pleasure, and Buller could now continue for his. The rapids were safely shot, but the incident was remembered. Buller's outspoken manner did not desert him when he became adjutant, even when dealing with Hawley. On one occasion, when differing about the promotion of a sergeant, Buller told his colonel that he could, of course, do as he liked but his action would destroy the sergeant's company. It was a couple of weeks before Hawley indicated that he had been forgiven.

So it was that when the 4th Battalion returned home in the summer of 1869, Hawley had inculcated in Buller a proper interest in soldiering. Probably also he had smoothed off just a few of his adjutant's rough edges.

2

THE RING

In the summer of 1869 Buller at last returned to England, his battalion's overseas tour having ended. In the following year he was senior enough to buy his captaincy, but, because no vacancy existed in his own unit, he was posted to his Regiment's 1st Battalion, then assembling in Thunder Bay on Lake Superior for what was to be known as the Red River Expedition. Convinced that there would be no fighting, Buller was reluctant to return straight away to Canada, having now spent no less than eleven of his twelve years service abroad.

For several years each separate Canadian province had been steadily gaining control over its own affairs, a process that culminated in 1867 with their federation into the Dominion of Canada, the British Empire's first self-governing nation. In 1869 this new Government bought out the rights of the Hudson Bay Company to administer its vast North-Western Territories, but did so without consulting the local people. Although the fertile prairies around the Red River had been first colonised by Scottish Highlanders, some half of the population was now made up of métis – individuals of mixed Indian and French blood – who accurately foresaw their sparsely settled country being thrown open to English-speaking outsiders.

Justifiably indignant at the lack of consultation, and encouraged by their Roman Catholic priests and the Quebec press, these métis formed a so-called 'Provisional Government'. Acting under its instructions, in November, 1869, a handful of armed men ignominiously expelled the Lieutenant-Governor designate despatched from Ottawa to take control of these new lands. Louis Riel, secretary to this 'Government' then seized Fort Garry, the Hudson Bay Company's headquarters on the Red River, half a mile from what was then the small village of Winnipeg. With some 500 armed men, the now 'President' Riel replaced the Union Jack flying over Fort Garry with a new flag, ominously a combination of the fleur-de-lys and the shamrock. The stocks of weapons, ammunition and stores in the Fort were seized, the annexation of the territory to the United States was mooted and several opponents imprisoned; one, a Mr Thomas Scott, was brutally and capriciously executed.

There was an immediate outcry in the English-speaking provinces of Canada to avenge Scott and restore the Queen's authority. For the use of Imperial troops, the sanction of the Home Government was speedily granted. The commander for the proposed expedition almost chose himself. The senior staff officer in Canada was the now Colonel Garnet Wolseley, whose arrival in Canada had coincided with Buller's first posting there.

Wolseley's time in Canada had been well spent. On a two-month leave he had paid unofficial and adventurous visits to both sides fighting the American Civil War. When it ended he had taken a major part in the expulsion of the Fenian-led invasion of Ontario by Irish unemployed ex-soldiers. In charge of the first cadet-training college for the volunteer Canadian militia, he had trained them for war rather than the parade ground. And, in the meantime, he had written for the War Office what was to be his famous *Soldier's Pocket Book for Field Service*, a much-needed practical handbook, marred only by over-dogmatic statements which gave needless offence.

Even before he was appointed to the Red River expedition, Wolseley had completed the detailed planning.[1] The problem was to get the troops there. Fort Garry lay only sixty miles from the United States border and the usual method of reaching the area was through North Dakota. But there was no question of an armed body of troops being permitted to travel that way. The sole alternative was by water through a wilderness of lakes and rivers. From Toronto the expedition would travel first by rail, then by steamer across Lakes Huron and Superior, then for a short way by road, and finally for 550 miles to Fort Garry by boat across waterways that had previously never seen anything larger than a birch-bark canoe, a total of 1,200 miles in all.

The fighting men of Wolseley's force were to be two-thirds Canadian militia, and one-third British regulars – the 1st Battalion of the 60th – supported by a few Gunners (armed with four 7-pounder brass mountain guns), Sappers, Army Service Corps and Hospital Corps. One militia battalion was raised in Toronto, one with difficulty in Quebec, both organized (as was the 60th) in seven companies each of three officers and fifty carefully picked soldiers. To carry the 1,200 men, two hundred boats were specially built. Twenty-five to thirty feet long and some six feet wide, each was capable of carrying fourteen men together with their tools, tents, blankets and sixty days' provisions, a total of four tons in all. To man them 400 so-called 'voyageurs' were collected, most of whom, except for 100 Iroquois Indians, proved to be utterly useless. Such were the administrative complications that the expedition was allocated no less than eleven Commissariat officers.

The force was small, but Wolseley's problems vast. The newly recruited militia had to be equipped and trained almost from scratch; as well as building the boats, ships had to be chartered for the long journeys across the Great Lakes; wagons, carts, saddlery, fodder and draught animals had to be procured for the fifty-mile road journey; and sufficient provisions collected to last for the summer. At first the United States Government, worried as ever by the Irish vote, refused to allow the passage of troops and stores even through the canal between Lakes Huron and Superior, and equipment unloaded for the resultant portage had to be protected against a threatened Fenian raid. A further difficulty was the split control between the Imperial and Canadian Governments, especially with the acting Dominion Premier, Sir George Cartier, opposed in principle to the expedition's objectives, as were most of his fellow French Canadians who envisaged the foundation of a western French province as a counter-balance to the increasingly powerful Ontario.

Although preparations for the expedition did not start until mid-April, 1870, Wolseley and his staff with five companies of the 60th left Toronto on 21 May for Thunder Bay at the western end of Lake Superior. Landing there four days later, Wolseley found that thirteen of the fifty miles of road, promised for 25 May, through the hilly and thickly-wooded country to Shebandowan Lake had still to be built; much of the rest was in a poor state. Immediately the troops were set to work unloading stores, extending the road and constructing base camps, one fortified and mounting two of the brass guns to counter the threat of a Fenian attack against the expedition's rear.

Despite everything, on 28 May the first companies of the 60th were able to start moving forward. However, it quickly became obvious that the 150 draught horses and eighteen span of oxen were not enough to drag the boats and supplies over fifty miles of half-made road, especially when it was discovered that the hurriedly enlisted and undisciplined civilian teamsters, some of them bar-keepers, some clerks, some 'decayed gentlemen', 'knew no more about the care of horses than they did about kangaroos'.[2]

Connecting Lakes Superior and Shebandowan, however, was a series of rivers, declared unnavigable because of rapids and waterfalls that together rose vertically for a height of 800 feet. To relieve the road transport, Wolseley determined to try this alternative route, and on 4 June the first half-dozen boats crewed by the 60th started up the Kaministiquia River. There, nineteen days later, Buller caught up with his new company, having already sweated for eight days to push nine boats overland for the equivalent of twenty-one road miles. It was a foretaste of the future: at each waterfall the soldiers had to drag the heavy boats on rollers and hump the stores on stretchers or their backs; at rapids three or four men would help haul their boat uphill by ropes, sometimes waist-deep in the river, while the rest poled.

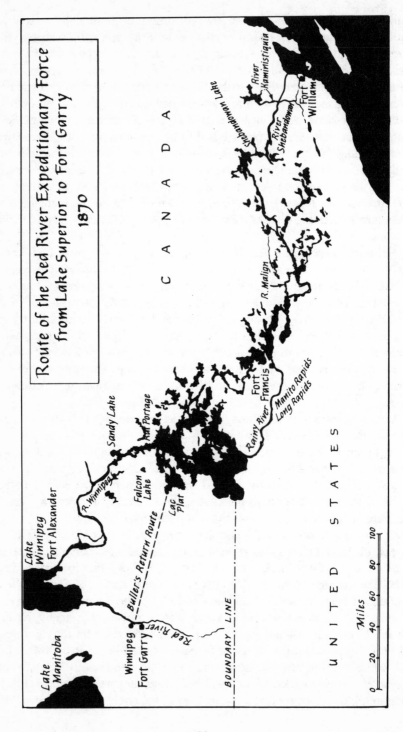

Route of the Red River Expeditionary Force
from Lake Superior to Fort Garry
1870

14

And all day they were plagued by the ubiquitous black-flies and all night by mosquitoes. For most of the time it rained. Food was simple and barely sufficient; officers ate and dressed like their men – unusual at the time. When the General Officer Commanding from Ottawa visited to judge progress, he was received by a bare-footed company commander of the 60th dressed in duck trousers rolled up to the knee, a woollen nightcap and an open-necked flannel shirt.

After seven weeks of this back-breaking toil Wolseley managed to accumulate 150 boats and two months' supplies at Lake Shebandowan. Having kept to schedule, despite the appalling difficulties, on 16 July the first two companies, each carried in six boats, began to row across the lake, followed the next day by Buller's. And so, to avoid jams at the portages, each day single companies in turn began their boat-journey proper. Buller, in a long letter to his sister Henrietta, written when he reached his destination, described the start:

> The next day our troubles began. No guide had been forthcoming; & Wolseley had said Oh! you have your map, keep the right hand shore all the way & you cannot miss the portage. Shebandowan is over 20 miles long, full of islands and all bays & inlets . . . We rowed till about 11 when I happened to notice that the water in front about 4 miles was then visible right ahead calm, while through an opening we were passing I could see rippled water. I at once judged that that must be the longest part, & turned sharp to the right; & by this lucky accident we were the only detachment (without a guide) that came direct to the portage and escaped rowing about five miles up a bay and back again.[3]

That first portage was to be one of the worst. Even after the hard physical toil of the past seven weeks, Buller's crew were still comparatively new to work that involved first dragging their boat and then carrying loads that included twenty-eight barrels of provisions over a distance of three-quarters of a mile; Buller himself humped five loads averaging about 100 pounds each. Wolseley wrote afterwards.

> All the officers with the expeditionary force soon became expert in making portages and in mending their boats, no one more so than my very able friend and valued comrade Redvers Buller. It was here I first made his acquaintance, and I am proud to feel that we have been firm friends ever since. He was a first-rate axeman, and I think he was the only man with us of any rank who could carry a hundred pound barrel of pork over a portage on his back. He could mend a boat and have her back in the water with her crew and all her stores on board whilst many,

under similar circumstances, would have been still making up their minds what to do. Full of resource, and personally absolutely fearless, those serving under him always trusted him fully.[4]

Wolseley did not know it all. In the final stages of the journey, coming down the Winnipeg River, a fully fit Buller averaged 180-pound loads over twenty-seven portages; in all, the journey involved no less than forty-seven, the longest 1,800 yards.

Another of Wolseley's future close colleagues was to make his first impact during the Red River expedition. William Butler, a year older than Buller, from whom he had taken over the border 'Look-outs' two years before, was the seventh child of an impecunious but well connected Catholic family from Tipperary. This future Lieutenant-General Sir William Butler, poet, prolific author and husband of Lady Butler, the famous artist of vigorous Victorian battle scenes, had already served around the world, made friends with Victor Hugo and spent a long leave exploring the prairies of Nebraska. Always amusing, highly intelligent, often aggravating, prone to philandering, his rich Irish brogue was said by Wolseley to have become more marked the older he got[5].

In a wealthy regiment such as the 60th Rifles it was unusual for an officer to lack the funds to buy his next step in promotion. Buller had jumped only two other subalterns when he bought his captaincy, but Butler had no way of raising the the £1,500 needed for his[6]: by 1870 five or six men junior to him had already overtaken him on his regimental list. His future seemed bleak indeed when he learned of Wolseley's expedition. Here was the chance of active service with its opportunities for distinction. Cabling the expedition's commander from Ireland, 'Please remember me'[7], he rushed back to Canada to meet Wolseley, then 'in the prime of manhood, somewhat under middle height; handsome, clear-cut features, a broad and lofty forehead over which brown chestnut hair had curled; exceeding sharp, penetrating blue eyes.'[8]

All official vacancies had been filled, but Wolseley secured for him the risky task of travelling through the United States to discover what he could about possible Fenian activities against the lines of communication and about the rebellion itself. In the course of an adventurous journey, Butler worked his way through Minnesota to reach the Red River. There at Fort Garry he even met a now alarmed Riel, uneasy about the consequences of his precipitate action.

That interview over, Butler continued his journey by canoe up the Winnipeg River and onwards to Fort Frances, a Hudson Bay Company post at the head of the Rainy River where he was met by Wolseley on 4 August, just as had been planned, with the words 'Where on earth have you dropped from?'[9] Butler brought with him several valuable Indian boatman who knew the Winnipeg, as well as the intelligence that the British and French settlers were equally afraid of one another but even more so of the Indians, and that Riel was very anxious for an amnesty. He carried also the first news of the outbreak of the Franco-Prussian War and the early French reverses.

Meanwhile the expedition had made steady progress. In a long letter to his sister Henrietta, Buller described how:

> . . . the work went on a portage long or short rough or smooth as the case might be, & then a hard row down a lake or river; never any rest . . . Down the River Maligne there were some heavy rapids to descend & here my special labours commenced; the voyageurs who had been sent with us to manage our boats, instead of being skilled boatmen were simply Canadian adventurers who wanted a free passage to Red River to see what it was like. I can fearlessly state that not one of them was as competent to manage a boat as I am myself.[10]

Although boats continually hit rocks and needed repair, the one steered by Buller himself escaped injury. His skills as a carpenter were now put to good use as he 'had to do all the tinkering' of his company's boats; this included mending gaping holes with tin and white lead.

Despite being constantly soaked and subject to unending toil, the soldiers stayed healthy and cheerful. Crime was utterly absent, the result so their officers decided of Wolseley's decision to deny them 'spiritous liquors'; black sugared tea was the sole drink, one that all ranks devoured with zest.

At Fort Frances, Buller's company had hoped for fresh provisions and a day's rest, but they obtained neither, although the Company manager was able to give Wolseley's small headquarters staff the run of its teeth among the green peas, cabbages and young potatoes in his garden. The troops who arrived later were rather more lucky: glorious fresh bread awaited them from a bakery set up by Wolseley. For Buller,

> After Fort Frances came two days down Rainy River 80 miles of sluggish water densely wooded with aspen and poplar and filled with starving Indians without end who bothered us day and night for pork and biscuits, of which as a liberal government allowed us one solitary pound apiece a day you can imagine they did not get much. Then came Lake of the Woods, a stormy inland sea . . . at the end of this there was Rat Portage another H.B. post where we found a most charming Mr Thompson who thought that nothing was too good for us, and more than that he really had something to give us in the shape of potatoes and onions and what I wanted and appreciated most, treacle. You may

laugh but you can have no idea how much it is liked in the bush; remember all we got for the day was 1lb of fat salt pork, a lb of hard biscuits or 1½lbs of flour 1 oz of tea 2 oz of sugar and ⅓ of a pint of beans things bye the bye which I hate. Now treacle is portable and goes well with flour pancakes or fried biscuits which under these circumstances were our only delicacies.[11]

Rat Portage brought them to the Winnipeg River (which flowed down into Lake Winnipeg), long dreaded for its 27 portages and 180 miles of rapids, waterfalls, whirlpools and angry rushing water about which they had been fully forewarned; through it all Buller was to be helped by one of Butler's Indians, 'a man of few words but a splendid fellow'[12].

By 19 August the worst of the unending drudgery was over but not the discomfort of the perpetual rain. The 60th Rifles had reached Lake Winnipeg and the portages were behind them. There they learned that Riel and his followers intended to resist, news that cheered everyone, anxious as they all were for the excitement of a fight after so much toil. Two days later, sails were hoisted in some fifty boats to make good use of a fair breeze to carry them across the corner of the lake to the mouth of the Red River. It was described as a magnificent and invigorating sight.

At last, on 24 August, again according to plan, the 60th disembarked at a point just over a mile from Fort Garry. Visible through the pouring rain as the troops drew near were its barred gates and cannons mounted in the stone bastions. But no flag flew and no shot was fired. Staff officers, mounted on some wretched ponies picked up nearby, were sent round only to find the south gate open. Riel and his last followers had fled some ten minutes before at the sight of the approaching troops. On the far side of the river, two figures were identified as being the 'President' and his Irish secretary.[13] There was to be no fighting after all.

Buller's sense of anti-climax matched that of his fellow officers and riflemen. After firing a twenty-one gun salute, the troops were marched into the Fort and the officers devoured the remains of Riel's breakfast. As he wrote to his sister, 'It does so disgust one to have come all this way for the band to play God save the Queen'[14]. The voyageurs and others got drunk on the local firewater and remained so until Wolseley started the 60th back on its long return journey on 29 August, after a short five-day respite, leaving the Militia in occupation.

After wandering around Winnipeg and talking to its citizens – both loyal and disloyal – a cynical Buller decided that they had come a long way to take part in an utter farce. Riel, he was told, had been incited to his rebellion by the Hudson Bay Company which wished to embarrass the new Canadian Government and delay the settlement; unfortunately the man had so overreached himself that the Company had been obliged to ask for help. Among his papers were found documents that suggested that the local bishop and Cartier himself had been implicated in it all[15]. Buller decided that 'to hang a few priests up here would probably have a good effect; but I imagine that the whole business is a political job of that scoundrel Cartier's and that everybody will be pardoned'[16]. His views undoubtedly reflected those of the rest of the weary and frustrated troops.

Buller had not appreciated how he had made his mark as a leader of men and an organizer. His qualities had impressed Wolseley, as had Butler's; others whom he had marked down were the brilliant Captain G. L. Huyshe, who had served as A.D.C. and was to write the history of the campaign, and a young cavalry officer and fine pianist, Lieutenant Hugh McCalmont, who, like Butler, had made his way at his own expense across the Atlantic and insinuated his way into the expedition at Lake Superior. With others, their names were to be added to the list of able officers kept by Wolseley in his notebook.

The first immediate mark of Wolseley's appreciation was to send Buller and his company, first with carts and then with pack-horses to open up a fresh 110-mile cross-country route direct from Fort Garry to the head of the Winnipeg River, so cutting out the laborious upstream portages; the reaction of the riflemen to this long trudge, partly across the soft, spongy muskeg has not been recorded. Wolseley also put forward the names of Buller and one other captain of the 60th Rifles for brevets to major, a step in the Army but not regimentally. Even though such appointments were used to mark merit and bring on the deserving, the War Office decided that, as there had been no fighting, the promotions should go to the two senior captains.[17]

After a short leave in England, Buller returned to Canada. His stay was, however, brief. In the meantime he had gained a place at the Staff College which he entered at the start of 1872. Never again was he to serve with his own, or any other British regiment. But the years he had spent with the 60th, culminating in the ardours of the Red River Expedition, had displayed to the full his human qualities – his magnetism, his sympathy towards those under him, his great strength and his ability to 'muck in' (to use an anachronism) that were to make his name a byword among the officers and riflemen of his regiment.[18]

Wolseley also returned to England. His reward for the success of the expedition, in which not a single soldier had died from any cause, was a KCMG and reversion to half-pay. His attitudes and his pen had not endeared him to officers of the old school, foremost among whom was the Commander-in-Chief, the Duke of Cambridge, cousin to the Queen.

That Buller should have even contemplated entering the Staff College was a measure of his fresh attitude towards his profession, so rarely did officers of his background do so. Wolseley certainly encouraged him, as was his habit with able young men; although he was never there himself, he was to make a practice of employing officers marked in the Army List by those letters '*psc*' – 'passed Staff College'. To do so was as yet unusual. Set up at Camberley in 1856 to remedy the deficiencies among both staff and commanders revealed by the Crimean War, the Staff College was not for decades to make a major impression on the Army. Funds were short, prejudice against change still intense, and the place lacked prestige, largely because staff appointments continued to be filled by nepotism rather than ability. Even in the next century some regiments were still reluctant to allow officers to compete for vacancies there.

But Prussia's defeat of France had, at the time of Buller's entry, given a fresh impetus towards Camberley's updating. The then commandant, Colonel Edward Hamley, was a thinking, literate and vigorous officer who was making some progress towards raising its status. Work became more practical and the emphasis on academic subjects – especially mathematics – was lessened. As a student, Buller was said to have been a 'wonderfully clever, clear-headed man, and endowed with a rare fund of anecdote'.[19] Certainly he worked hard[20].

Nevertheless, he did not complete the course. It happened thus. During the August of his second year he was spending some leave on the Continent, combining fishing with a tour of the Franco-Prussian War battlefields. As can happen, he had neglected to leave a contact address, but when on two successive nights he dreamt that Wolseley was standing at the foot of his bed saying 'Buller, where are you?', he packed and returned home.[21] There he found that his old commander was about to appoint someone else to supplant him on the staff being assembled for an expedition against the Ashantis on the West African coast.

Buller rightly saw that prospects were poor for a captain of fifteen years' service who had never distinguished himself in action. This then was his chance: appointment as Deputy Assistant Adjutant and Quartermaster-General on active service[22]. It did, however, involve, leaving Camberley before the end of the course, but the Duke of Cambridge decreed that he should be considered as having graduated. Alas for such promises. Buller was never to receive his *psc*, but it hardly mattered.

This war against the warlike Ashanti kingdom lying inland from the Gold Coast (the modern Ghana) marked the start of the late Victorian expansion of the British Empire and the involvement of other European powers in that 'Scramble for Africa'. The problem in West Africa, as elsewhere, was to maintain a strip of trading stations on the cheap against the threat of powerful and hostile forces up-country. 'Gold Coast' it may have been named, but until the end of the eighteenth century the primary cargoes shipped through the forty or so fortified factories, owned by a variety of European countries, were slaves for the New World; these the traders bought at the factory gates from other tribes which had kidnapped them in the unknown forests of the interior, a feature of Africa's economy that long predated the Western entrepreneur.

Eventually the European liberal conscience rebelled at the horrors, with Britain setting an example, first by abolishing the trade itself in 1807 and then, in 1834, by making the ownership of slaves illegal throughout its Empire. The consequence for the Gold Coast was that the turnover in other commodities barely justified the cost of maintaining the forts and protecting the coastal tribes – a responsibility that had accrued over the years – from the depredations of the Ashanti.

When in December, 1872, Ashanti armies invaded the coast, slaughtering and torturing local tribesmen and threatening even the small fort garrisons, prestige alone demanded that something be done, reluctant though William Gladstone, then heading his first Liberal administration, was to commit the country to adventures overseas. On the other hand, the British public – over-enthusiastic for war as ever – was well informed by both missionaries and the press about the unpleasant customs of the Ashanti, whose fetishes demanded a regular toll of sacrificial victims – thousands at a time on such occasions as a new king's installation at Kumasi, the capital. Paradoxically, the near destruction of the overseas market in slaves had so reduced their value as to render the butchery affordable.

Chosen to lead the expedition was the thirty-eight-year-old and now Sir Garnet Wolseley. He had not been unemployed for long. In May, 1871, the Secretary-of-State for War, Edward Cardwell, whose widespread reforms were to include the abolition of both purchase and flogging, together with the introduction of short-service and linked infantry battalions, had brought the iconoclastic young officer into the War Office as an assistant adjutant-general to help him complete his task. This close acquaintance resulted in Wolseley being put in charge of the expedition, for which he was gazetted as civilian administrator as well as military commander. As he had ensured before the Red River, his plans for the expedition were ready even before it was sanctioned.

On 2 October, 1873, the expedition arrived at Cape Castle on the Gold Coast after a foul journey in a stinking little ship. It consisted of no more than seven staff and twenty special service officers, a couple of doctors and seven Control Department civilians. Awaiting their arrival at the Coast were just a few Royal Marines and a battalion of the West India Regiment, most of them freed slaves, famous for their bible-carrying piety. Otherwise Wolseley was to rely upon locally raised levies, commanded by the special service officers. That was the theory, but this officer-only force was a

SCALE OF ENGLISH MILES.
10   20   30   40   50

22

subterfuge. Unknown to Gladstone and his Cabinet, Wolseley had arranged with Cardwell for two British battalions to be held in readiness and sent for after he had cleared the coastal areas. The European troops would then be used for the main thrust against Kumasi, the Ashanti capital.

Wolseley had selected his own people. As well as Buller, he was taking Huyshe and McCalmont, together with Colonel J. C. McNeill, his Chief of Staff on the Red River, and Mr M. B. Irvine, the Deputy-Controller, both of whom also had served him well there. His Military Secretary was Captain Henry Brackenbury, an ugly, untidy and rather affected desk-bound Gunner, but the owner of a clear, logical mind; his Private Secretary was another Gunner, the studious and equally scruffy Lieutenant J. F. Maurice, who had taught at Sandhurst. Literate himself, Wolseley had a penchant for officers who could write as well as fight. Huyshe, Brackenbury, Maurice and Butler, who joined later, were all from the same mould, while Buller, although no author, had a lively pen and was as well read as his commander. Among the special service officers, attracted to this unhealthy coast by the prospect of active service and an extra guinea a day, were Lieutenant-Colonel Evelyn Wood (like McNeill, a VC) and Major Baker Russell. With Major T. D. Baker, the Assistant Adjutant-General, these officers were the foundation members of what was to be known as 'The Wolseley Ring', 'The Ashanti Ring', or sometimes 'The Wolseley Gang', a body of able men who moved with their master from one scene of action to another, often the object of dislike and jealousy to the less favoured.

As soon as they arrived at Cape Castle, Wolseley placed Buller in charge of intelligence. It was a challenging task. Although every available Colonial Office Blue Book, report on previous expeditions, volume of memoirs or map had been collected and pored over before and during the voyage out, the Intelligence Department at the War Office had only just been created and even geographical information was sparse and often inaccurate.[23]

Buller straightaway set about enlisting a corps of interpreters, consulting traders and their contacts, examining escaped Ashanti prisoners and finding anyone bold or avaricious enough to spy on the enemy. Not least of his problems, as he wrote to his sister, was that 'it is the – to deal with a language that has no written character and as many patois as there are inhabitants'; two different officers, he complained, spelt the same place as Yamakind and Jareah, both having heard it correctly pronounced.[24] Although he reported that 'No offers, either of gold to the poor, place to the ambitious, or freedom to the prisoners, can induce anyone to approach the Ashanti camp, such a step being regarded as certain death'[25], he did succeed in recruiting four reliable spies, two of them women and one a boy. His notebook contains meticulous details on local personalities and topography[26]. As Brackenbury recorded, Buller had 'from the beginning, shown a skill and judgement worthy of a trained detective'[27]. Such was the quality of Buller's intelligence reports that one of his first was to find its way to Queen Victoria's desk.[28]

In intelligence gathering, needless to say, the Ashanti had every advantage which they used to good effect.

The information Buller had so quickly garnered enabled Wolseley to deliver a preliminary blow against the Ashantis, some 30,000 to 40,000 of whom were encamped a few miles inland from Fort Elmina which lay six miles to the west of Cape Castle. But they were short of food, dysentery was rife, and they were meditating a retreat home across the River Prah. On 13 October, therefore, a force of about 800 Royal Marines, Bluejackets, West Indians and newly-enlisted Hausas (tough and warlike Muslims hailing from what is now Northern Nigeria), was landed at Elmina in the greatest secrecy. Its task was to destroy a number of villages from which the Ashantis were obtaining food and whose chiefs, contemptuous of the white man's ability to venture into the bush, had refused any form of co-operation.

Wolseley, remembering Buller's expertise as a woodman, had put him in charge of 30 axe-bearing labourers, their task to cut tracks through the dense bush. However, when the shooting began, Buller quickly got himself mixed up in the fighting, taking over from Colonel McNeill when the latter was seriously wounded. After a sharp little action and at a cost of some twenty casualties, the villages were duly burnt. More important was the fact that white troops had covered twenty-one miles in the space of twenty-four hours, so demonstrating to the Ashanti that they could operate in the bush, contrary to popular belief, and convincing them of the need to withdraw.

Morale rose throughout the Protectorate. It was an effective start, one used by Wolseley to obtain Cardwell's agreement to the despatch of the regular battalions, now increased to three, an essential step because it had proved all but impossible to enlist more than a handful of effective native troops, such was the deep-rooted terror of the Ashanti.

The Gold Coast, the original 'White Man's Grave', soon took its toll of Wolseley's small band of officers. During November he nearly died of fever himself and half his subordinates were out of action. Among them was Buller who made light of it in letters home[29], but Evelyn Wood, who encountered him in Elmina, remembered differently. 'Please order me a cup of tea,' asked Buller, 'and then give me some information as quickly as you can.' 'Why the hurry?' Wood demanded. 'Because,' came the response, 'I feel I have fever come on and I am not certain how long my head will last.' He was right. Soon afterwards, in a fit of delirium, he drew his revolver and fired three shots at his Fanti hammock bearers, mistaking them for Ashanti. Fortunately he missed.[30] Captain Huyshe when afflicted in the same way attacked his servant with a sword, slicing off an ear; remembered by all for his sweet-tempered and gentle nature, he was among those who did not recover.

Buller's duties as Intelligence Officer were taken over for the time being by Butler (at long last a half-pay captain) who arrived just as Buller went sick. Butler had not wasted the interim years. A journey to the Rockies had been followed by a visit to the bloody aftermath of the repression of the Communard insurrection in Paris, and yet another sojourn in the Canadian wildernesses. News that Wolseley was embarking on another campaign had resulted in a further successful telegram.

Meanwhile preparations for the arrival of the British battalions were going ahead, Wolseley's plans being based upon limiting their stay in the country to the dry period between December and March when disease was less prevalent. Speed then was of the essence. A forward hutted base had to be built at Prahsu, the crossing over the Prah, seventy miles from the coast and sixty from Kumasi, and a road from the coast constructed. Because medical opinion blamed malaria on damp rather than the mosquito, dry sleeping conditions were considered essential. To cope with this, 400-man hutted camps with raised sleeping platforms, each with a small hospital, water-purifier and stores, were set up at ten-mile intervals; at each, teams of hammock-bearing porters were stationed to rush the sick and wounded down to the waiting hospital ships.

Vast numbers of labourers and porters were needed. The men, who were averse to physical labour, were hard to attract, thus rendering compulsion necessary; women, used to work and eager for the money, were easier to come by and just as strong. The control of this human transport was a matter of immense complexity, far beyond the capability of the civilian commissaries, competent though they were. Wolseley arranged, therefore, for Lieutenant-Colonel George Colley, professor of military administration at the Staff College, to be sent out to take charge of these complicated lines-of-communication, but working under Mr Irvine, a radical step indeed. An outstanding staff officer, military thinker, artist and linguist, Colley enthused fresh life into the obtaining and organizing of the 17,000 porters he calculated were needed. Desertions never ceased, but somehow or other Colley kept the machine working.

The problems matched those of the Red River. Supply and transport were equally complex and time was limited – on the Red River by the end of the spring river spates and the start of the winter freeze, in Africa by those few weeks when disease was a just acceptable hazard.

Soon after Buller recovered, he was sent forward to the Prah to organize a company of native scouts and, with the help of the senior doctor and Sapper, select the site for and plan the forward base. It was his first sight of the magnificent trees of the African forest proper, 'mahogany, coco-nut, banyan, in fact a tropical forest in all its luxuriance of foliage and creepers'[31] Despite illness, pressure of work and even at times a lack of writing materials, wherever he was Buller managed to find time to pen long letters to his sisters on every imaginable topic – natural history, the strategy of a campaign, battles fought in all their detail and the often daily mundane round.

From the first, Buller displayed what was to be a lifelong antipathy towards reporters, a common outlook at the time, and an inheritance from Wellington and Raglan; Kitchener, in his abusive 'Get out of my way, you drunken swabs' just before the Battle of Omdurman, reflected the attitude. Such an ambitious publicist as Wolseley lived to regret his criticism of correspondents in his *Soldiers' Pocket Book* as 'the curse of modern warfare', who 'eat the rations of the fighting men and do no work at all'[32]; outwardly polite to them, the large number of newspapermen who flocked to the Ashanti disgusted him. Afterwards, Winwood Reade of *The Times*, G. A. Henty for *The Standard* and the utterly unscrupulous H. M. Stanley for *The New York Herald* all produced 'instant' but readable books. Among others *The Daily Telegraph* and *The Illustrated London News* also sent their men. All carried weapons and sometimes used them.

Buller's comment that there was 'a *Daily Telegraph* correspondent here now . . . who will probably write some live lies about it. The great M Stanley of the NY Herald never leaves this [sic] and trusts entirely to fancy'[33] summed up his outlook. Stanley recounts a conversation with an unnamed staff officer 'who thoroughly shares Sir Garnet's hatred for newspaper men' to whom he had suggested that if an officer trusted to a correspondent's honour not to write anything that would furnish information to an enemy, no *gentleman* of the press would disappoint him. 'Trust in his honour!', came the response, 'By heavens! I would trust to nothing less than his back. On the first publication of anything I thought not proper, I would tie him to the triangle and trust to fifty lashes well laid on his bare back not to do the like again'.[34] It was almost certainly Buller, talking with his tongue rather in his cheek for he strongly opposed flogging. But he never curbed his views on the press, a prejudice that in the end caused him untold harm.

Since that first engagement in October, Wolseley's small force of Marines, West Indians, Hausas and a few local levies, had fought several hard actions to defend the seventy-mile line of communications. Nevertheless, by 15 December the by then half-starved Ashanti army was back across the Prah. The first stage of the war was over.

In the meantime a further battalion of the West Indian Regiment had arrived, and on New Year's Day the three European units began to land, dressed in the drab but business-like grey homespun Wolseley had settled upon before leaving England. As each sub-unit came ashore, it began its march up to Prahsu, where Wolseley himself had moved on 2 January. With him was Buller, surveying, gathering intelligence and taking a major part in the negotiations with the Ashanti King. These proved abortive but did secure the release of a number of captive missionaries. At the same time three subsidiary columns of native levies, one commanded by Butler, began to move towards Kumasi by more southerly routes, their object to distract the attention of the main Ashanti army.

On 20 January, 1874, the European troops began to cross the Prah. Ahead went an advanced guard of native troops, skirmishing against light resistance and often accompanied by the ubiquitous Buller. His intelligence organization had accurately foretold that the Ashantis would give battle first at Amoafu, some fifteen miles short of Kumasi, and again outside their capital.

On 30 January, near Amoafu, the Ashantis laid their ambush. The Black Watch were ahead, hacking parallel paths through the thick jungle, when the first shots were fired. Wolseley's succinct instructions for coping with such an attack were remembered. 'Be cool; fire low, fire slow and charge home.' Disciplined courage, 7-pounder guns and the short Snider rifle were too much for the enemy hordes, the slugs from whose antiquated weapons wounded but rarely killed. It was an untidy, scrappy battle: little could be seen and small isolated parties of men coped as best they could. But, after a long day's fighting, the Ashanti, still fighting hard, drew off, leaving only four British dead, but no less than 194 wounded, 113 of them Black Watch.

All day Buller had gained little respite, rushing to and fro with Wolseley's orders. Then, when the force started to push forward again on Kumasi on 2 February, once more he was with the advanced guard, which again saw heavy fighting as it approached the city. Outside it, as forecast, the final battle was fought. Casualties were again high, but just before dusk on 4 February the leading Highlanders entered the capital, a fine place of broad avenues and well-built porticoed houses. The King had flown, but large crowds, among them many still-armed men, watched Wolseley ride in mounted on one of the few available mules – his old leg wound still troubled him.

The following morning the city was almost deserted. There was nothing more Wolseley could do but but march home: the rains were near, sickness was mounting and the tenuous supply line was threatened. So the next day the city was made ready for burning; at the same time, prize agents, under Buller's control, ransacked the riches of the treasury, collecting solid gold masks, necklaces and ornaments, gold dust and gold and silver-mounted weapons, the quantities limited only by the scarcity of porters. Meanwhile the war correspondents and parties of soldiers had been examining the horrors of the 'Place of the Vultures', an acre of stinking corruption into which the bones and bloated carcasses of the tens of thousands of sacrificial victims were piled, many freshly slain.

The following morning Kumasi flared as the long columns of troops and porters started for the coast. The Europeans were already worn to skeletons, their features haggard and drawn. Like many, Buller was near collapse. In a letter written on 14 February from the coast, he admitted:

We had rather more fighting than we wanted, for out of a grand total of about 2,000 men of all ranks [he was counting only the Europeans] we lost, killed and wounded, 390, or nearly 1 in 5, a heavy percentage, to say nothing of the sick . . . I shall be very glad to get back home . . . I cannot help feeling that I lose energy daily.[35]

Once again he was making light of his illness. Carried in a hammock during the later stages of the journey, he was by then desperately ill, so delirious that he failed to recognize his cousin, a naval captain, into whose ship Wolseley arranged for him to be embarked; horribly dirty, ingrained with mud and dirt, he was gently tubbed. Like others, Butler among them, it was months before he completely recovered; recurring bouts of 'coast fever' were to plague him for years.

Both Stanley and Winwood Reade faulted Wolseley's handling of the campaign, the former for not taking more decisive action when he reached Kumasi, the latter on a variety of grounds, many unjustified. Certainly Wolseley had failed either to capture the King or establish any form of long-term control over his dominions. And although the Ashanti had learned that their jungles were no longer invulnerable, two further expeditions were needed towards the end of the century before the Gold Coast could enjoy for a time both peace and a measure of just administration.

In nearly every way Wolseley's campaign had, however, been a model of its kind. He returned to find himself a popular hero, the recipient of both the GCMG and the KCB, and a useful £25,000 grant. As for Buller, he had pulled himself out of the ruck, having made his mark, as Wolseley reported, as 'an excellent staff officer' to whom his commander was indebted[36]. His rewards were a brevet majority and a CB. It was perhaps surprising that certain correspondents should have been rather more than luke-warm in their praise, Stanley writing of his 'traits of character which, on a more intimate acquaintance with them, will prove him not unworthy of filling posts of the most onerous and most responsible nature'[37]; Winwood Reade merely suggested that 'his talents are best displayed on active service'[38].

3

SOUTH AFRICAN ACCOLADE

As Buller slowly convalesced at Downes during the summer of 1874, his family was shocked by his physical weakness, from which he recovered only slowly. On the other hand his sister Henrietta noted that 'he had gained enormously in self-confidence': when he left for the Ashanti War he had been worried that Wolseley would expect too much of him, but he now knew that he had more than realized expectations[1]. Henrietta marked especially his changed behaviour at social gatherings. 'There was an indefinable – not self-assertion – but self-dependence in him, which had never been his before'. Nevertheless, to make a speech was torture, and he steadfastly refused to appear at banquets as a 'distinguished guest' until his family insisted that he could not possibly refuse local invitations.[2]

To savour again the delights of the Devon countryside and the riches of the Downes library helped speed his recovery. Wild flowers were at their best and his mother, an ardent botanist, had instilled in him a deep love for them, one that had expanded when, as an ensign at Winchester, he explored the nearby river-banks.[3]

He read both rapidly and voraciously. On this leave he immersed himself in Tennyson's newly published *Enoch Arden*, 'the most perfect thing he had ever read'.[4] Books always formed a large part of his travelling baggage – a cabinet edition of Shakespeare, Charles Lamb, Milton, Macaulay, Arnold and Ruskin. His taste in fiction lay with such as Meredith, Dickens, Stevenson and Trollope; George Herbert was another favourite poet, while a retentive memory enabled him to quote yards of light verse such as *The Ingoldsby Legends* or cap a Latin quotation. His personal literary style should not be judged by his lengthy and hurried letters to his family, often written when exhausted by fighting or staff work. As he grew older he expressed himself in writing with the lucidity with which his speech had always been marked. Sir John Fortescue, the British Army's great historian, was to recall that, while Wolseley's biography of Marlborough had taught him nothing he did not already know, Buller, that great commander, as Fortescue described him, had at once in conversation thrown a new light upon his character.[5] But despite the example of Wolseley, who wrote continually and omnivorously, even trying his hand as a novelist, Buller never himself attempted authorship, unlike so many of his colleagues in the 'Ring'.

His convalescence sadly coincided with the mortal illness of his elder brother James. They were a close and affectionate family, but of all his brothers, 'Jamie' was dearest to Redvers, perhaps because he had much of his mother in him, while Redvers took after the father with whom he had so little in common. On 13 October, 1874, James died; long afterwards Buller confided to Henrietta that it had been the greatest grief of his life, but had resulted in his greatest happiness[6]. Heir now to over 5,000 acres in Devon and Cornwall with a rent roll of £14,137,[7] Redvers became squire of Downes. His deep attachment to his home, combined with his love of country life and sports, tempted him to follow custom by retiring from the Army and devoting himself to the management and enjoyment of his estates, together with the wide local responsibilities he had also inherited. But Redvers, having proved himself both as leader and staff officer, had now developed a taste for serious soldiering; moreover he had also fallen under Wolseley's reforming spell.

So it was that Buller decided to stay on at the desk he was now occupying at the War Office, that of DAAG in the Adjutant-General's department. In the half-dozen or so confused and decayed Pall Mall buildings which housed the War Office, communicating with one another by devious stairways and corridors, Buller saw much of William Butler, who arrived the following October, as well as other old Ashanti friends, whose ability and Wolseley's influence had brought to the hub of affairs. Not that the hub spun especially quickly: to reorganize does not, as a matter of course, make for efficiency. Nor could Buller find much sympathy for his advanced views on unit training. As ever the financiers controlled the place, and as Butler complained 'a corporal and a file of men could not move from Glasgow to Edinburgh' without the sanction of the War Office.[8]

Frustrating though life was, in his three years there Buller learned how the system worked and what was needed to better it. He also took on such tasks as the running of the 'Ashanti Club',[9] founded under Wolseley's auspices, and the reorganization of the Naval and Military Club in Piccadilly, more commonly known as the 'In and Out', on to a sound social and financial basis.[10] Moving now in wider circles, he dined at Marlborough House with the Prince of Wales, later King Edward VII, an evening ruined by a recurrence of the fever.[11] It was all a far cry from the Staff College, where, only three years or so earlier, the Commandant had found a need to rebuke him for 'riotous behaviour'.[12]

When the chance came to leave, Buller seized it. Offered employment in early 1878 under Major-General the Hon Frederic Thesiger, later Lord

Chelmsford, who had been posted to command in South Africa, he accepted, even though the time seemed inopportune. For Europe was close to general war. The previous year, Russia's intervention in the Balkans to protect Turkey's Slav Christian minorities from brutal persecution had brought Turkey near to defeat; Russia threatened Constantinople, and Britain, fearful for her position in the Mediterranean, was herself making warlike noises against Russia.

However, after carefully weighing the alternatives, Buller correctly concluded that it would all come to nothing, and on the 1st of February he sailed with Thesiger for the Cape. Also on board was his old friend, the now Brevet-Colonel Evelyn Wood, together with a number of untrained drafts, most of whom had less than four months' service and had still to fire their rifles. Cardwell's linked battalion system, with the home unit reinforcing its fellow overseas, had yet to settle down.

With him Buller carried a letter from Wolseley, which suggests that he, then on leave in England, had been consulted before Buller accepted this new appointment:

I have written to Sir T. Shepstone [the Commissioner for Native Affairs in Natal, of whom more later] telling him of you: I thought this a better plan than enlarging upon your merits in the letter of introduction which I enclose – at least I spare your blushes by this plan – you know already the high opinion I have of you, and how I should always like to have you with me when I may have the good fortune to be employed in the field.

Should you hear of our having a war in Europe I would advise you to come home at once.[13]

When Thesiger landed, what became known as the Ninth Kaffir War had been in progress for five months, its very name an indication of the frequency of these conflicts. (The Arabic 'Kaffir', denoting 'unbeliever', had yet to gather its derogatory connotations.) The arrival in a near empty country of the Bantu people, moving down from eastern Africa to seek fresh grazing grounds and escape from Arab slavers, had almost coincided with the landing of the first Dutch at the Cape of Good Hope in the mid-seventeenth century. As the Boers increased in number and sought fresh farms to the north-east, confrontation was inevitable. The transfer of the Cape to Britain after the Napoleonic Wars, followed by the arrival of the first British settlers, encouraged the Boers to inspan their oxen and trek northwards to escape. The result was a century of unceasing conflict, Boer against Bantu, Boer against Briton, but more often Bantu against Bantu or Boer and Briton allied against Bantu.

Thesiger, accompanied by Wood and Buller, immediately moved to King

William's Town, in what was known as British Kaffaria and around which the fighting was centred. The conflict, starting as a brawl between Fingoes (Zulus who had fled from the exactions of their chiefs) and the Xhosa Galeka, had spread into a serious anti-white rising. Other than the 90th Foot (later the 2nd Bn The Cameronians), Thesiger's troops consisted of Colonial units of very variable quality. Moreover, the effective prosecution of the war was impeded by the refusal of the Cape Government to allow Thesiger, an Imperial officer, to control their units, and by a certain ill-feeling between the British private soldier on a shilling a day and the local volunteer paid five times more.

Buller's first job was staff officer to a Commandant Frost, an able Colonial officer. It lasted only five or six weeks, but gave him a grounding in bush warfare and the characteristics of the irregular troops, both Boer and British, an invaluable preparation for his next task, command of the 250-strong Frontier Light Horse, which he took over on 22 April, 1878. This, his first independent command, consisted of a mixed bunch of often disreputable characters, Boers, British and others, its Regimental Sergeant Major a deserter from the 80th Foot. They were 'in terribly bad order', as he told his sister in his still rather diffident manner on the day he took over, 'and I fear there is not much credit to be got out of being associated with them, but I will do my best.'[14]

His best was good indeed. By encouragement, example and hard discipline, Buller quickly moulded these irregular volunteers into shape. He suffered no nonsense. Early on, having given his men some time off after a tough patrol, he warned them to be on parade two days later, sober and fit for service. A single trooper paraded drunk and threw abuse at him. Apparently ignoring the incident, Buller marched the unit off. Then, a few miles into the veldt, he ordered the man to dismount and clear off.

The workmanlike dress and equipment of the Frontier Light Horse should have set an example to the regular units alongside whom they fought, still decked out in tight-collared scarlet and blue. Leather-patched brown cord breeches and high leather gaiters were worn with an open-necked, coloured flannel shirt and a loose-fitting many-pocketed and usually disreputable light jacket, the whole surmounted by a red-puggareed and wide-brimmed felt hat. (In the horse-lines in the early morning, Buller would himself appear bare-legged in slippers still wearing a red scarf as a nightcap.) Weapons were a mixed bag of long Martinis, Martini-Henry carbines and Sniders, but every man also carried a revolver and a hunting knife.

What appealed to Buller's men was the stark, seemingly fearless courage of this unorthodox British regular, pictured by a seventeen year-old trooper as 'tall and wiry, with rather small, keen eyes'.[15] Tough and brusque he was, but his troopers also discovered that he was both accessible and sympathetic.

'If we were lying in the rain, so was Buller. If we were hungry, so was he. All of the hardships he shared equally with his men. Never did Buller, as commander, have a patrol tent to sleep under, while his men were in the open. He was the mainstay of Colonel Wood's column, and the idol of all.'[16]

During May they operated as one of several mixed columns of white troops and Fingo auxiliaries, all under Evelyn Wood, and fighting often among precipitous, bush-covered cliffs. In one of these engagements, Wood remembered watching Buller leading his men under heavy fire down a forty-foot toboggan-like cliff slide, shouting 'Frontier Light Horse, you will never let those redcoats beat you'.[17] The enemy fled before Buller arrived, but it was an unhappy day for him, parsimonious as he always was with the lives of his men: both his captains had already been hit, one killed and the other severely wounded, and half a dozen troopers had died with them.

This was but one of the several small battles the Frontier Light Horse fought that May. By the month's end the tribes had capitulated, but there was plenty more work awaiting the now toughened unit.

Although there was widespread unrest among a number of South African tribes, the principal danger lay with the warlike Zulus, who lived to the east of the Orange Free State and the Transvaal, the two Boer republics, and to the north of the British colony of Natal. The Zulu king, Cetshwayo, commanded a superbly trained army of 40,000 warriors, organized into twenty-six disciplined regiments, armed with assegais, knobkerries but, as yet, no more than a few firearms. Although the intelligent Cetshwayo tried to avoid an open confrontation with his white neighbours, his warlike state represented a permanent threat to their safety. Especially threatened was the Transvaal, some of whose 6,000 Boer families had stimulated trouble by encroaching over their ill-defined borders well into Zulu territory.

Into this morass of conflicting races and interests Sir Bartle Frere had arrived in April as Governor of the Cape and High Commissioner for Native Affairs. Lately Governor of Bombay, widely experienced and exceptionally able, for such a pro-consul South Africa hardly posed an adequate challenge, but his covert task, as revealed to him by Mr Benjamin Disraeli's Colonial Secretary, was to unite the colonies, republics and independent African kingdoms of South Africa into a prosperous and peaceful confederation, similar to the new Dominion of Canada.

Soon after landing, Frere heard that the Transvaal, bankrupt and threatened by its warlike neighbours, had been annexed without opposition, a short-lived coup but one that encouraged Frere to tackle the Zulus. Using the pretext of a border kidnapping, on 24 November he issued an ultimatum to Cetshwayo, among its terms a number of clearly unacceptable provisions, including the disbandment of his army, the bedrock of Zulu society.

Cetshwayo, reluctant for war, temporized and offered concessions but to no effect, and on 11 January, 1879, the first of five British columns crossed the Tugela River into Zululand, three of them directed to converge upon Cetshwayo's kraal at Ulundi. Preparations for the invasion had been in hand for over six months, Buller having learned as far back as August that war was probable[18]. During July he had marched his regiment north into the Transvaal, where in some further skirmishing, his servant, a fellow Rifleman, had to his great sorrow been killed; by January, having enlisted a further 100 men in Natal and acquired equipment and remounts to replace his heavy losses from horse-sickness, he was near Utrecht, on the Blood River, part of Evelyn Wood's No 4, or left-hand column, which also included the 13th (later the Somerset Light Infantry) and the 90th Foot, together with some 400 natives, a total of 2,100 men, with six 7-pounders and a couple of rocket troughs. In all Lord Chelmsford (Thesiger had succeeded to the title during the summer) commanded nearly 17,000 troops and auxiliaries, among the former seven battalions of British infantry.

The tragic fate of the larger part of the centre column, which Chelmsford had accompanied, is well known. After crossing Rorke's Drift over the Tugela, it established a camp at Isandhlwana, about fifteen miles to the east. There, two days later, while Chelmsford and about half the force was absent on a foray, the ill-prepared camp was attacked by 15,000 Zulus. When Chelmsford returned that evening, he found the naked bodies of over 800 British soldiers and 900 natives, their bellies ripped open as was the Zulu custom. Only a handful of mounted men had escaped.

Horrified by such an unparalleled disaster, Britain straightaway scraped together some 10,000 reinforcements and despatched them to the Cape. To replace the unsuccessful Chelmsford, Wolseley was uprooted from Cyprus, in which freshly acquired Protectorate he was serving as High Commissioner. Meanwhile, with the victorious Zulus threatening to overrun the small towns and scattered homesteads of Natal and the Transvaal threatened, the British were thrust back on the defensive.

News of Isandhlwana reached Wood the following day. Immediately he built a strongly entrenched camp on Kambula Hill. There he concentrated his force, and to Buller's men fell the task of skirmishing and patrolling outside its walls. Buller wrote:

In the saddle for 80 hours a week does not leave one much time for writing, and sleeping . . . for I have nearly 160 square miles of country to patrol with a very inadequate force.

'Terribly weak in men', his regiment had been reduced to 150 effectives, largely because many troopers had taken their time-discharge[19] just a week after Isandhlwana – as was their right. This was a problem that nearly always beset irregular units and especially during the coming Boer War of 1899 to

1902. Men joined with an enthusiasm that for many was soon dampened by the rigours and dangers of war.

Buller had few secrets from his two sisters. The letter he wrote after Isandhlwana reveals that at this time in his career he was still far from unambitious:

> . . . still the General writes that he has specially reported me to the S. of S., and every little helps, for if I am to get anything out of the Zulu War in the way of further promotion I must do a big thing otherwise I have not got a chance. Small brevets are easy enough to get, but the plum of a full colonelcy is another matter.[20]

That 'small brevet' did now arrive, a lieutenant-colonelcy.

Wood, who had received his brevet to colonel after the Ashanti campaign, was far more ambitious, an unfashionable characteristic then and later among army officers, acceptable though it was in most other callings. A year older than Buller, Wood – oddly enough – had begun life as a midshipman in the Royal Navy. Badly wounded while serving ashore in the Crimea, he had switched to the Army and by the age of twenty was commanding an irregular cavalry regiment in the Indian Mutiny, where he won the VC. Far from prepossessing, dumpy and with a straggling moustache, he was a martyr to ill-health, attracting every available disease.

The arrival of a few small irregular and mounted infantry units at Kambula slightly lightened the load of the Frontier Light Horse, but they still had little or no rest, raiding, reconnoitring and harrying any Zulus nearby. Rarely out of the saddle himself, and never seen asleep, Buller's restless stamina was to become legendary.

On one occasion work of a rather different order came Buller's way. Cetshwayo's hold on his subordinate chiefs was in no way complete, and in mid-February one of them, a certain Uhamu, passed word to Wood that he wished to surrender. The challenge was to ensure that his clan's families, among them 300 of his own wives, were brought safely in to Kambula. Wood decided to tackle the job himself, taking with him Buller and 360 troopers, together with a couple of hundred of Uhamu's warriors. Reaching their destination after sunset, the usually insomniac Wood slept off the effects of sunstroke while the women were collected. Buller, for his part, was said to have never even lain down. The return journey the next day, with Zulus loyal to Cetshwayo dogging the column's flanks, was purgatory for the children and the many pregnant women. As Buller wrote:

> Poor things they were very tired, and during the last two hours begged to be allowed to lie down and die but we kept them going and got them through, only 4 of the stragglers being assegaied.[21]

Buller, after declaring that he would not touch the verminous little brats, was later seen riding with six toddlers clutching his back or saddlebow.

But far sterner work awaited him. Aggressive though his patrolling had been, the Zulus and their allies were constantly raiding the British communications and the isolated white farmsteads along the disputed Transvaal border. One especially troublesome clan had as its stronghold the formidable 600-foot-high Hlobane Mountain, some thirty miles east of Kambula. It was, as a trooper wrote:

> The western terminus of a . . . range, the south, north and west boundaries being protected by steep cliffs, quite inaccessible except – at some spots – by baboons. On the eastern side the high cliffs ended where the plateau joined the next hill, which was boulder-strewn, very steep, and narrow on the summit.[22]

Towards the end of March Chelmsford had asked Wood to make a diversion so as to draw some of the Zulu forces towards his area while he attempted to relieve his fifth column, besieged since Isandhlwana at Eshowe in southern Zululand. Near impregnable though Hlobane seemed, and held by some 4,000 Zulus, Wood decided to tackle the enemy stronghold, using only his irregular horse and native levies. Although it has been often said that Wood's intentions were to launch a determined attack on the stronghold, his orders make it clear that he planned no more than 'a reconnaissance . . . to be pushed if possible to the top of the mountain'. Reports had, in fact, already reached him that Cetshwayo's main army was moving towards Kambula[23].

Wood decided that his main assault would be carried out by some 400 colonial horsemen and 300 native auxiliaries, commanded by Buller, who would tackle the eastern end of the plateau, while a smaller party, which included only 120 white men, under Lieutenant-Colonel John Russell, made a diversion at the western corner, which Wood had decided was just practicable for men on foot. Behind Russell was to come Wood with more friendly Zulu auxiliaries.

After bivouacking a couple of miles short of the mountain on the night of 27 March and leaving his camp fires burning so as to deceive any Zulu scouts, at 3 a.m. Buller began his climb, his men slipping and stumbling among the jumble of six-foot-high boulders as they led their sure-footed 14-hand Basuto ponies, the clatter of their ascent blanketed by a fierce and lengthy thunderstorm. Only at the last moment did the Zulu outposts hear them, but their few scattered shots killed two of Buller's officers, as well as a trooper and several horses. Meanwhile Russell, having scaled the lower plateau at the western end and confirmed that there was no way up for horses on that flank, sent twenty dismounted men to contact Buller.

As Buller's troopers and Africans rounded up the Zulu cattle, their owners began to rally and hit back, causing him to collect his force and plan his return; at the same time he sent on ahead his second-in-command and close friend, Captain Barton, with thirty men, their task to bury their three comrades who had been killed. No sooner had Barton left than there appeared below them some 20,000 white-plumed Zulu warriors, their assegais gleaming in the sun, moving in five long columns. Wood's information had been correct. It was the main Zulu army. Then Buller made a tragic error:

We were 30 miles from camp. Our horses had been under saddle since 3 a.m. It was then 10 a.m. & they had had nothing to eat really since the previous morning. I saw that we had not a chance of getting back the way we had come, so I at once sent two men after Barton, telling him to return by the right of the mountain. Alas for the use of careless words! [By right] I meant the north side. Poor Barton, going down the Mt. with his back to it, understood that he was to turn to his right, and so went to the left, or S. side, on which was the Zulu impi.[24]

Joining up with the fifty-strong Border House, which had started out with Buller but been delayed by losing touch during the night march, Barton was caught between the Zulus of the main army, many now armed with Martini-Henry rifles captured at Isandhlwana, and others following on his heels from above. He and half his men were to die, together with the larger part of the Border Horse.

Undoubtedly Buller was to blame, but this sort of thing occurs only too easily in war when instantaneous decisions are made by weary men under enemy fire, something little understood by armchair critics. The error might not have been committed had adequate maps been available, together with a proper system for pinpointing places on them. Imprecision in orders was, in any case, far from uncommon in the British Army in the days before a common staff drill for their form and content had been introduced.

The only other practicable way off the plateau was that by which Russell's few dismounted men had ascended, a series of rock ledges some four feet or so high and eight to ten wide, interspersed with giant boulders. Sending his native levies and most of his horsemen off ahead, Buller, with some of his Frontier Light Horse, stayed to cover their withdrawal. Soon the Zulus were among them, clambering down and around the flanks of the retreating column, shooting, stabbing and propelling boulders on top of them. Retreat turned into rout.

Last away were Buller and seven troopers, four of whom died as they turned to leave the plateau. Among the hideous confusion and panic, he was one of the few who kept his head, steadying and reassuring those near him. The seventeen-year-old, having dropped his horse's bridle in order to save himself, felt a clout on the ear, an iron hand gripping his shoulder, and heard Buller's roar of 'where's your horse?' Ordered to go back and get it, he did just that.[25]

Even when they reached the lower slopes at the foot of the cliffs, their danger was far from over. Many horses had been killed or maimed; no trooper on his feet could outrun a Zulu. Those still mounted dragged a comrade up behind them. Buller himself managed to save in turn four of his men, galloping back each time into the mêlée to rescue yet another horseless man.

At the foot of the mountain Buller managed to rally his disheartened troopers and begin the long march back to Kambula. But his day was not over. When back in camp a solitary horseman reported that a number of stragglers were lost out on the veldt, he collected half a dozen volunteers and rode out into the pitch-dark night to find and bring them in. By then he had already been in the saddle for nearly 100 hours.

When the roll was finally taken, ten of Buller's officers and eighty troopers failed to answer their names; another eleven were wounded. Also dead were two officers and several men who had been with Wood. Among the many friends Buller had lost was Piet Uys, the commandant of the only party of Transvaal Boers who had joined Chelmsford, together with two of his sons. Uys was, Buller wrote to his aunt, 'my guide, counsellor and friend' and his loss was 'a most serious one to all South Africa & irreparable to me. He really was the finest man, morally speaking, I ever met. . . . It was a bad day. I hope I shall never see such another.'[26]

Five Victoria Crosses were to be awarded for the day's work, the best deserved of all of them undoubtedly Buller's. It was said of him that he earned the coveted decoration twenty times over during the war. Throughout the day he had displayed the reckless bravery that everyone now expected from him. Courage with most men is an expendable commodity, the product of the sublimination of fear. But fear seems to be lacking in the make-up of a few individuals, and for others battle can even be pleasurable. Buller was such a man, as was Wood. But the naturally brave can often be unimaginative and sometimes insensitive, and this Buller was not.

The survivors were given no time to recover. The next morning, as they were sadly musing over their losses, the main Zulu army, still in its five threatening columns, came in sight below the ridge on which Wood had built his camp. It was a strong position, protected by a laager of chained wagons, backed by an earth and stone wall. As well as his two British battalions, mounted infantry and irregular cavalry, there was also a battery of 7-pounders.

Wood had feared that the Zulus would by-pass Kambula to attack the almost undefended white settlements further south, but, as he had hoped, they deployed, a fearsome ring of warriors, to encircle his camp. Concerned that he might be attacked simultaneously from every direction, he was relieved to notice that a single regiment had taken up position about a mile away but far closer to his camp than the others. At Buller's suggestion, he allowed him to take his mounted men out and attempt to goad this body into an independent attack. Dismounting a few hundred yards from the regiment, Buller's troopers let loose a volley and then fell back as they charged, repeating the manoeuvre until their opponents came within range of the 7-pounder guns, the signal for his now hotly pursued men to gallop for the safety of the laager.

The Zulus' attack lasted for nearly four hours, during which they flung themselves time and again against the volley fire of the 13th and 90th Regiments. Only once did they manage to come to close grips with the British defenders, most of whose losses came from the captured Martini-Henrys. When, towards the end of the afternoon, the Zulus drew off, wavering and disheartened, Wood let loose Buller's horsemen at their heels.

Buller's men showed no mercy. The pursuit was undoubtedly brutal, and later evoked some controversy at home. But it was not the African custom to take prisoners, except for use as slaves. The wounded could expect to be butchered, and it was with this in mind that at least one trooper shot himself on Hlobane: bleak stories of the aftermath of Isandhlwana abounded. Revenge in such circumstances was inevitable.

The British losses at Kambula numbered no more than twenty-eight killed and fifty-five wounded. 785 mangled Zulu bodies were collected from the immediate vicinity of the camp; probably 2,000 or more in all had died. The defeat had a shattering effect on the Zulu nation. It was the last time their army took the offensive.

In a letter a week later to Alice, his other surviving sister and always addressed by him as 'Lucy', Buller tells of a war correspondent who turned up two days after the battle. 'The rascal tried three times to interview me, but I knew too much for him, and he had to send off his report without so much as getting a question into me.'[27] Another – possibly the same man – who rashly told him that he considered himself justified in reading and making use of any private correspondence he might find, was surprised the next day to be turned out of Buller's tent. 'I was much amused at the concluding paragraphs of your letter, telling me to be civil to correspondents,' a later letter reads, 'as the day before I received it I had had to pull one through a thorn bush to teach him manners . . . if he revenges himself in caricaturing me buy a copy of his paper & keep it for me.'[28] These are yet further instances of his obsessive and often unreasoning dislike and distrust of reporters. Unlike some of his fellows, of whom Wolseley was the prime example, he hated to an exaggerated degree any form of self-advertisement, a characteristic that was never to leave him. Nevertheless, the press still eulogized him with labels such as the 'Bayard of South Africa', one paper depicting him in a later skirmish as:

> Leading his men at a swinging canter, with his reins in his teeth, a revolver in one hand, and a knobkerrie he had snatched from a Zulu in the other, his hat blown off in the *mêlée*, and a large streak of blood across his face, caused by a splinter of blood from above, this gallant horseman seemed a demon incarnate to the flying savages, who slunk out of his path as if he had been – as indeed they believed him – an evil spirit, whose very look was death.[29]

A rather more sober account describes his workmanlike garb, contrasting so strikingly with the tight-collared scarlets and blues of officers sweating with their regular regiments, and he bestriding:

> . . . a stout pony of fourteen hands that looks barely up to his weight . . . For armament Buller preferred a carbine, with the ammunition carried *en bandolier*. Sabres he would not be troubled with, saying that he was sure that, if his men had been so armed on Inhlobana, they would never have got up the hill, and if they had would certainly not have come off it alive.[30]

Not only contemporary illustrators but reputable modern writers also tend to depict a sabre-wielding Buller winning his Victoria Cross.

That earlier letter after Kambula was written by a man weary both physically and mentally, and mourning the deaths of several close friends, for one of which he held himself responsible. 'As for the Zulu War,' he wrote, 'I begin to fear that it will never be over.'[31] But ahead of him lay three months more hard riding and heavy fighting.

The expected strong reinforcements now arriving from England had enabled Wood's force to be increased by a further infantry battalion and by several more small units of mounted troops which increased Buller's command to 1,400 horse, the equivalent of a cavalry brigade. (In his own regiment he still ranked as no more than a captain.)

When Chelmsford's final advance into northern Zululand began at the end of May, before the arrival of Wolseley, ahead moved what was now known as the Flying Column, Wood's augmented command. With it was the young Louis Napoleon, Prince-Imperial – and Emperor of the French if the Bonaparte dynasty were to be restored. A refugee in England, the Prince had attended the Royal Military Academy at Woolwich and been reluctantly allowed by Disraeli to further his military knowledge by seeing something of active service. He was a lively and popular young man, but had proved so foolhardy that Buller, in whose charge he had been placed, asked for him to be removed elsewhere, a request Chelmsford agreed.

Then, on 1 June, as the Flying Column was trekking from Kambula to link up with the main force, Wood and Buller, riding together and examining the countryside, suddenly picked out an officer galloping madly towards them. 'The Prince – the Prince Imperial is killed,' the breathless man gasped as he reached them. 'Where – where is the body?' asked Buller, but the rider could only gasp and point to a distant hill. 'Where are your men, sir? How many did you lose?' demanded the enraged Buller, turning on him savagely with the accusation 'You deserve to be shot, and I hope you will be. I could shoot you myself.'[32]

The officer was a Lieutenant Carey who had been out with the Prince on a patrol which, having failed to take proper precautions, had been surprised by a party of Zulus. In the subsequent *sauve qui peut* the Prince had been slain.

Carey was court-martialled at his own request so as to clear his name, but found guilty, a verdict subsequently overturned. Inevitably his reputation and career were blighted, but Buller, who had reacted with such wrath in the heat of the moment, afterwards excused him, reasoning that it was the officer's first time under fire. Buller, according to a previous biographer, 'to the end of his career refused to condemn a man for one mistake'[33].

As Chelmsford advanced slowly towards Ulundi, over-cautious after the tragic errors that had led to Isandhlwana, Buller's light cavalrymen scouted ahead of the ponderous columns of marching men. Cetshwayo, now fully aware that his warriors could not withstand his enemy's modern weapons, made increasingly anxious efforts to negotiate some form of peace, but Chelmsford was bent on the total destruction of the Zulu military machine: Isandhlwana had to be revenged, the threat to the white settlements permanently removed and his own reputation restored.

From the defensive laager built five miles short of Ulundi, on 3 July Buller and his horsemen were despatched to pick a suitable position just short of Cetshwayo's capital where the Zulus might be provoked into attacking. Having chosen the place, they were then ambushed by some 3,000 Zulus, now well equipped with fire-arms, but, fortunately, liable to fire too high. Extracting himself in copybook fashion with units covering one another in turn as they withdrew, Buller lost only seven men. That day another two officers and a sergeant were to win the Victoria Cross – again for rescuing unhorsed men.

The following day Chelmsford's force started out from its laager, again with Buller scouting ahead. Approaching Ulundi, the 5,000 men formed themselves into a hollow rectangle as they neared Chelmsford's chosen battleground, and there, just to the west of the capital, they halted to receive the Zulu attack, Gatling guns and artillery at each corner of the square, bands playing and the Colours of the 2nd Royal Scots Fusiliers uncased, the last but one occasion the British Army would fly them in battle.

After harassing the Zulus as they had at Kambula, Buller's scouts galloped back into the security of the square with their enemies at their heels. The final destruction of the Zulu *impis* then took place. For thirty minutes they threw themselves into the storm of bullets and shells that poured out of each side of the square, displaying courage that aroused the admiration of even the young British soldiers they failed to reach. But after their experiences at Kambula they were that less resolute, and when parties were seen to be drifting away from the battle Chelmsford launched the 17th Lancers out of the square. The pursuit, in which Buller's troopers joined, was to resemble the slaughter after Kambula. The military power of the Zulus had been destroyed, but Kambula had been the decisive battle.

Needless to say, Wolseley and his staff, who had arrived at Cape Town ten days earlier, received the news of Chelmsford's victory at Ulundi with rather mixed feelings: all that now remained was to find and capture Cetshwayo, and deal with a certain Sekukini, an independent and troublesome chieftain who controlled a near inaccessible region of north-eastern Transvaal. Wolseley had hoped that his two tried friends, Wood and Buller, could be used for these tasks, but he was to be disappointed. Two weeks after Ulundi he was obliged to report to the Duke of Cambridge:

> The men who have been the life and soul of this war are Brigadier-General Wood and Lieutenant-Colonel Buller. If their advice had been steadily acted upon, I believe that no further operations would have been necessary now . . . I am extremely sorry that I have been obliged to allow both Brigadier-General Wood and Lieutenant-Colonel Buller to return home. Both are pretty well worn out, and both require rest for mind as well as for body. I feel their loss beyond measure, as I had looked to them to finish this business.[34]

Wolseley also noted in his journal that Sir William Russell, the famous *Times* correspondent, who had exposed the iniquities of the Crimea and who was now reporting for the *Daily Telegraph*, had told him:

> Chelmsford leant entirely on Evelyn Wood & that Buller influenced Wood . . . but that Buller is in his opinion far the better man of the two. I concur in this view myself, judging from my Ashanti experience.

I think Wood ought to be made a General Officer. If he be not so promoted it will be a scandal, for we are as an Army very badly off for Generals & Wood will make a really good one although not in my poor opinion a first class one. Buller would certainly make the better General of the two.[35]

In contrast, when Wolseley stayed with his two old friends, he received an uninhibited report on his predecessor. 'I put up with dear old Wood: both he and Buller say Chelmsford is not fit to be a Corporal'.[36] For all that, Chelmsford was an extremely likeable person, as even the acerbically critical Wolseley was obliged to admit.

A young Gunner subaltern, Arthur Bigge, a close friend of the Prince Imperial, had fought alongside Buller for much of the campaign. Then and later, he remained a devoted admirer of the older man, whose kindness and good company in camp he had enjoyed and about whom he wrote:

It would be impossible to exaggerate what he accomplished with 'Buller's Horse', a curious conglomeration of humanity representative of varied nationalities, of every class of society not by any means excluding the criminal! But by his marvellous personality that unstable volatile body consolidated itself into an effective and dependable force, yet almost spontaneously disintegrating itself into its heterogenous elements with a consequent loss of efficiency the moment the inspiration of the leader was removed . . . I shall never forget how we all looked up to and admired him.[37]

Lieutenant Bigge, later Lord Stamfordham, was to become Private Secretary to two sovereigns, Queen Victoria and King George V.

Buller's 'Five Bob Colonials', as the British regular derisively knew them – they were paid five times more than him – , had made a great name for themselves. Even after the subsequent two Boer Wars, men would point out a veteran and say, 'He was with Buller in Zululand'.[38]

But as ever, yet another of Buller's characteristics had made itself felt in South Africa. To the Military Secretary at the Horse Guards, Evelyn Wood felt impelled to write, 'I hope you manage to keep him in the Service, his very frank tongue notwithstanding.'[39]

Buller's physical deterioration dated back to Kambula and was noticed by Chelmsford who, on asking Wood what he had been doing to him, received the answer, 'Working him to death and giving him nothing to eat.'[40] So ill was he that he never fully recovered. One serious affliction was veldt-sores. These so crippled his hands that his writing was permanently affected, but, exhausted and disabled though he was, such was his determination that he would still write many-paged letters home the day after Hlobane and Kambula. Depicted as 'tall, gaunt and serious with a long thin nose' by the Queen's Private Secretary[41] when he returned home, it was from this time that his large frame is said to have begun to thicken.

4

RESPONSIBILITY

Writing to Buller before he sailed from the Cape, Wolseley had forecast the welcome he would meet in England:

I am very sorry to hear you arnt up to the work at present, but you have had a hard time and one cannot go on for ever – a [?] will soon set you up and you will find that both you and Wood will be received in England with open arms as you so well deserve. You two are looked upon as the heroes of the war, whose actions have [?] us through the mess and redeemed the reputations of the Army.[1]

He was right. Recognition, honours and a long convalescence all awaited Buller when he landed on 26 August, 1879. The appointment of A.D.C. to the Queen, a distinction which carried with it the rank of colonel, was that further jump in Army rank he had hoped for; to his CB he now added the CMG. In Devon, he received a welcome which today would be given to the winners of the Football Association Cup: at Crediton Station, fog-signals fired a *feu-de-joie* and a cheering crowd dragged his carriage to the front door of Downes. A month later the county honoured him at Exeter with a banquet and the resultant anguish of speech-making.

Shortly after reaching home, Buller, together with Evelyn Wood, was commanded to Balmoral where he and the Queen immediately took to one another. Five years earlier, on his return from Ashanti, he had been commanded to dine at Windsor Castle,[2] but he does not appear to have attended, probably because he was ill. Before they met, he was apt to express his disapproval of his Sovereign with comments such as, 'What can you expect with a woman on the throne,' but after their first meeting he became her lifelong admirer. 'I could talk to her for ever, and as if I had known her all my life,' he told his sister.[3]

Chelmsford had recommended both Wood and Buller to the Queen, telling her, as she wrote in her journal, that he considered them the:

. . .'2 best officers' in my service. Col. Buller he thinks 'one of the finest soldiers of the century', so modest, & reticent, – that it was in fact very difficult to say for what individual deed he had got the Victoria Cross, as he had been doing acts worthy of it, all along the line . . .'[4]

A week later, after she had met and pinned his Victoria Cross upon him, she wrote:

Col. Buller is reserved & shy, with rather a dry, gruff manner. He also, though naturally averse to talking, told me much, that was very interesting. He is very downright, when he does speak, & gives a very direct answer . . . Col. Buller was very modest about himself, saying he got far too much praise.

Evelyn Wood, on the other hand, she thought 'wonderfully lively', attributing his unceasing talk to his deafness; this, she thought, made him unable to hear any general conversation.[5]

Buller had impressed everyone and was 'clever and intelligent and so modest about himself', as the Queen directed a lady-in-waiting to inform his aunt, Lady Suffolk.[6] An exceptionally warm personal note the Queen herself wrote to him after he left is remarkable for her error in twice addressing him as 'Sir Redvers Buller', an honour that still lay in the future.[7] All had been startled by his frankness with his Sovereign and by his even differing from her at times – unlike her courtiers whom he perceived as being 'absurdly afraid of her'.[8] One of them, Sir Henry Ponsonby, her Private Secretary, was to tell his wife that Buller's 'silence – for which he was known – has quite disappeared and he talks away only not so much as Wood'.[9] (This 'silence' was no more than a shyness among strangers. In the company of friends he was what was known as a 'clubbable' man, a member not just of the Naval and Military but Brooks's, the Athenaeum, the Beefsteak and Grillons as well – the last two distinguished by the variety of the interests and callings of their inmates.

Buller had noticed that the Queen always saw Wood and himself separately, and he presumed, undoubtedly correctly, that she did so in order to discover the extent to which they contradicted one another.[10] Their talks certainly touched upon Wolseley, whose radical attitude towards reform she abhorred, as, of course, did the Duke of Cambridge, and whose supercession of Chelmsford had been strongly opposed by them both. In some way Buller and Wood between them seem to have managed, for the time being at least, to have modified the Queen's dislike of their patron: Wolseley's wife, as ever vigilant in watching her husband's interests, was able to inform him that 'The Wood and Buller visit to the Queen and their championship of you did you great good'.[11]

A few days after his Balmoral visit Buller received this letter from Disraeli – by then Lord Beaconsfield:

The Queen wishes me to see you, but it is not merely in obedience to Her Majesty's command, but for mine own honour and gratification, that I venture to say, that, if your engagements would permit you, I should be happy to see you here on the 25th inst.[12]

Seldom can a still youngish soldier have received a more flattering letter from one so distinguished, but the invitation was refused. It was not a question of politics: old-fashioned Whig though he was, Buller's views on imperial matters matched his Prime Minister's. What had upset him was Beaconsfield's refusal to receive Chelmsford on his return to England, a slur that conflicted with Buller's innate loyalty to a chief of whom he was fond, despite his contempt for his professional abilities.

In the general election a few months later, Buller was asked to follow the family tradition and stand as a Liberal in North Devon.[13] He was tempted to do so, but, much as he admired Gladstone in several ways, on some matters he was his vehement opponent.

His leave over, Buller was posted to the 2nd Battalion of the 60th, then serving under Sir Frederick Roberts in the Second Afghan War, but as he was about to embark a peremptory order from the Duke of Cambridge stopped him. Still no more than a regimental captain, Buller's army rank of colonel made him liable to find himself commanding the brigade, a not altogether uncommon but potentially invidious situation. Instead he was despatched to Scotland in April, 1880, as Assistant Adjutant and Quarter-master-General, but after no more than a couple of months he was moved to Aldershot in a similar post. During his time there he attended the German manoeuvres, the first time he had seen armies deployed on a European scale. However, his stay in Aldershot was also short. Early the following year he was on his way back to South Africa where a full-scale war against the Boers was under way.

Much of the blame for this unnecessary conflict can be traced to Wolseley, whose reputation rests on his military abilities both in the field and at the desk rather than his showing as an imperial pro-consul, work for which he had little appetite.[14] His first experience of South Africa dated back to a six-month tour as Governor and Commander-in-Chief of Natal in 1875, hardly a prize for the man whom Disraeli, who had come to power the previous year, was to label as 'our only general'. But it was the first of the steps in Disraeli's grand design to bring together the disparate South African states and tribes into a single British-ruled federation; moreover, it enabled the Duke of Cambridge to rid himself for a time of the bothersome reformer he so thoroughly disliked and distrusted.

To assist him as Governor of Natal, Wolseley took with him several talented members of his 'Ring' who had served him so well in West Africa. Among them were Colley, considered by Wolseley and many others as the ablest man in the army; Brackenbury, mediaeval historian, journalist, part-time war correspondent, military reformer and *Punch* versifier; Lord Gifford who had displayed great skill and gallantry against the Ashanti; and, of course, the irrepresible Butler. All of them outstandingly able, they slipped into their role of government advisers with consummate ease; the last three equally made their mark as philanderers among the not overmodest colonial ladies, who, to Wolseley's despair, found his officers irresistible.

Having recommended the annexation of Zululand, a simple task as Wolseley portrayed it, and having made soundings in the two Boer Republics on the question of federation, he returned to the War Office in the September of the same year to resume his duties as Inspector-General of Auxiliary Forces. As already touched upon, yet another backwater, that of Cyprus, awaited him in July, 1878. Again he was able to select his staff, and although Colley and Butler were not available, he collected Brackenbury, Gifford, McCalmont, Baker Russell and others, much to the rage of Cambridge, from whom both Wolseley's appointment and the selection of his staff had been kept secret.

The Duke had a strong case in his criticism of the exclusiveness of what enemies were describing as the 'Wolseley Gang'. Other able men were being denied their chance to develop their skills, a misfortune for the Army as such; nor was there much encouragement to attend the Staff College when the best staff jobs seemed always to go to a small self-perpetuating coterie. Nevertheless, as is always the case, Wolseley liked to have men around him whom he knew and trusted, and who were used to working together. The reporter, Archibald Forbes, who accompanied him to Cyprus, has described how the hurriedly assembled staff:

> . . . met, blended, and set to work in the saloon carriage between Dover and Calais, as if they had stepped into it out of a department in which they had been co-operating for years. While they settled minor points of detail, their chief meanwhile slept serenely, easy in the perfect assurance, based on experience, that his subordinates would deal with these as he would desire they would be dealt with.[15]

It would be another quarter of a century before the Army's adoption of the General Staff system made such methods standard.

In an eulogistic essay on Wolseley, published in 1885, Forbes postulated that the general's secret was to choose his staff officers so that their abilities matched their individual tasks, but that not all were of exceptional military ability: some, in fact, were dull. In describing each man's qualities, without mentioning their names, Forbes's pictures one of them with 'seemingly no attribute at all, save inertness, a love for gazing on the wine when it is red, and the cultivation of strong language'; in action, however, there arose 'a veritable god of battle – a lambent thunderbolt of war'.[16] This seems to have been a dig at Buller. The names of the several correspondents with whom the latter clashed so vigorously in Zululand have proved elusive, but Forbes was there, working for *The Daily News*. Six years earlier, however, and immediately after that war, in a lecture given at Bradford, Forbes flattered Buller in much the same way as he did Wolseley;[17] perhaps the journalist was then swimming with Buller's current tide of popularity.

To return to Wolseley's second visit to South Africa. When he was switched there from Cyprus to clear up after Isandhlwana, he had taken with him the four members of the 'Ring' already in Cyprus, together with Maurice, to join Buller, Wood and Butler who were already there, the last-named serving on the staff. From India, where he had been expanding his expertise and reputation as private secretary to the Viceroy, came Colley to be chief-of-staff. With the aftermath of Ulundi settled and most of the British troops sent home, much against his will Wolseley was then compelled to remain out there, once again High Commissioner, to further the move towards a federation.

A major step towards British hegemony in South Africa had already been taken with the 1877 bloodless annexation of the Transvaal, two years after Wolseley's first visit. Now, with the Zulus no longer a danger, the Boers were seething with discontent, aggravated rather than alleviated by Wolseley in turn bullying and cajoling them in patently insincere and bombastic terms. Soon, they were refusing to pay their taxes and threatening violent resistance. Such was the state of the country in April, 1880, when Wolseley was at last allowed to hand over to the now Major-General Sir George Colley and return home.

In December, 1880, matters came to a head. The Transvaal Boers proclaimed a republic and with considerable misgivings decided to challenge the might of the British Empire, ambushing a column of troops on its way to Pretoria and besieging several of the small garrisons scattered around the country. In January a 1,000-strong British relief force was defeated at Laing's Nek, the sole viable route from Natal into the Transvaal. British losses were heavy: Boer marksmanship and fieldcraft, and especially their courage, had all been grossly underestimated. Then, a month later on the night of 26 February, 1881, in a further attempt to force the Boer positions Colley himself with 750 men seized Majuba, a towering table-topped hill commanding the Nek. Many of his troops were raw and drawn from a variety of units. In the subsequent disaster when the Boers counter-attacked the hill, Colley, brilliant at a desk but inexperienced and inadequate as a field commander, died. His British regulars broke and fled; a third had been killed or wounded, eighty-nine were made prisoner. The Boers had lost just six men. Evelyn Wood, who had arrived in Durban eighteen days earlier and been despatched north as Colley's second-in-command, subsequently reported to the Duke of Cambridge:

> I start by saying the men did not behave well. They failed to do what our soldiers have so often done, retrieve the bad handling of the officers by indomitable courage.[18]

One officer who had distinguished himself but been seriously wounded was a young Gordon Highlanders subaltern, Ian Hamilton.

By the time Majuba was fought, strong reinforcements had either arrived or were on the way, among them Buller, despatched as senior staff officer to the general commanding at the Cape but hopeful of being diverted up-country to the fighting. However, he consoled himself, as he wrote from the ship, that even if he stayed in Cape Town, his new post should allow him to save enough money to buy new curtains and carpets for Downes – his income, though large, was clearly not unlimited. Frequently his letters home contain mention of plans for improvements to his much-loved house, but against this, he took care how he spent his money.

Buller arrived at Cape Town on 27 February, 1881, only to learn that Colley had been killed that very day – the electric telegraph by then accelerated the receipt of both news and instructions, not just within South Africa but by undersea cable to Whitehall also. The magnitude of the disaster, which he accurately saw as threatening British rule in South Africa, and his sadness at the loss of a dear friend, the grief for whose young wife sitting alone in Government House in Pietermaritzburg was still with him three months later.[19] There, to Natal, he had straightaway been sent as second-in-command to Wood, now Governor and Commander-in-Chief, High Commissioner for East Africa and, perhaps optimistically, Administrator of the Transvaal as well.

Buller's initial reaction was to collect all the available troops, now numbering some 14,000, and attack the Boers. Knowledgeable as both Wood and he were regarding South African warfare, he was confident of success, even though, as he wrote home, 'I hardly think we shall beat them as easily as we ought to,' adding that it was 'easier to persuade a man to fight when he does not want to than it is to keep a man quiet when he wants to fight.'[20]

This tempered optimism was probably justified, but there was small doubt that, before such a war was over, the Orange Free State, as well as many of the Cape Boers, would have been drawn into the conflict. Moreover, the Transvaal Boers had gained in confidence as a result of their successes, although some who had recently served under Buller against the Zulus declared that his presence was worth 10,000 British reinforcements. Gladstone, who had formed his second Liberal administration in April, 1880, so displacing Lord Beaconsfield as Prime Minister, had been violently critical of the annexation of the Transvaal while in opposition and had hinted during his election campaign that its independence would be restored. This naturally raised Boer expectations, which were then flattened after the Liberal success at the polls, when they were offered no more than a measure of self-government.

Majuba, however, proved to be the final battle of that small but – for the British – inglorious war. Impassable communications brought about by continuous heavy rain, combined with the near starvation of one of the isolated British garrisons, led Wood to negotiate a twelve-day armistice starting on 6 March. Nevertheless, he informed the Government that he intended to renew the advance at its conclusion. Like Buller, he sympathized with the Boer case, but recommended that 'decided though lenient action' must be taken[21]. With the granting of independence now a near certainty, Wood saw it as important to British prestige that the Boers should first be driven off Laing's Nek, a part of Natal. Buller, thinking along similar lines, foretold in a letter home that a more serious conflict with the Boers would be inevitable when their independence was restored.[22]

On Government orders, the armistice was prolonged while Wood conducted tortuous negotiations with the Boer leaders. At one such meeting, on 13 March, Wood and Buller were received by a guard of honour composed of former troopers of the latter's old regiment, the Frontier Light Horse; with rather less chivalry, the two British officers seized the chance to view their enemies' positions. At a further meeting, Buller, growing weary of the wrangling over the past, declared, 'Well, it does not really matter what you said; the question is what are you going to do now,' a remark that found favour with some of his opponents. Among them was Paul Kruger, whom Buller recognized as the Boer strong man; another was the suavely sophisticated Piet Joubert, whom Buller described as 'not altogether trusted' by his compatriots and having 'cruel-looking hands' and eyes to match, adding that he feared that 'the Boers have killed a great many Transvaal Kaffirs and have oppressed the rest . . . that has always been their custom'.[23] This was a time when he was giving much thought to the question of so-called just wars, 'those condoned by God to remedy evil,' a theory with which he found fault, contending that mortals can do no more than regret the past and do the best they can for the future.[24]

With both the Boers and Gladstone's government anxious for peace, on 23 March Wood, as directed from home, signed provisional peace terms which were ratified in August; again the Transvaal was a republic, but subject to a vague British 'suzerainty' which was abolished three years later. Meanwhile Major-General Sir Frederick Roberts, on leave in England after his victorious march from Kabul to Kandahar, had been despatched to South Africa to restore British arms. Landing at Cape Town, he had to suffer the ignominy of being rushed out of the country twenty-four hours later by the next available ship. Again Buller and he had failed to meet.

Evelyn Wood's role in all this was to arouse much unmerited obloquy in army and even wider circles, a fate that his second-in-command escaped. Promoted temporary Brigadier-General and acting Major-General on 29 March, four jumps in rank in three years, Buller's reactions were in several ways revealing:

> You will have been surprised at my being made a Major-General; so was I myself, and in truth rather sorry. It puts me over the head of T.D. Baker who will I fear feel it very much, and as I like him and feel he is quite as good if not a better man than I am I think it rather hard upon him, besides he has everything to get from the Army, while as for me I could leave it at any time.[25]

Appointed as Administrator of Natal during Wood's absence in Pretoria as a member of the Royal Commission settling the peace terms, Buller then found himself confined to an office, from which he could escape only at intervals, coping with uncongenial political problems, both complicated and taxing, but which provided him with sound experience for the future. Portrayed at the time by a Natal newspaper as 'A tall, muscular, wiry-looking man, with bronzed face and grizzly beard, clad in an ordinary dark-blue service tunic – the left breast of which blazed with bright-coloured ribbons,'[26] he was fit enough to ride 360 miles from the border to Pietermaritzburg and back in four days, spending fifty-five hours in the saddle.

It was, then, with some relief that he sailed from South Africa in December, 1881, leaving the country at the same time as most of the reinforcements which had arrived with him. A letter, written just before his departure, summarizes his attitudes towards the war:

> I never looked forward with any great keenness to fighting the Boers. I did not mind going out from England for it. I thought then, and still think, that they had begun treacherously, and should be punished. But now it is different. We have condoned their offence, and I really like a good many of them, besides that they have in the long run justice on their side. It would also have been a war from which little credit could be gained, and which would have been an unpleasant one to fight out; for as the Boers had no strategical point the occupation or destruction

of which would render a continuance of the struggle hopeless, we should have had to reduce them by harrying their farms and burning their homesteads: cruel work at the best of times and very cruel against a much-married and much-scattered population like the Boers. So on the whole I am really glad it is over.[27]

A not unperceptive forecast.

Another long leave was his due when he arrived home early in 1882 and reverted to his permanent colonel's rank. While he waited for his next posting, he immersed himself in the care of the estate, every stone of which he knew and loved.[28] Then, at the age of forty-two, he took to himself a wife, one five years younger than himself. Lady Audrey Howard was the daughter of the 4th Marquess Townshend and the widow of Redvers's cousin, the Hon Greville Howard, who had recently died leaving his widow with four small children, two boys and two girls.

Although Buller had long known his future wife, to whose children he was guardian, their friendship changed course only during his three-day visit to her home at Castle Rising in Norfolk, just before he left for that First Boer War. As he admitted to Henrietta, he found Audrey 'so desolate and lonely, poked away in a corner of England, one may say without a friend within reach', that he was concerned that any approach would be mistaken for pity; thus it would be resented were he to declare his affections – which he rather coyly admitted to his sister.[29] Afterwards she noted that although he had women friends, enjoyed the society of some women, and felt that he should marry, he had until then never really fallen in love.[30]

When a man delays marriage into his forties, families can fuss and worry, as did Redvers's siblings. James, when near death, had asked his two surviving sisters to leave Downes as soon as he died because he feared that, if they remained, Redvers would feel the place was still their home and consequently never marry. To allow them to do this he settled an annuity upon them to pay for the rent of a house.[31] Living as mere appendages of the male members of their families, this could be the sad lot of maiden Victorian ladies, and Henrietta, in her journal, never complained at being uprooted from the house where she had been born and lived all her life, but she comments with some poignancy:

'When your brother marries, he is lost to you,' a man, to my surprise, once said to me. Undoubtedly this was in a great measure my case. I gained a sister, who has been a real sister to me. But all passed thro' her, & the fact of her having children of her own took away the right of confidence about their welfare which would have been mine if they had been his own.[32]

But she was able to watch with admiration how Redvers gradually made his wife's children his own, to the surprise and the pleasure of their grandmother and his aunt, Lady Suffolk, who had dreaded the effect on them of the arrival of a step-father.

At the end of the twentieth century a man who fails to marry or delays finding a wife until mid-life is likely to be marked as homosexual; the memories of too many famous men have been scarified by today's writers who allow only a single interpretation of close friendship between two men, especially those of different ages. But in the past government officials and service officers often married in their late thirties and forties: many lacked the money to support a wife; many lived such isolated lives that they rarely met an eligible woman; some were deterred by the inevitability of long separations. Some, of course, were homosexual, but, like their heterosexual colleagues, they often managed to control their desires – in their case because of the abhorrence and disgrace that awaited discovery. Considering the calumny to which Buller has been subjected, he is, perhaps, fortunate, to have escaped being so branded. It could well be, of course, that as with many men, Buller lacked a strong sexual drive, unlike the other members of the 'Ring', whose escapades in South Africa and elsewhere were chronicled with such exasperated amusement in Wolseley's letters to his wife. At no time was Buller numbered among them.[33]

They made a fine looking couple, he in his prime, she a distinguished but demurely modest dark-haired woman, with lovely eyes, a sensuous mouth and a firm nose that matched her husband's. Dr Norman Dixon, the author of a somewhat celebrated work, *On the Psychology of Military Incompetence*, has described as a 'mature and motherly woman' this charming and most attractive woman of the world, whose literary and artistic tastes matched her new husband's. He then proceeds to draw the near unwarrantable conclusion that the marriage was the consequence of Buller's over-devotion to a dead mother whose photograph 'he always carried' (a sinister habit?) and who had kept him 'passive and dependent', a mother-fixation which led to his being over-protective towards his men.[34] The mature can surely be bored by young girls and good officers are protective of their soldiers.

Henrietta commented how her father and Redvers, both shy, reserved and undemonstrative, were attracted by women of a warm, impulsive and demonstrative nature who met them more than half-way, and that both married accordingly.[35] Certainly Redvers was as devoted to his wife as she was to him, and it was to be a supremely happy marriage.[36]

After their wedding, which took place quietly and by special licence at St Margaret's, Westminster, on 10 August, 1882, the couple left for their honeymoon in the Low Countries. That their happiness was clouded by the outbreak of yet another war is made clear by Lady Wolseley's warning to her husband, 'Colonel Buller was married to-day; which I luckily heard of in time to send him his present yesterday. He writes that he has avoided seeing us lest he should express a wish (he feels the wish he says!) to go to Egypt.[37]

When Britain had a war to fight, the cry was 'send for Wolseley'. Hailed by the press as 'our only General', a description coined by his great admirer, Disraeli, he was being affectionately satirized in Gilbert and Sullivan's *The Pirates of Penzance* as 'the very model of a modern major-general'. So it was that when an Egyptian mob massacred 150 Europeans in Alexandria on 11 June, 1882, this popular soldier-hero was straightaway charged with securing the safety of the Suez Canal and ensuring the lives of the 90,000 other Europeans living and working in Egypt.

The opening of the Canal only thirteen years before had even further enhanced the importance of Egypt as the crossroads of the Middle East and the defile that linked Britain with its eastern possessions and interests. Vassals of the Ottoman Empire, the near independent Khedives of Egypt were Albanian in origin and they, together with their land-owning classes, had almost nothing in common with the peasantry, or *fellahin*, whom they savagely oppressed to keep themselves in exorbitant luxury. When the Khedive's international debts at length brought the country to near bankruptcy, Britain and France intervened to protect their investments and set up a system of Dual Control to run the country's finances, so increasing the resentment of the middle-ranking army officers, many of them *fellahin* in origin.

This dislike of both their rulers and foreign intervention led first to a Colonel Arabi Pasha virtually deposing the Khedive and then to a combined French and British fleet entering Alexandria harbour to overawe Egypt's new rulers, a display of force that contributed towards the subsequent June massacre. When Arabi's men so strengthened Alexandria's harbour defences as to threaten the security of the fleets, on 11 July British ships bombarded the defences. Then, as the Egyptian Army withdrew, leaving the mob to loot and burn, parties of sailors and marines were landed to police the city. The French, however, wary of further trouble from Germany, sailed away and took no further part.

Meanwhile, and with startling speed, a British expeditionary force was being collected from the Mediterranean stations, from India and the United Kingdom. On 17 July two regiments from Cyprus landed in Alexandria; thirteen days later the first of a fleet of transports carrying a hastily improvised force of two divisions and corps troops, made up to strength with reservists, sailed from England, followed on 9 August by an Indian cavalry and an infantry brigade from Bombay.

Around Wolseley – now a lieutenant-general and acting general – who reached Alexandria on 15 August, soon collected most of the members of the 'Ring', as always to the aggravation of the Duke. Butler was one of two assistant adjutant and quartermaster generals with Maurice as his assistant. Baker Russell was commanding a cavalry and Evelyn Wood an infantry brigade, with McCalmont serving as Baker Russell's brigade major. But missing were Brackenbury and Buller. The former, having worked in turn as military secretary to the Viceroy of India and military attaché in Paris, had then been switched to a civilian post running the Irish police; almost at once he resigned in the hope of joining Wolseley, but instead found himself on half-pay in his substantive rank of major. It was no more than a temporary set-back to a scintillating career. The newly-wed Buller, on the other hand, needed by Wolseley to head his intelligence, was more easily caught.

So it was that the Bullers' honeymoon was interrupted almost before it had begun by a letter from Wolseley, received in The Hague on 21 August and probably sparked by his wife's news about the wedding. In it Wolseley emphasized that he did not wish to throw temptation into Buller's path so soon after his wedding, but hoped that marriage would not be allowed to interfere with a career of which he prophesied Buller would be proud. '. . . if I had my way I should have given you a Brigade, but the Duke would have all General Officers'. If, nevertheless. Buller wished to join him, he would certainly find something for him to do as a special service officer, abjuring him at the same time 'do not go near Horse Guards nor mention this to anyone if you mean to come.'[38] Wolseley took small pains to avoid annoying his Commander-in-Chief.

It was an invitation impossible to refuse. That night the Bullers returned to England, spent the next day buying his campaign kit, and paid a flying visit to Downes. Four days after leaving The Hague, Buller was able to set out by the swift overland route to Brindisi and arrive in Ismailia by 1 September. 'I confess,' he wrote to his sister, 'I never left England with so heavy a heart.'[39]

Wolseley's problems were much the same as those that confronted the Anglo-French expedition which in 1956 invaded Egypt also to safeguard the Canal (an operation that took months to mount as opposed to Wolseley's weeks). Should operations be confined to the Canal or should Cairo be occupied? Should the initial landings be at Alexandria or should they be directed towards Ismailia, the terminal both for the railway and the Sweet Water Canal, upon which any force on the Canal would depend for its water supply? Unlike 1956, however, the occupation of the Egyptian capital, or for that matter the Canal, would not provoke international outrage.

Assuming that the British would develop their toe-hold in Alexandria and then take the shorter and easier route to Cairo, Arabi Pasha had massed the larger part of his forces in that area, but he had also built strong defence works at Tel el Kebir, between Ismailia and Cairo. For Wolseley secrecy was

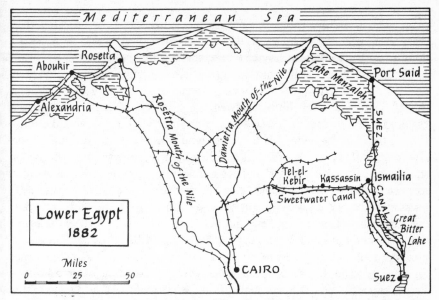

Mediterranean Sea

Aboukir — Rosetta

Alexandria

Rosetta Mouth of the Nile

Damietta Mouth of the Nile

Lake Menzaleh

Port Said

Suez Canal

Tel-el-Kebir   Kassassin   Ismailia

Sweetwater Canal

Great Bitter Lake

Lower Egypt
1882

Miles
0   25   50

CAIRO

Suez

paramount in order to prevent the Egyptian troops being shifted to the Ismailia route and the Sweet Water Canal or even the Canal itself being blocked. Surrounded by a vast corps of inquisitive pressmen, Wolseley took the precaution of avoiding taking even his senior generals into his confidence: careless talk was only too common in the Victorian army, and Alexandria was crammed with spies.

Small probing operations by Wolseley outside Alexandria so successfully deceived Arabi Pasha that when the Royal Navy occupied Suez on 2 August he saw it as no more than a diversion. Then, on 20 August, the British seized Port Said, at the northern end of the waterway, and twenty-three transports, crammed with troops, started south down the Canal for Ismailia. Wolseley's deception had worked.

As the build-up of his force at Ismailia progressed, Wolseley's plan, conceived before he left England, was to move troops and stores forward along the line of the railway to Kassasin, just short of Tel el Kebir. There he would concentrate sufficient strength to destroy the Egyptians barring his way to Cairo and then strike swiftly with his cavalry for the capital, an operation similar to his Ashanti campaign but with mules and railway trucks substituted for porters' muscles. And this time his British troops would be sweating, not under the West Coast's damp heat but the grinding heat of an Egyptian summer, with some still dressed in their thick serge.

Wild exaggerations of Egyptian strengths had made Wolseley increasingly exasperated with his intelligence staff[40], over whose seven officers Buller was put in charge when he arrived at Ismailia. In a letter to his wife written the following day, 2 September, in which he gave her full details of his general's

57

plans (a far from unusual habit among senior officers that did not altogether cease even after 1914), he accurately forecast that there would be much to do but that he would probably be home for the winter.[41]

On 5 September Buller moved up to join the small garrison by then holding Kassasin, his task to reconnoitre and map the Tel el Kebir positions to which Arabi had now himself moved. That night he rode out with a small cavalry escort, so placing himself that at dawn he was just over a mile from the centre of the enemy position and could observe it in the light of the rising sun. This he repeated the following day, but with a couple of squadrons of cavalry, enough to drive in the enemy picquets, and allow him to sketch their southern flank defensive works. Before dawn on the 9th, making a further foray with but a single officer to glean more accurate measurements of distances, he found himself at daybreak on the wrong side of a large body of Egyptian cavalry. As the two fled, Buller's horse began to play the fool and managed to buck him off, but his grip on his reins was fortunately secure. The Egyptian cavalry proved to have been part of a strong force of some 13,000 men making what was to be an unsuccessful attempt to drive the British out of Kassasin. Buller, as ever looking for a fight, mounted a fresh horse when he reached camp and attached himself to the cavalry.

This sortie was Arabi's sole attempt to check the British build-up. Luckily for his enemies, he was a man of small imagination. Traffic along the Canal, the tenuous supply line to Kassasin and the newly-laid pipes bringing water from Ismailia to Port Said might all have been cut or harassed but he did nothing, waiting instead behind the entrenchments at Tel el Kebir, now manned by 25,000 men, for the coming British attack. Against him Wolseley had concentrated rather more than half that number, together with sixty guns. It was now two weeks since the British landing at Ismailia, a seemingly slow rate of progress and one that the press, nettled by the way Wolseley had deceived them, took delight in criticizing. But, as ever, Wolseley was making sure that his preparations were as complete as could be made before he struck.

Because a direct attack over open desert in daylight would clearly be costly, Wolseley decided to advance under cover of darkness, a type of operation unprecedented since the Peninsular War and hazardous indeed for a large body of troops quite untrained for night work who would have to cover four miles in the dark. The boldness of Wolseley's concept aroused misgivings even among his immediate circle and led Buller to recall that he knew of not a single campaign when Englishmen did not fire on Englishmen, and that even in daytime.[42]

But it was upon the accuracy of the intelligence about the massive Egyptian earthworks and the detailed topographical measurements obtained by Buller and his officers that Wolseley depended for success. Precise they proved to be. Buller was also responsible for marshalling the columns and giving each of them their detailed directions, a task which, he confessed to his wife, had made him horribly nervous,[43] understandably so when the outcome of the battle depended so completely on his previous work. Although there were mishaps, the inevitable outcome of such an operation, as dawn broke the British foremost troops were almost into the defence works before the Egyptians had even raised the alarm. Despite stubborn resistance in many places from the Sudanese and *fellahin* soldiers, within an hour the battle was over. Although it ended in a rout, the ever-generous and poetical Buller was to write, 'They died the good death . . . They did not desert the desert, and Egypt will not forget them'.[44] Habitually, during the subsequent century, the British of all classes made a habit of mocking the military qualities of Egyptians, only to be surprised by their courage when they were well led or had something worth fighting for.

British killed and wounded numbered under 500, the exact number Wolseley had forecast beforehand; some 2,000 Egyptian corpses lay strewn about the desert. Arabi's main army had been smashed. By the next afternoon, British and Indian cavalry had reached Cairo, where a further 10,000 Egyptians straightaway surrendered. It was just as Wolseley had planned.

Before the battle Buller had written to his wife, urging her to remember that if anything happened to him:

'The Lord gave, the Lord taketh away, blessed be the name of the Lord.' Let this console you, and the recollection that you have made me inconceivably happy, that during the last year and a half I have known you I have been an altered and am an altering man, and an immeasurably happier one, and this has been your doing . . . this I know that I shall go under fire tomorrow with as light a heart as ever I did.[45]

When describing the battle to his wife afterwards, Buller was to confess that 'he thoroughly enjoyed' the sharp fighting,[46] but after he had mulled over his feelings, he confessed in a further and introspective letter, written just before he returned to England:

I did not somehow feel at all as if I were likely to be shot. It really was very odd. I felt like two people; when I thought of the coming fight my spirits rose and I felt so happy, and then I thought of you and that you might be made miserable, and I felt that it was really wicked to be glad there was going to be a fight. I do believe that it is very wicked and very brutal, but I can't help it. I become just as if I were aerated. I always feel very much ashamed of myself afterwards, but I cannot help it.[47]

One writer drew this aberrant conclusion from Buller's words:

Letters that Buller wrote to his wife reveal that, for him, fighting brought relief to a terrible lust for which he candidly confessed shame. Like a virgin youth lured into a brothel, he suffered agonizing remorse after shooting and killing had apparently given him a form of orgasm, emotional or physical.[48]

As is the way with such material, this odd conclusion in a little-known book was to be repeated by other writers, among them Dr Norman Dixon, both a professional psychologist and a retired soldier, as evidence with which further to denigrate Buller. Laying emphasis on the words 'candidly confessed shame' Dixon adds his professional authority to the suggestion that Buller may have experienced an emotional (whatever that may be) or physical orgasm in battle. The writer further proposes that Buller's love of a fight stemmed from the aggression he had shown as a small child being blocked by 'the gentle injunctions of his anxious mother'; this blocked aggression was as a consequence re-routed in adulthood into violent behaviour towards the 'dark-skinned races whom without distinction he labelled "savages"'.[49]

How many men who have killed in the fear or excitement of battle have not felt shame afterwards? Nor is the enjoyment of fighting uncommon. What is more, it is hard to visualize a rather inhibited and shy late Victorian English gentleman confiding such sexual aberrations to a bride with whom he had enjoyed no more than a fortnight's honeymoon. Buller may have been confessing, but to no more than shame at his enjoyment of battle and to his thoughtless disregard of the unhappiness his death would bring to a wife to whom he was devoted.

But Dixon then goes further, comparing Buller with Himmler, and describing both as having 'a lust for killing and resources of murderous hostility when set against "inferior peoples"'. Both of them Dixon saw as comparable because, among other characteristics, they both had the capacity for efficient administration, together with a proneness to fits of compassion and excessively over-protective feelings. Both Buller and Himmler, he suggests, also possessed a compulsive desire for status and social approval, and the use in times of stress of food and drink as an anodyne for anxiety,[50] failings from which Buller in no way suffered.

But to return to the battle. There had been no rest for Buller after Tel el Kebir. First he was busy arranging the collection and examination of the hordes of prisoners in the immediate aftermath of the battle. Then, the morning after the cavalry occupied Cairo, he reached the city himself, accompanying Wolseley in a captured train and travelling on the footplate with a Sapper so as to keep an eye on its Egyptian driver. Once there, he and Butler, both starving, took a cab to find a restaurant.[51] For so recently captured a city, Cairo was tranquil indeed.

What would today be termed 'military government' then fell to Buller's lot, one in which 'Pashas, Effendis, Prefects, Mudirs, Bimbashis, Beys and all other Turks, Egyptians, infidels and heathen, were hard at me'. Cairo itself did not appeal to him as a city, but the people did, the 'ever-varying ceaseless current in the narrow streets . . . I could look at them for ever'.[52]

Less than two weeks after the battle, British troops were lining the streets of the city for the formal entry of the Khedive, at whose reception the next day Buller admitted to his wife to having been tempted to pocket his gold coffee cup, set with diamonds.[53] In a peaceful atmosphere race meetings were already being organized and Wolseley was able to stand by his promise that Buller would be one of the first to go home.

By early October he was back with his wife in England, having been away for no more than a crowded six weeks.

5

DISTINCTION

The pattern of Buller's inter-campaign breaks in England continued unchanged: honours, a long leave in which to recuperate and enjoy Downes, and then a not too lengthy staff appointment. The reward for Tel el Kebir was a KCMG, the leave lasted until July, 1883, and the staff appointment was that of Assistant Adjutant General at the War Office, again under Wolseley, Adjutant-General since 1881, a post that carried with it much of the power wielded by future Chiefs of the Imperial General Staff (in the next century the by then redundant word 'Imperial' was to disappear).

As for Wolseley, the peerage he had long sought arrived, but disappointingly a mere barony, not the expected viscountcy; with the title came a grant of £30,000, essential to help support its dignity, together with the permanent rank of general. Both as Adjutant-General and Quartermaster-General, the posts Wolseley had previously held, he had fought tenaciously for reforms such as the retention of the short service system, still under fire because some young troops had done badly in South Africa, and officer promotion based on merit rather than seniority. Now after his success in what he saw with justifiable pride as the tidiest little war the Army had ever fought, he began to relax a little, devoting much time to opposing plans to tunnel under the Channel and thwarting the Government's attempts to pull virtually all the British troops out of Egypt.

Buller's previous leave had been marked by his marriage. This one was to see the birth of his only child, a daughter, christened Audrey Charlotte Georgiana, a joy for one with his love of children, but not one for too open enthusiasm. 'The baby is decent,' he wrote, 'and an addition to the household; I am told I ought to admire the Rose of Devon [a prize heifer], but I prefer the baby.'[1] However, a settled family life was still a long way off.

After Tel el Kebir, the problem of Egypt appeared to have been solved, but this was far from so. The Sudan, a vast and near waterless land except for the Nile valley and the equatorial south, produced little but slaves for the markets of the Middle East. It had been conquered after a fashion by Egypt some sixty years before, and since then the northern Sudanese, whose mixed Arab and negro blood had produced a race marked by intelligence, courage and endurance, had smouldered in discontent under the harsh yet inefficient rule of their northern neighbour. Then, the year before Tel el Kebir, a young member of one of the mystical dervish sects whose members boasted descent from the Prophet had proclaimed himself as Mahdi, the redeemer or messiah, who would establish an Islamic kingdom of perfection, a universality of religion and law, in which all opponents, whether Christian, Islamic or pagan, would be slain. As a start the Mahdi's followers began to slaughter the largely ineffective Egyptian garrisons scattered around the country. Worse was to come. After Arabi Pasha's defeat, the new and over-confident Egyptian ministers had despatched in November, 1883, a virtually untrained force of something short of 10,000 *fellahin* soldiers under a retired Indian Army officer, Hicks Pasha, to deal with the Mahdi. Their fate was to be slain, almost to a man.

Sir Evelyn Baring, the future Lord Cromer and previously an *avant-garde* young Gunner officer, one of Cardwell's advisers, and later Finance Member to the Viceroy of India's Council, had been appointed Consul-General in Egypt, in theory to watch British interests but in practice as virtual dictator. His recommendation that the Sudan should be abandoned was accepted with alacrity by Gladstone. But to do so without loss of both face and the large Egyptian and Sudanese garrison of Khartoum posed a near insoluble problem. So it was that the Government sent off to Khartoum in January, 1884, Major-General Charles Gordon, a gallant but too independent a soldier who ten years earlier, in Egyptian service as Governor-General, had given the Sudanese a brief taste of sound and honest rule. His instructions from the British Government were ambiguous, his interpretation of them selective, but to evacuate the garrison was the core of his task.

Meanwhile one of the Mahdi's followers, a prominent slave-trader named Osman Digna, had created havoc among the garrisons in the eastern Sudan, around Suakin. His successes culminated in the slaughter near Trinkitat, some fifty miles south of Suakin, on 3 February, 1884, of yet another large but untrained Egyptian force. In command had been Colonel Valentine Baker Pasha, sent from Cairo to relieve the besieged garrison at Tokar and secure the route from Suakin to Berber, a camel-track to the sea by which both the garrison of Khartoum and its inhabitants, threatened equally by massacre, might be brought to safety.

The widely forecast slaughter of Baker's rabble now obliged the Government, much against its will, to use British troops, as it should have done in the first place. From the Cairo garrison and from units diverted from troopships voyaging home, two regiments of cavalry and five of infantry, together with some Royal Marines, Gunners and mounted infantry, in all about 4,000 men, were collected at Trinkitat. In charge was Major-General Sir Gerald Graham and it was a measure of Buller's reputation that he was now rushed out to the Sudan as Graham's second-in-command and chief-of-staff.

Buller hardly expected the summons. In a letter to his wife, written on 8 February, he had discussed the Cabinet's dilemma:

The Government appears to be quite nonplussed by events in Egypt, and do not know what to do. I must say they deserve their troubles. By crass ignorance, or unreasonable temerity, they have got themselves into a hole whence there is no good avenue of exit, short of sending a force to Suakin, or being turned out next Tuesday, when the vote of censure [in the House of Commons] is moved. If anybody goes to Suakin it will be from Egypt and will not affect me.[2]

The following day he was showing Lord and Lady Wolseley around 29 Bruton Street, his newly acquired London house. Eighteen days later he was in Trinkitat after a slow and wearisome journey in a variety of ships and trains, concerned all the time that Graham would have finished the job before he arrived.

It was a pity that he did not reach Trinkitat sooner. The organization he found there was hardly up to his standards. For example the 65th York and Lancasters, landed the day after he arrived, had been ordered through the Royal Navy to leave their kits on board. It had been assumed that they would be on shore for no more than a day or two as baggage guards, but instead they set off immediately for Fort Baker, three miles inland across a swamp, some of their officers wearing only light boots. That night the tentless and baggageless battalion suffered a savage downpour after a meal of tea and biscuits.

The next day, 29 February, the 65th, ravenous, wet and wretched, set off with the rest of the force to capture a position occupied by Osman Digna at El Teb, some four miles away. Moving in a single large square, half of which Buller had in his charge, Graham's troops took a slightly indirect route so as to avoid the stinking remains of Baker's soldiers littering the ground.

Well armed with captured weapons, including no less than four Krupp guns, three howitzers and a Gatling, the Sudanese opened a brisk and effective fire on the unwieldy square as it neared their position. But when the enemy showed no signs of taking the offensive themselves, Graham gave the order to attack, and slowly and steadily the well-drilled ranks trudged forward through the sweltering heat towards the shallow earthworks. Eventually they were cleared, but not before what Buller described to his

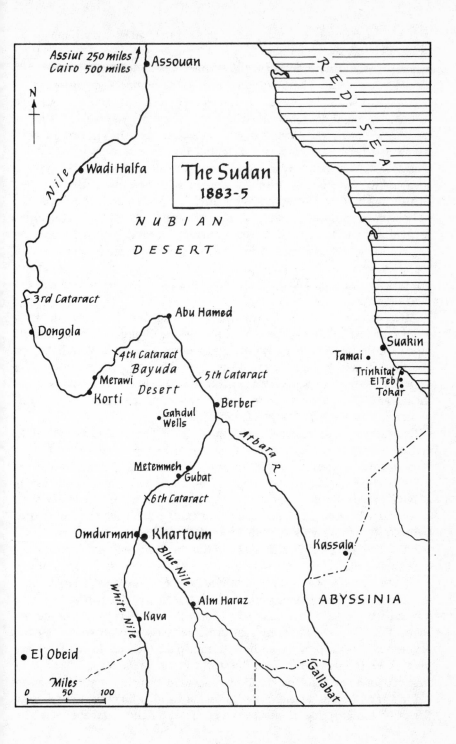

Assiut 250 miles
Cairo 500 miles
●Assouan

N

Nile

●Wadi Halfa

The Sudan
1883-5

NUBIAN

DESERT

RED SEA

⊢3rd Cataract

●Dongola

Abu Hamed

⊢4th Cataract
Bayuda
●Merawi   Desert
Korti

5th Cataract

Tamai ●

Suakin●

Trinkitat●
El Teb●
Tokar●

●Berber

●Gakdul
Wells

Arbara R.

Metemmeh
●Gubat

X6th Cataract

Omdurman● ●Khartoum

Kassala●

ABYSSINIA

Blue Nile

White Nile

●Alm Haraz

●Kava

● El Obeid

Miles

0   50   100

Gallabat

wife as 'a very pretty bit of hand-to-hand fighting'. It was a scrimmage he would like to have joined but could not, because, as he put it to her, 'for a general it would have been *infra dig*, and I had to look on. I told you I should be quite safe. I shall never have any more fighting, I am afraid!'[3]

Not only had the Sudanese fought with their customary courage, but they had shown sound discipline, their retreat being in no way a rout. What is more the British cavalry, commanded by Brigadier-General Herbert Stewart, which had been held outside and behind the square, ready to tackle the Sudanese as they retreated, suffered heavy casualties through charging too soon and too impetuously. Although the two sides were about the same size, British losses at El Teb numbered nearly 200. Later 825 Sudanese bodies were counted, probably 1,500 died. Few prisoners were taken. No Sudanese surrendered and the wounded would attempt desperately to spear or knife any British soldier who came within reach, shamming death in order to do so. They were, as Buller afterwards wrote to the uncle of a young cavalry officer who had been killed, 'the smartest savages I have ever seen and the most desperate'.[4]

After occupying Tokar, evacuated by Osman Digna's men, Graham's force returned to Trinkitat on 5 March, where Buller, reverting to staff officer, spent the next four days and nights embarking for Suakin the troops and the 850 camels – a far more taxing task. After a few days to eat, wash off in the sea the filth of a week's campaigning and sleep in the tents awaiting them, on 11 March the force set off for Tamai, fifteen miles to the south-west, to strike another blow at the Sudanese.

Because the square formation adopted at El Teb had proved hard to control, Graham now arranged his force into brigades, each moving in a separate square with the cavalry outside. After a night being sniped at in bivouac – the Sudanese shot well – the two brigades moved out across ground broken by dry watercourses to assault the enemy positions with Buller's 1st Brigade echeloned about 700 yards behind the leading square, the front face of which was made up of three companies of the 42nd Royal Highlanders (the Black Watch) and three of the York and Lancasters.

Soon the British soldiers were able to pick out the black forms of the Sudanese ranged along the hills ahead and, as they approached a deep ravine, the 2nd Brigade came under fire. It was then that Graham, who was with this square, displayed his incapacity. Some 200 yards from the ravine, he shouted 'Forty-second, charge', an order obeyed only too readily by the aggravated Highlanders whom he had unjustifiably criticized to their faces for their performance at El Teb. But it was a trap. Graham had lifted the lid from his solid box of infantry, and into it poured a horde of several thousand hidden dervishes, spear and sword in either hand, who curved around the flanks of the charging Highlanders and Yorkshiremen, flooding into the square. Several parties stood firm, fighting for their lives, but the rest fell back, a struggling mass, the confusion furthered by the thick black smoke hanging in the still air. It was the occasion later to be commemorated in Kipling's stirring lines:

An' ere's to you, Fuzzy-Wuzzy, with your 'ayrick 'ead of 'air –
You big black bounding beggar for you broke a British square!

A debacle similar to Hicks's and Baker's threatened.

But Buller's 1st Brigade, although attacked on all four sides, was to save the day. Handling his units in a masterly manner, Buller directed a heavy cross fire into the flanks of the massed dervishes, so slackening the pressure on the 2nd Brigade that its shattered units managed to rally and re-form. Buller's Brigade then successfully assaulted the now disheartened Sudanese. What seemed almost certain disaster had been turned into victory. In the end British killed and wounded again numbered little more than 200, one tenth of the Sudanese losses.

In this second action Buller had been far more closely involved than at El Teb, something he failed to reveal to his wife, although he did admit that he had once again been lucky: a bullet had penetrated his charger's ear, one from a random volley fired by Royal Marines in the other square which so unsettled his men that he had been forced to ride out in front to rally them. At no time was Buller ever seriously wounded on a battlefield.

Despite the exhilaration he gained from battle, he was as always sympathetic towards whoever he happened to be fighting. A letter to his wife after El Teb, read:

I cannot believe there will be another fight. I really hope there will not be, for these poor devils are plucky fellows, and one of them is worth a dozen Egyptians, and I would much rather be on their side than on the Egyptian one.[5]

This was not an uncommon attitude. A press report remarked on a similar sentiment current among the officers of the York and Lancasters.[6] It was their adjutant's first taste of war, something he had longed for. But the death of close friends and soldiers he knew well shocked him. Like Buller, in the future he was to be known for the way he husbanded men's lives. His name was Herbert Plumer, victor of Messines, viscount and field-marshal.

Writing after El Teb, Wolseley encouraged his friend:

You know without my saying so, how proud I am of your success and how glad I am when you have the opportunity of showing the stuff you are made of. I have kept Lady Audrey informed of all the news we received – that has not however been enough, as Graham tells us as little as possible – a very wise precaution *before* fighting but one that might with advantage be dispensed with after such a success as he has had.

The letter ended with advice to send a long account of the battle to the Duke of Cambridge, as 'he loves to receive letters from officers in the field'.[7] But Buller had already done so;[8] again, after Tamai, he wrote a further uninhibited account of the battle to the Duke, in which he spared no one except General Graham, and was especially blunt about the Royal Marines, who 'behaved very badly'.[9]

Despite much arduous marching and counter-marching, for the time being fighting in the eastern Sudan was at an end and the British troops left as planned. As a contemporary historian was to write: 'The ill effects of the withdrawal . . . upon the rebellious tribes cannot well be exaggerated. Notwithstanding their repeated defeats they easily persuaded themselves that they had driven the English out of the country.'[10]

So Buller was home by mid-April, having been bored during his last few days in Suakin through a lack of reading matter. In his rush of departure, he had left behind his 'constant campaigning companion', a cabinet edition of Shakespeare, but at the last minute he had pushed into his baggage two volumes of Charles Lamb.

The qualities Buller had displayed were well summarised by Graham, who gave him full credit for his success. The official despatch describes:

. . . his coolness in action, his knowledge of soldiers and experience in the field, combined with his great personal ascendancy over both officers and men . . .[11]

His reward was promotion to the permanent rank of major-general at the remarkably early age of forty-four. At last the Army was recognizing talent, not mere seniority.

Another example of Buller's unfortunate foibles was again displayed in the aftermath of the campaign. A journalist who tackled him for an interview soon after he landed received this:

Sir, I have been handed your letter of the 22nd, and have to thank you for the compliment implied therein. I trust you will not think me discourteous, but I hold such very decided views as to the impropriety of Officers on the Active List communicating their opinions to the Press that I must ask you to allow me to decline the interview you ask for.

'Impudent scoundrel' and 'rascal' were the soubriquets with which he abused the poor man in private.[12]

Once again Buller's stay in England was short. On 26 August he was off, back again to the Sudan. There Gordon, instead of evacuating the country, had manoeuvred the British Government into despatching a large expedition to rescue him from Khartoum. There he was now besieged, the Nile, his only escape route, barred to him because his steamers could hold no more than a handful of his troops, let alone the many civilians whom he refused to abandon to the Mahdi's mercies.

The decision to send the expedition had been delayed by Gladstone's Cabinet vacillating until late August, despite an emotional parliamentary and press campaign. Nevertheless, Wolseley, as Adjutant-General, had since February been drawing up his plans. A three-man committee, its members Buller, unemployed since his promotion, and two other Red River veterans, Butler and McNeill, mulled over the different routes by which a force might reach Khartoum. The shorter one was by Suakin and Berber, a mere 245 miles, but across near waterless desert. The alternative was the Nile valley, 760 miles by rail and river steamer to Wadi Halfa followed by a further 666 miles to Khartoum. Expert opinion, both in Egypt and Whitehall, was split on the subject, but it was hardly surprising that Wolseley's rather over-weighted committee came down strongly in favour of the river route.

So it was that a Red River type operation was set under way, albeit on a rather different scale and influenced much by the administrative lessons learned against the Ashanti. Over 11,000 men were collected, but of these it was planned to deliver only three battalions at Korti, eighty miles beyond Dongola. From there the assault on Khartoum would be launched. With these three battalions would be an 1,100-strong Camel Corps, raised in England from volunteers, forty from each of fifteen cavalry regiments and Foot Guard battalions, together with 300 from the three regiments of Household Cavalry as well as small numbers from several line regiments. The balance of the 11,000 would be tied down, garrisoning Cairo and Alexandria and guarding the long communications. The proportion of 'tooth' against 'tail' foreshadowed the future.

As had been done in Canada, special boats were built, four hundred whalers, each to carry a twelve-man crew up river from Wadi Halfa onwards. They were to be strong enough to tackle the six reaches of cataracts through which the Nile poured and each would carry supplies for 100 days, packed in sixty-pound loads for the many portages that lay ahead. These loads were to be delivered intact at Korti, supplies for the journey being found from a series of depots set up along the line of march. And, as on the Red River, Canada was to provide *voyageurs*, some 400 of them; ignorant of the trade though many were found to be, on the whole they were to perform a sound job of work, as did the Kroomen who had served Wolseley well in the Ashanti and who were also brought in as boatmen.

Not until the last moment did the Cabinet decide who was to command the expedition. The Duke of Cambridge favoured the appointment of one of the generals already in Egypt, leading Wolseley bluntly to declaim:

> To select for command of this contemplated expedition General Earle, of whose capacity for command we know literally and absolutely nothing, and whose name is totally unknown to the Army and will not therefore impress our rank and file with confidence, whilst you could give that command to General Buller, whose name is known to every bugler in the Army, who has proved his capacity as a leader in war . . . This a policy that is incomprehensible to me. How many of our worst disasters are traceable to the adoption of such a policy.[13]

The compromise reached was that Major-General Earle, who was much senior to Buller, would command any force that moved south of Wadi Halfa with Buller as his Chief-of-Staff; in overall charge would be General Sir Frederick Stephenson, commanding in Egypt.

Buller agreed with Wolseley. He had dined with the Queen at Osborne five days before he left; as her journal shows, his manner was unchanged:

> I had some conversation with Sir Redvers Buller, who was very plain spoken. He is not pleased at being sent out to Egypt under Gen: Earle & would rather not go out at all, or else, have had the command of the whole.[14]

However, the clash that had developed between Stephenson and the Adjutant-General over the Nile route was such that Gladstone agreed at the end of August to Wolseley himself being given the job, much to the displeasure of the Duke and the Queen, the acclaim of the general public and the recipient's happy surprise.

The news of Wolseley's appointment, which reached Buller before he left, inspired him with confidence. Just six days after he reached Cairo, Wolseley overtook him and the next day announced that his old colleague was to be his Chief-of-Staff and Evelyn Wood his General in Charge of Communications south of Assiut. With Brackenbury, Butler, McCalmont and the polymath Herbert Stewart all there, the Ring was gathering. But it was no longer the same smooth machine. As Wolseley put it in his journal:

> All my old companions, men whom I brought on – E Wood – Redvers Buller, Brack, Butler &c are now reaching that age & standing in the service when it is difficult to place them in a small Army in the field, and when there, each and all are so jealous of the other, that the team is difficult to drive.[15]

Both this journal and Wolseley's letters to his wife are marked by harsh and often bitter criticisms of staff and subordinates, sometimes merited but often ungenerous towards old comrades loyally serving him. They reveal someone under great strain, coping with what seemed near insuperable problems and usually living in what was considerable discomfort for a man in his fifties.

It was William Butler, impulsive, bumptious and dogmatic, who first aroused Wolseley's ire and who first suffered the rough edge of his tongue. Butler, in charge of the boats, an onerous task, complained to Wolseley that Buller 'did not consult him more . . . and follow his advice', and also that he was 'determined . . . to be an outsider'.[16] Butler's talent, Wolseley decided, was erratic and he 'can neither work in any ordinary groove, nor work in harmony with other members of a team'.[17] For Buller's old and close friend not just to complain directly to Wolseley, but to go so far as to suggest also that some of the staff were determined that the expedition should fail suggests that the strain upon him had become too much.

Buller's further problem was Wood, another very old friend. The absence in the British Army of a proper staff system resulted in the respective duties of Chief of Staff and General in Charge of Communications being ill-defined. Nor did Wolseley clarify them. The result was a series of disagreements between Buller and Wood, culminating one evening in an open clash in front of Wolseley who noted that Buller appeared to have 'had a little too much liquor on board for he entered into a noisy altercation with Wood'.[18] But it was for Wood that Wolseley reserved his special venom, prejudiced, as he did admit, over what he described as the 'disgraceful peace he made with the Boers in 1881'.[19] Wolseley always acknowledged Wood's gallantry, but the journal is scattered with largely unjust accusations of vanity, cunning, flattery, puzzle-headiness, intrigues with the press, popularity seeking and administrative incapacity.

Wolseley was right in deploring this concentration of too many senior and ambitious officers, but he had himself brought it about.

At first Buller was not among those Wolseley disparaged. In a letter to the Duke of Cambridge, Wolseley wrote:

The longer I live, the more I realize how very very few men there are with brains so organized as to enable them to look at affairs from a war point of view. It is a peculiar organization of the brain . . . a rare gift . . . with difficulty if at all acquired by education. Sir Redvers Buller has it, and therefore is invaluable as a Chief of Staff; but I could count over on the fingers of one hand all the men I know of in the Army who possess this invaluable gift.[20]

But as problems proliferated in the coming weeks, Wolseley began to complain about Buller too, going so far as to declare that he would never have him again as his Chief of Staff. 'He always raises objections to every proposal, although in the end he comes round to it . . . No one does right but himself: he thinks of everything . . . in fact all the world are fools & he alone is wise. He would make a much better fighting General than a Staff officer . . . He is too fond of argument.'[21] What especially annoyed Wolseley was Buller's habit of 'crabbing' the ability of Herbert Stewart, Wolseley's closest personal friend and an officer whom he held in particular regard.[22] Perhaps Buller remembered Stewart's inadequate handling of the cavalry at El Teb.

This remark in a letter to his wife, written some weeks after he arrived is both characteristically modest and also reveals his capacity for self-awareness:

> . . . Wolseley allows me as much responsibility as I choose to accept. I think I have the situation that about suits me best, one, that is, involving all the responsibilities of execution with those of invention and preliminary organization. I never have credited myself with much ability on the inventive side; all mine, if I have any, is on the executive side, and possibly if I have a strong point it is resource, which is a great help in execution.[23]

He had made a very similar comment to his sister, Lucy, when he was serving under Wood in Natal. 'Chief of the Staff', he wrote, 'is a very nice position you have all the power of the General & none of the responsibility although of course I have to try to save Evelyn trouble as far as I can and when ever I can'.[24] The immodesty of his words to the Queen before he left had been quite out of character.

As he coped with the preparations, Buller at times seemed to be less than enthusiastic about the campaign. Despite his relish for the danger and excitement of battle, together with the satisfaction he found in exercising his profession, he disliked war as such, abhorring the suffering it entailed both for soldier and civilian. In a letter written four weeks after he arrived, he declared that he was convinced there would be no fighting, a remark described by an earlier biographer to have been 'an illustration of a besetting foible' – his habit of making similar comments before campaigns, the wish being father to the thought.[25]

It has also been said that this luke-warm approach was due to a lack of sympathy for Gordon so pronounced that he went as far as to query whether 'the man was worth the camels'. There is small doubt, however, that the 'man' to whom he referred was an officer who early in the summer had produced a hare-brained scheme to use a small force of camel-riding volunteers to bring Gordon out of Khartoum.[26] Although the two had never met, Buller certainly admired Gordon's fine military qualities and his ability to win the loyalty of the Sudanese, whom he had governed – to use Buller's own words – by 'the summary and almost irrational exercise of arbitrary power'.[27]

During their journey up the Nile to Wadi Halfa, begun on 27 September, Wolseley and Buller, after an initial glow of interest, soon became bored with the sameness of both the river and the antiquities, comparing the latter to their disadvantage with an English cathedral. At the same time, the plight of the Egyptian peasants, ground down by an iniquitous land tax, evoked Buller's deep compassion.[28] But their arrival at Wadi Halfa brought them sharply back to the realities of the campaign. There they learned that Gordon's three European officers, sent out of Khartoum with his diaries and code-books on 10 September in a steamer, had been murdered six days later. From the scraps of messages which Gordon still managed to smuggle through, it was now clear that his position was critical and that Khartoum might well fall before the relief force could arrive.

Little, however, could yet be done to hasten matters. The first of the 800 whalers had arrived at Alexandria from England on 22 September, only six weeks after the orders had been placed with the builders. From there they were moved by train to Assuit, by barge to Assouan, and in tow behind river steamers to Wadi Halfa. Egyptian soldiers then portaged the craft around the Second Cataract at Wadi Halfa; there the troops were embarked, together with their Canadian so-called 'voyageurs' – Indians, lumbermen, even middle-class professionals, but far better material than their Red River predecessors. From the Second Cataract onwards the troops struggled to sail, row and pole their craft upstream towards Dongola. Thither Wolseley moved on 24 October, so losing touch with his Chief-of-Staff, who was to see him for no more than eight hours in the next two months, so adding to the latter's many problems.[29]

Delays now occurred, one of the more serious being the halting of all steamer traffic for five days in October through a lack of coal. In a startling innovation, all transport between Cairo and Wadi Halfa had been left in the hands of the travel agents, Thomas Cook & Sons, who charged the Government £21 per passenger for the full journey. As happens, the contract between agent and War Office had been loosely written: the inevitable argument ensued. Buller, who had not been told the facts, learned of the possible delay on 18 October and time was lost in a barren discussion with the Senior Commissariat Officer before the matter was resolved. Wolseley blamed Buller, and himself as well, for not having checked personally:

In dealing with a Chief of Staff in whom one has every confidence I feel too much inclined, I know, to give him a free hand . . . The result has been in this one respect unfortunate.[30]

But the root cause of the delay lay again in the British Army's lack of system and Wolseley's failure to clarify responsibilities, particularly those of Wood and Buller. Lower down the hierarchy it was much the same. Wolseley had removed from his Senior Commissariat Officer responsibility for transport and attached him, not to Buller's but to Wood's staff; at the same time he had appointed a separate and inexperienced officer as Director of Transport, suggesting but not making it clear that the functions of supply and transport had been separated.[31] It is perhaps surprising that Buller, faced with such split roles and a faulty War Office contract, took no more than four days to get the coal moving again.

On 13 November a message reached Wolseley from Gordon that his food would be finished by mid-December, news that made it plain that relief by the river route could not reach him in time. This Buller had already foreseen, recommending to his chief only the week before that a force should move directly across the desert by camel from Korti to Metemmeh on the Nile, some 100 miles north of Khartoum, so cutting off the great loop made by the river as it swung east to Berber.

As ever, Buller's thoughts on this were spelt out in a long letter that ends:

The objection is that we would reduce our fighting force to 3,000 men at the outside, and it is a question whether that is enough. I think it should be. I have not an idea what Wolseley means to do, but I think he must do something of that sort.[32]

That complaint was based upon Wolseley's failure to keep him properly in the picture during their long separation. Not until Christmas Eve, when he joined Wolseley at Korti, where the infantry battalions were now collecting, did he learn that his chief had at last made up his mind to act on the lines he had recommended seven weeks before. The Camel Corps and supporting troops, under Stewart, were now to move directly across the desert to Metemmeh, while three infantry battalions, with Earle in charge and Brackenbury as his second-in-command, continued their river journey. Again Buller confessed his misgivings, the clarity of his English collapsing as often happened in those long personal letters written when hurried or stressed:

I am sorry that Wolseley did not make up his mind sooner. I could have done him much better than he will be now, but he has so persistently said that we must go by water and that he must put at least 5,000 men at Shendi, that I have been put off my idea, and have been doing my best to prepare for his. Consequently he has not here either the men, the camels, or the food I should have liked to have had for the operation he proposes . . . The expedition we are going on will be severely criticised, and partially justly so, for Lord Wolseley has, I think, quite forgotten that I was not in touch with his mind during the last two months, and consequently it was out of my power to follow his line of thought . . . one does not like to do bad work, when one is conscious that one could have done better. However, I have patched it up as well as may be, and we shall do pretty well, I think.[33]

The main problem was the shortage of camels, only 8,000 having been bought before Wolseley and Buller arrived – some 2,000 to 4,000 less than were needed. The purchasing officers were also quite ignorant of the abstruse art of camel-buying from Arabs: many animals were already old and worn out. Of the rest most were to be ruined by the ignorance of the cavalry troopers, one matched unfortunately by the Commissariat and Transport Corps.[34] But, as Buller had anticipated, it was he who was to be criticized for the camel shortage.[35] Later he tried hard to buy or hire extra camels at Korti, but could obtain no more than a few.

The consequence was that Stewart lacked the animals to move his force and his supplies in one body. Leaving Korti on 30 December with 1,100 men and 2,000 camels, he established a base three days later at the Gakdul Wells, ninety-five miles away, before returning to Korti with the animals to pick up a further 1,400 men with more supplies and be back at Gakdul on 12 January. From there two days later he set out on the final eighty-one mile march to the Nile with 3,000 camels, many now half-dead from over-work and lack of food, carrying 1,600 men, their equipment and their supplies.

Sixty waterless miles further on, just short of the wells at Abu Klea, Stewart found the Sudanese barring his way. The next morning, 17 January, on foot and formed into square, his force advanced towards the water upon which existence depended. Once again the impulse of the dervish charge broke the British square, once again the Gardner gun jammed, but once again units rallied and drove their enemies out. Losses, however, numbered eighteen officers and 140 soldiers, a high proportion of the small force.

That night the parched men of the Camel Corps, their thickened tongues filling their mouths, quenched their thirsts in the muddy, yellow water of the wells. The following day they reached the Nile, but only after another grim battle in which Stewart was mortally wounded in the groin.

The Household Cavalry had relished the chance of showing their fighting qualities in this, their first battle since Waterloo. Nevertheless, Buller, with all the infantry prejudices, was to be critical of the performance of some of the cavalry, reserving his praise for the few Mounted Infantry present and commenting, with some justification, that Wolseley had been unwise to 'pick Cavalry men to do Infantry work'.[36]

With Stewart dying, command of the force had passed to Colonel Sir Charles Wilson, in the opinion of Percival Marling, a young cavalry officer, 'rather an old woman who doesn't know anything about drill, and funks responsibility',[37] a not too uncharitable comment. On 24 January, a week after Abu Klea, Wilson embarked with a party of men for Khartoum in two of Gordon's steamers he had found waiting for him. On 28 January he came level with the city, only to be met by shouted imprecations and shell-fire. Three days earlier 40,000 Mahdiists had stormed and sacked the place. Gordon had been speared on the steps of his palace: Wolseley's expedition had failed.

Meanwhile Wolseley, when at last he learned of Stewart's wound, despatched Buller on 29 January to take charge of the desert column and appointed Wood as Chief-of-Staff in his place. Wolseley's orders to Buller – the preamble to which read 'Above all things don't get wounded. I can't afford to lose you' – were merely to clear the enemy out of the Metemmeh neighbourhood, without locking too many men up in holding the place, and to be ready to co-operate with Earle in an attack on Berber.[38]

As Buller rode out to take over his new command, now based upon the village of Gubat, near Metemmeh, behind him marched a battalion of the Royal Irish Regiment, whose speed and stamina on their feet suggested that the Camel Corps had all along been an unnecessary and expensive luxury. With him travelled a young Sapper, Major Herbert Kitchener, his burgeoning reputation based upon his intelligence work in Arab disguise; another future field-marshal who at the time caught Buller's eye was a cavalryman, the then Major John French.

On 3 February, while Buller was still at Gakdul, the news of the fall of Khartoum reached him on its way through to Wolseley. The latter's subsequent letter to Buller reveals how badly shaken he was:

The news of the fall of Khartoum has indeed been a blow to me – poor Gordon. Practically with its fall my mission ends, and its fall leaves me without instructions. If we were two months earlier, to go on and engage the Mahdi would be easy, but to do so now would mean to keep all my force in the Sudan for the hot weather, which would I think be a dangerous risk to run. I think it is quite certain we shall be ordered back to Egypt, surrendering the Sudan to its fate . . . This is a sad end to all our hopes and work. I feel like a beaten cur. Your sincere friend, – Wolseley.[39]

So began a rain of often daily and sometimes twice-daily letters with which Wolseley bombarded Buller, instructions at times imprecise and at others conflicting. First Metemmeh was not to be attacked lest the number of wounded awaiting evacuation should be increased, then Buller was being told to tackle it as a preliminary to capturing Berber and opening up the Suakin-Berber route to the interior. And so it went on, but at the same time, as the man on the spot, Wolseley gave his old colleague a free hand, his personal affection clear from the informality of letters ending in terms such as 'God bless and protect you, my dear Buller'. On 12 February he writes: 'I can't do without you . . . Evelyn, anxious to serve and always cheery don't suit me as C of S';[40] four days later he was insisting 'It is not only me but everyone in this army and at home, all look to you as the coming man in the army'.[41] Criticize Buller as Wolseley often did in his waspish journal, there is small doubt that he liked, admired and valued him as staff officer, fighting soldier and friend.[42] But Wolseley's criticisms, often quoted out of context, were to be put to good use by Buller's detractors.

However, when Buller reached Gubat on 11 February he found the remnants of the desert column short of supplies and their few remaining camels almost as worn out as their shoddy boots – bayonets that bent against bone were among the complaints about other shoddy stuff. Dejected by the conditions and the expedition's failure, morale was poor, but as always Buller's mere presence invigorated the weary troops; typical was the young Marling, who, after Stewart was wounded, would write, 'If only Buller had been with us'.[43] Nevertheless, with an estimated 5,000 to 6,000 dervishes in or near Metemmeh, Buller wasted no time in deciding that there was no question of attacking the place and that he must fall back to Abu Klea.

So it was that on 12 February Buller sent off his sick and wounded to Korti, escorted by 300 of his best men; two days later the rest of his force was back at the Abu Klea wells, sniped at effectively by the dervishes and rationed to a quart of stinking water daily. In one of his long letters to his wife, which like so many others, seem to have been written with the object of preserving a detailed record of the campaign, and with which he enclosed almost everything he received from Wolseley, Buller wrote of his amusement at:

> the way some of these gay young men who have come out here medal hunting have got sold. There are some real good soldiers among them but there are others who would never have been here had they the least idea they were going to be kept here for the summer.[44]

One whom Buller had spotted as a 'real good soldier' was the thirty-three-year-old Earl of Dundonald, in command of the 2nd Life Guards detachment, who had guided back the first column of wounded after Abu Klea. In this, his introduction to war, he had been shattered by the battlefield's horrors and Wilson's subsequent failure to provide firm leadership. On meeting his new commander at Gakdul, he had:

> . . . remarked to Sir Redvers, who was a very kind-hearted man . . . that much seemed to be very wrong in the world, for here were the Arabs practising fearful acts of cruelty and enforcing slavery on the black people, and here was this same black people whom we wished to liberate fighting against us with fanatical hatred, and it seemed impossible to get into their minds that we were friends.

Buller, Dundonald recorded, agreed with him, but suggested that perhaps it was better not to think too much about it all, but just do their duty.[45]

Bemused by Wolseley's instructions, the aggravated Buller in the end let his temper slip and penned Wolseley an ill-tempered and sarcastic letter, in which he discussed how Berber might be taken with bootless men and a few half-dead camels.[46] Aggravated though he was, Wolseley replied sympathetically:

> . . . The taking of Berber this season is out of the question . . . I want you back here. No tent, the want of a professional staff, the dust storms, and my cypher have ruffled you somewhat, but a glass of Nile water with a little of my horribly fiery whiskey in it will set you up. I envy you being fired on all night. I believe that even the distant smell of gunpowder would brighten me up more than anything else at the moment.[47]

Those discomforts were to some extent self-inflicted because, to the exasperation of those around him, Buller insisted on sharing the hardships of his men – as he had done on the veldt. On the other hand, when he could do himself well, he did. At Wadi Halfa his table was known for its excellence. Forty camels were said to have been needed to move his baggage, but he was not alone in this: Wood's tents, camp furniture, food and wine filling ninety-six packing cases.[48] Even as far forward as Korti Buller could still offer his guests champagne and quite lavish food.[49] Much has been made of this, for there is small doubt that Buller was becoming self-indulgent and starting to put on weight. But in the field he lived hard, unlike others. Officers of one fashionable regiment were said even to have smuggled wine[50] as far forward as Gubat – almost certainly champagne, then judged a near essential stimulant and tonic. For years to come British officers would boast that 'any fool can be uncomfortable', and usually suit the action to the word.

By the time Wolseley's gently worded reprimand reached Buller, he was back in Gakdul, having evacuated Abu Klea on 23 February, just as 8,000

78

fresh enemy reinforcements appeared in front of the vital wells. During the three-day march, Buller's steady and untroubled demeanour inspired his almost barefoot, but now confident men. Nonetheless, it was fortunate that the dervishes failed to follow up the retreat. This was in part due to the British having filled in the Abu Klea wells, so depriving their enemies of water. For this Buller was later to be harshly criticized, interference with wells being judged unethical. He had, in fact, only agreed under pressure from his more hard-headed subordinates, among them Kitchener. In any case, Wolseley had actually ordered it to be done.[51]

Having extricated the battered desert column to Gakdul, a task Buller described as the most difficult he had tackled,[52] Wolseley brought him back to Korti on 27 February, once more as his Chief-of-Staff, having already despatched Wood to complete the evacuation, now no more than routine work. Buller's critics were to accuse him of vacillating both at Gubat and at Abu Klea.[53] This is hard to justify. At Gubat he had acted with speed and decision. A six-day delay at Abu Klea was due to the need to wait for camels to be brought up for the sick and wounded, and the stores needed for the journey back.

The River Column had already been ordered back as well, with Bracken-bury now in command, Earle having been killed in a sharp battle fought when it was still 150 miles short of Berber. Among its officers was that young Ian Hamilton, who had been badly wounded at Majuba, and was later to be remembered as the unsuccessful commander of the hurriedly prepared and ill-equipped 1915 amphibious landing at Gallipoli, with which his reputation was so unhappily to be linked. Versifier, essayist, military thinker, artist and humorist, Hamilton, in an autobiographical volume, has left a light-hearted account of the Nile campaign. A confidant of Roberts, whom he had served as Assistant Military Secretary in India, as an outsider – an 'Indian' – Hamilton viewed with a mixture of awe and envy 'that awful enemy Ring', of which Buller was 'the evil genius'.[54] Jumping his leave-bound ship at Cairo, Hamilton nevertheless discovered an unexpected generosity in Buller, who, recognizing ability, allowed him to join the expedition. At the time Hamilton found it hard to avoid admiring this 'evil genius', both as an administrator and for his handling of troops, which he likened to that of his patron, Roberts. What is more, he was to discover that Buller had insisted that his new commanding officer should take him up river and not leave him at base.[55]

Hard desk work was Buller's lot on his return, coping with the manifold problems of a weary and beaten force strung out along the Nile valley. Because the Government failed to decide finally until June to abandon the Sudan, the decision being taken largely because of a renewed Russian threat to India, preparations were in hand for a further campaign, either in the grinding summer heat or the autumn. Life for Buller was made even more difficult by Wolseley's departure for Cairo, leaving him again out of touch and in the dark as to his intentions. This lack of contact resulted at one point in the Secretary of State signalling Buller direct for his opinion. In his reply, as he admitted to his wife, he had described them as

> military madness, political suicide and sanitary murder . . . it seems to have fetched them as rather an over-coloured criticism on their plans [sic], but one cannot be picking and choosing one's words in a temperature of 100°. However, I cannot help fearing that I have been rather like a bull in a china shop.[56]

He probably had. However, Wolseley had bequeathed the final evacuation of the Sudan to him:

> . . . who can estimate what a loss to our nation Sir Herbert Stewart will be? He was out and away the ablest man all round I had here. Redvers Buller in some respects and in some qualities ran him close, but, all round, Buller was not by a long way Stewart's equal. Buller is far the best man we now have. His manner is against him, but as a fighting soldier, and an organizing staff officer he is A1. I have left to him all the details of the withdrawal from the Upper Nile.[57]

One aspect of that withdrawal much troubled Buller. It was the unpleasant future that awaited the many Sudanese who had thrown in their lot with the British.[58] It was a problem that his countrymen would face again and again a century later, and one to which no solution was ever found.

Not until August did Buller reach England, his reputation even further enhanced. Straightaway he left with his wife for their 'third honeymoon' in three years of married life, as she put it in her amusing but near illegible diary.[59] Through South Wales the couple travelled to the south-west of Ireland, where they stayed with friends, some living under death threats from evicted tenants. By November, with a KCB added to his other honours, the now Sir Redvers Buller was again occupying a War Office desk, this time as Deputy Adjutant General, Wolseley's right-hand man.

The campaign, Wolseley's last, had tarnished his record. His picked force had suffered defeat by what was seen as a horde of savages, its inadequacies revealed in a flood of books and articles from the returning participants. It was also the effective end of the 'Ring'. Its members were now mature and experienced officers, subject to rivalries and hard to control, for whom their commander had failed to provide proper direction and leadership. The strains of the campaign, both physical and mental, had borne too heavily upon an ageing man.

6

IRISH INTERLUDE

After less than a year in the War Office Buller opened a surprising letter. Dated 16 August, 1886, it was from the newly appointed Conservative Secretary-of-State for War, Mr W. H. Smith, son of the similarly initialled founder of the well-known newsagents, who had, before entering politics, himself overseen the expansion of the family business. The terms of his letter were not altogether clear. After a preamble about the disturbances in the south-westerly counties of Ireland, it continued:

It is therefore contemplated to appoint an officer of rank as a kind of Special Commissioner or Magistrate and to give him control through the County Inspector and Head Constables of Police, and the assistance of the Divisional Magistrate, and to place at his disposal such a force of Cavalry as he might deem necessary for night patrol duty, and it is believed that in a very short time indeed by this kind of vigorous action, complete discretion resting with the Commissioner, whose only superior would be the Chief Secretary, Sir M. H. Beach, that these outrages would be put an end to.

The letter then said that both Brackenbury and Buller – the two men both suitable and available – were being asked whether they would accept the appointment, one as Smith admitted, 'about as unpleasant a job as I could propose to anyone'.[1] At the same time he wrote to the Duke of Cambridge:

Redvers Buller goes to Kerry to restore law and order there. We think it possible that a new and strong man . . . may bring a fresh unprejudiced mind to bear on them, infuse a new spirit into those who are responsible for law and order, and by vigorous activity in the use of the existing processes of law, he may be enabled to put a stop to the moonlighting which is going on.[2]

Interviewed two days later by Smith and Hicks Beach together, Buller was offered and accepted the task, stipulating only that he should be allowed to resign at any time if his military interests demanded it – a further war would almost certainly bring a demand for his services.

That same day Buller himself wrote to the Duke that 'though I dislike it above all things I do not see how from motives of simple patriotism alone I could do otherwise – Ireland is the sore now most affecting the country and I deem it my simple duty to do what I may to heal it.' Nevertheless, as he had told the Chief Secretary, he had 'grave doubts of my competency for the duty'.[3] Possibly he never knew that five months earlier the then Home Secretary had decided that he was the best available candidate for the even more challenging post of Metropolitan Police Commissioner.[4]

This new Conservative government, led by Lord Salisbury, had taken office in early August after Gladstone's administration had been forced to resign after the defeat of its Home Rule bill in June, ninety-three Liberal Unionists, all bitter in their opposition, having voted with the Conservatives. The fresh and vigorous approach towards violence which the new Government sought was badly needed, although Sir Michael Hicks Beach was over-optimistic in thinking that Buller might deal in a couple of months or so with a successful terrorist campaign which had rumbled on in one form or another for fifty years or more. Gangs of so-called 'Moonlighters', well disguised peasants armed with rudimentary weapons and successors to the 'Whiteboys' of the earlier years of the century, were murdering landlords or their agents, burning houses, slaughtering or ham-stringing stock and intimidating anyone so foolhardy as to bear witness against them.

Both the Liberal Party and the Irish Nationalist Members at Westminster greeted with a mixture of derision and disapproval the appointment of a senior soldier to suppress the misdeeds of an unarmed peasantry, one that had, nevertheless, been responsible during the past year in Kerry alone for two murders, eighteen threatened murders, thirty-nine cases of arson, nineteen of cattle-maiming, fifty-two of levying money and goods, together with untold intimidation and boycotting.[5] Not untypical of the Nationalist press was a coloured cartoon in *Freeman's Weekly* of 4 September, depicting a red-coated figure on a tired horse waving his sword at a farmer and demanding, 'Now then, my man, tell me is this the way to the disturbed districts?' 'Bedad, its not, my nigger walloper,' comes the reply, 'If it's disturbances ye're looking for, just follow the fellow with the carpet bag, and you'll get them galore – But if it's disturbances ye want to *create*, then this road will do as well as any other.' The fellow with the carpet bag is, of course, a lawyer, following the signpost to Belfast and bearing a flag emblazoned 'ORANGE ROWDYISM'. (Since June riots in Belfast between Protestants and Catholics had resulted in a number of deaths and the army being called in to help the police.) Much of the press, including papers from as far off as South Africa and Canada, was, on the other hand, sympathetic towards a man faced with a difficult and thankless task that could well blight his career.

By 28 August Buller had set up his headquarters, such as it was, in the Railway Hotel at Killarney, his staff just a single officer, his private secretary, Lieutenant-Colonel A. E. Turner, who had served him well in the Sudan. An able officer, who knew Ireland intimately and was known for his sympathy towards Home Rule, Turner had worked previously as private secretary to the Lord Lieutenant.

The two counties of Kerry and Clare were Buller's responsibility, the entire south-west heel of Ireland and the most troublesome area of the island. His resources were sparse, no more than 149 policemen, all but thirty-nine of whom were employed on static protection duty when he arrived. Troops there were, but no record of their use appears in his correspondence. His long but lucid letters, handwritten to Hicks Beach every two or three days on stationery he had abstracted from the War Office before he left, have recorded in detail his frustrations and successes. Buller's third surviving letter sets out his two major problems:

The country is lawless. It has been badly and loosely governed . . . no man will give evidence, most of the law breaking that occurs are never reported [sic] and never heard of by the Police . . . On the other hand the Police are I think reasonably efficient and are doing their best, but they are a military body, they live in barracks and do not mix with the population, so they know little of what goes on . . .

Nor was there a proper force of detectives, other than the odd man taken off his normal duties, given 1s 6d daily extra pay, and called a 'special'.[6]

Ireland, he wrote, needed 'A wise, kind and strong government'. It certainly did. Only two days after he arrived, he had discovered that 'the real evil in this country is want of money', due, he wrote, to the fall in the value of store cattle by 50% – the agricultural depression of the 1880s was hitting hard on already poverty-stricken country. In this same letter he reported that his 'reign in Kerry had not opened auspiciously, one individual having been murdered, another fired on and wounded and a dwelling house fired into.'[7]

Buller's first action was drastically to reduce the number of policemen protecting threatened landlords and their property. It was an unpopular move with those affected, but one that allowed him to organize patrols and ambushes, and watch suspected Moonlighters, many of whom were known to the police despite the absence of a proper detective force.

And somehow Buller managed to better the flow of intelligence. The wide publicity his appointment had provoked resulted in ideas being volunteered to him by a wide variety of individuals, ranging from absentee landlords living in Northamptonshire to retired Metropolitan policemen.[8] Whitehall made enquiries for likely agents, but could turn up nothing better than a retired member of the constabulary who had emigrated to New York and could be brought back to Ireland under the guise of a cattle merchant. History does not relate whether he was used.[9] The classic means of obtaining such information was to buy it from informers, and it appears that Buller's arrival coincided with a large increase in the cash made available for such bribes.[10]

Buller's public reputation as a tough, fighting soldier, combined with the cool courage with which he tackled this new challenge, did much in itself to restore public confidence. Much of his time was to be spent in travelling around his area, seeing everything for himself and talking to everyone he could meet. At all times he wore civilian clothes and disdained protection. Hostile press cartoons and drawings depicted him closely escorted by soldiers and members of the Royal Irish Constabulary, but this was not so. The day after he arrived in Killarney he walked out of his hotel and noticed that he was being followed by a couple of men. On discovering that his shadows were policemen, he gave orders that he did not require such protection. In a long letter the Chief Secretary passed on to him a warning that at a series of meetings in Dublin his assassination had been planned.[11] This evoked:

> With regard to my personal safety, I am, I think, as careful as I should be. I am quite sure of one thing, and that is I can do much more good by going about quietly in the way I have than by parading the country with escorts of horse and foot which would excite the people, and I think do evil. I try to reduce the risk to a minimum . . . but such risk as remains I think I ought to run . . .[12]

Any such new broom will encounter antagonism and prejudice, especially when dealing with a body of men as dispirited by lack of success and overwork as the local R.I.C. But Buller's qualities appealed to those Irish policemen as they had done to his South African scallywags or his cockney soldiers. These attributes were described by a fellow officer as:

> His bluff, outspoken manner, his unvarying cheerfulness and sense of humour, above all his appreciation of hard work loyally performed, encouraged the men to persevere and stopped depression in case of failure. His power was soon felt throughout the police; he infused new spirit into the men under his command, and was always ready to take

responsibility, made allowance for failure, and revived the weary forces of law and order.[13]

Within a month of Buller's arrival, his methods began to produce results. Four policemen on night patrol duty in Castle Island, a notorious trouble spot some dozen miles from Tralee, surprised and apprehended a gang of young Moonlighters in the act of disguising and arming themselves with revolvers and other weapons. That same night in Killarney a party of eight was arrested when helping carry off a threshing machine. Another night, when a patrol bumped into a gang and both sides opened fire, one Moonlighter was badly wounded and the rest chased and caught.

Something new in the South-West, these and other successes, small though they were, had a psychological impact out of all proportion to their size. Magnified by the Tory press and denigrated by Nationalist organs, they were headline news. Violence in no way ceased, but outrages became fewer, and on 28 September Hicks Beach was able to write to Buller, 'I congratulate you on the success of the police against the moonlighters. They will soon begin to be afraid of the game.'[14]

Buller soon felt sufficiently on top of his job for his wife to join him. They met as guests at Viceregal Lodge in Dublin on 28 October where Lady Audrey noted in her intermittent diary[15] that it was 'a time to be remembered – He looked very well – I felt almost shy at the thought of seeing him again! Only two months, but somehow the circumstances were new and strange'.

It was unusual then for an educated woman to be cursed by such an appalling scrawl. She had started a new notebook when she left Downes by train a week earlier; arriving at Waterloo, she had walked up to 29 Bruton Street – even the upper classes of the last century retained the full use of their legs. Her onward train and boat journey was spent in the company of a newly married young woman, whom she found was also bound for Viceregal Lodge. Lady Audrey 'tried to make her talk about Redvers, but without success . . . she was too much interested in her new clothes and new husband to know much of the distresses of the country'. No sooner had her new acquaintance's husband joined them on the quayside than she again tried to turn the conversation to Redvers. Attending evensong at St Paul's Cathedral before she left London, she had been flattered that the mention of her husband's name had gained her immediate admittance to a seat in the choir. A rather naive but touching delight in Redvers and her marriage time and again light up the diary's pages.

Lady Audrey had 'a little dreaded' meeting Lady Londonderry, her hostess at Viceregal Lodge and a most formidable *grande-dame*. However, she found her pleasant, and Lord Londonderry even more so. He had 'very simple manners, no swagger or pomposity or self-consciousness – nor the affectation of extreme horsiness, which I'd a little anticipated – (tho' I like a tinge of horsiness).' Her comments on her fellow guests could be shrewdly humorous, often kind but sometimes devastating: one great lady was arrogant, peevish, vulgar and unpleasant; another exhibited just the right amount of 'fine ladyism'.

On the Saturday, their hosts left the couple alone, lending them a Victoria to enjoy 'a most delightful sort of little honeymoon' spent poking around among the old Dublin antique shops, visiting the museum and driving through Phoenix Park.

Monday evening found them at their Killarney hotel, which she found 'very delightful'. As someone who had climbed in the Alps around Zermatt as a girl, sleeping in mountain huts, she could enjoy a simple country inn and the company at dinner and anecdotes of a very Irish inspector of constabulary. Colonel Turner, 'a thorough Homeruler' had made her small sitting-room pretty with flowers and books. 'I am very happy,' she wrote that night.

She was embarrassed by the presence of a policeman outside their bedroom door, but she discovered that her husband always went abroad unescorted. It was as clear to her as it was to him that to gain the people's confidence – to use her own words – he had to show confidence in them, and that having reduced other people's protection, he must show them an example. And it was to Castle Island races, where earlier a murder had taken place on each of the four roads leading into the place, that Buller took his wife soon after she arrived in Ireland. He made no secret of his plans and afterwards wrote:

> Nothing could have been better than the bearing and behaviour of the people . . . Indeed there were serious thoughts of giving me a reception with the band, led by the Captain of the 'Revolver Boys': one ex-suspect was supposed not to favour this idea . . . but they were very civil; there were about 2,000 people there.[16]

The confidence Buller instilled by such behaviour and the successes his police were obtaining were not the only reasons for the reduction in the number of burnings and killings. Offsetting the drop in the price of cattle, there had been an abundant harvest and no signs of any widespread failure of the potato crop, a still present threat in Ireland. There was undoubtedly a general decrease in tension in the south-west.

Impetuous as always, no sooner had Buller arrived in Killarney than he had let Hicks Beach have his ideas for the political solution of Ireland's problems. As Buller saw it, a two-pronged attack was needed: the people must be forced to obey the law, but this was only possible if they were to be protected against the oppression of their landlords.

1. Downnes, the family home near Crediton in Devon. (*Mrs Peter Parker*)

2. 'A delightful little pencil sketch at Downes.' (p2)

Train
Sept. 1848.
M.B.

3. The Duke of Cambridge was Commander-in-Chief from 1856 to 1895.

4. 'The Black watch were ahead… when the first shots were fired.' (p27) (*Illustrated London News*)

5. 'Wolseley… had qualities which brought him near uniquely rapid promotion.' (p7)

6. 'Wood was… ambitious… an unfashionable characteristic among army officers.' (p35)

7. 'Hamilton… discovered an unexpected generosity in Buller.' (p79)

8. 'Sir Frederick Roberts had been despatched to South Africa to restore British arms.' (p51)

9. The act which won Buller the VC. From the *Illustrated London News*, October, 1901. (see pp37-40)

10. '… he took to himself a wife… Lady Audrey Howard was the daughter of the 4th Marquess Townshend.' (p53) (*Mrs Peter Parker*)

11. 'General Buller looking out for Tokar': from *The Graphic*, 29 March, 1884. (see p63)

Both Lord Salisbury and his Tory party were committed to firm government in Ireland, the preservation of the Union and the restoration of respect
for the rights of property. But Sir Michael Hicks Beach, the Chief Secretary,
was a man of moderate and liberal views. A previous Chancellor of the
Exchequer, he had refused the Leadership of the Commons in order to
assume a post of obloquy and danger which he had already held once. It may
have been rather more than a coincidence that he should have asked for a
soldier of known radical outlook to work for him in Ireland's most troubled
area. The sympathy and confidence that existed between the two, both much
the same age and near contemporaries at Eton, is apparent from their
correspondence.

They had this also in common: both were landowners and both were
known for the care with which they ran their estates. Hicks Beach, far from
wealthy and a man of the simplest tastes, did not even employ an agent to
manage his Cotswold acres; he attended to every detail himself, knew his
tenants and their workmen, and kept in sound repair his buildings and
cottages, replacing them when need be, even though he had to borrow the
money to do so. And this was at a time of severe agricultural depression,
when the newly built North American railways were enabling imported
prairie-grown wheat to undercut that of the European farmers.

Such men had little use for those Irish landowners, sometimes absentee
and living in England, whose agents extracted the last possible penny from
their impoverished tenants. Some, on the other hand, were as considerate as
they could be towards their tenants, near bankrupt though they might be
themselves. But they suffered for the sins of their fellows.

The underlying essence of the Irish problem, as Buller saw it, was that
produce prices – despite the recent and temporary increase in prosperity –
were not high enough to pay established rents; because of this the country
was lawless, the people had no faith in the Government, no one would give
evidence and few outrages were reported to the police. There was then a
need to:

> Take powers for the Government to stay evictions at will, and to deal
> with real property: especially it is necessary that special powers should
> be taken to deal fairly with heavily mortgaged estates. The police should
> inquire and report to Government before permitting evictions . . . A
> strong local Government in the West will make this a happy country
> quickly, I believe, but repression of the peasantry, unless there is a wise
> re-adjustment of landlords, will be useless.[17]

In essence Buller was suggesting that either the farms of near bankrupt
landlords should be compulsorily acquired by the Government for resale to

tenants, or that Gladstone's Land Act of 1881, by which a system had been set up for rents to be fixed for a fifteen-year period, should be modified to allow for further reductions to offset the effects of the depression.

Buller's daily forays into the countryside had straightaway opened his eyes to the realities of the injustices suffered by Irish peasant farmers. His sympathy was immediately aroused, but officially there was little he could do: as the senior police officer in the area, his role was merely to enforce the law. Nevertheless, he could also impose delay, and this he did. The two weapons used by the landlords against their tenants were eviction or cattle distraint; in both cases the agents, carrying out what was usually a dangerous task, were entitled to protection, a duty performed and loathed by the police because it inevitably led to further disorders. After a few weeks' experience of such work, Buller issued instructions that ten days' notice must be given if police were needed so as to allow time for any necessary enquiries. He then used this delay to try to settle cases informally, often suggesting to the landlord that he should avoid going ahead. Such was his reputation and force of personality that at times this worked. Evictions decreased appreciably.

With landlords such as the millionaire Lord Clanricarde, who never visited his estates, extracted every possible penny, and declared that anyone was mistaken who thought he could be intimidated by the shooting of his agent – a previous one had been – persuasion was ineffective. However, Hicks Beach did what he could, sending personally for the wretched agent and instructing him to inform Lord Clanricarde that 'if he did not make allowances to his tenants or parts of his property which the agent had himself persuaded Lord Clanricarde to make, I would postpone sending the police.'[18]

Although Buller disguised his true feelings in public, his letters to Hicks Beach were far from restrained. This is clear from the Chief Secretary's reaction to one on 5 November, in which he admitted that:

> My colleagues in the Cabinet were a good deal 'flustered' by your observations in your memo as to the state of Kerry and Clare, as to your having 'had a good deal of trouble with the Sheriffs, who have tried to effect seizures in a manner more like thieving than anything else.'

The memo had contained a request for measures to control the Sheriffs, something that Hicks Beach was obliged to refuse on legal grounds, telling him at the same time that the Cabinet was worried that he was exercising what they described as these 'discretionary powers' in providing police protection.[19]

The press rapidly seized upon Buller's sympathetic approach to his task. The Nationalists were delighted. Although *United Ireland* had published on

9 October a cartoon depicting Buller ordering a policeman to open fire on a family group waving a white flag, a couple of weeks later it was gloating over his instructions, duly leaked, regarding the ten days' notice requirement for police protection depicting it as a humiliation for the Government. The *Daily News* was, on the other hand, typical of many Unionist organs in likening Buller's actions to those that had cost James II his throne.[20] Another paper pointed out that his sympathy for the Irish peasant was similar to his attitude towards the Boers. With the Unionists wrongly accusing him of being an outright Home Ruler, Buller was getting little thanks from anyone. Misrepresented on all sides, Hicks Beach also felt obliged to warn him against unguarded speech, pointing out that he himself had said very little about the iniquities of landlords in the House of Commons because it would have been used as a general excuse for tenants not paying their rents, and that Buller must guard against similar misrepresentations.[21]

If Buller was not exercising these 'discretionary powers', he was certainly moving very close to it, and, as many papers hastened to point out, his instruction to the police had been issued on 14 October just after he returned from Dublin where he had seen the Chief Secretary.

In mid-November Buller managed to find the time to take a short break at Downes. Often in the past he had expressed himself forcibly to Hicks Beach, but now, in a letter written to his political master, he abandoned restraint completely:

> The bulk of the landlords do nothing for their tenants but extract as much rent as they can by every means in their power, and the law helps them; and the tenant, even if an industrious hard-working man, has no redress. Landlords are not evicting now in Kerry, but they are distraining cattle where they can; . . . What chance has a tenant under the present law? No – you must alter the law if you are to have peace. Of that I feel convinced. For 120 years British bayonets have backed up landlords in extracting excessive rents, and have supported them in grossly neglecting their tenants. What is the result of those 120 years? The tenants have combined against the injustice and persecution, and where are the landlords? Nowhere. Bankrupt in money and in moral power. Is there not a lesson in this? and do you think you can go back? I for one feel sure that you cannot, and that if you do not advance, and that quickly, the flood will overwhelm you; and Home Rule, with all its concomitant evils and miseries, will surely immediately ensue. You must not forget that the Kerry tenant is really unrepresented. He has no money to go to Court to defend a case. The landlord never goes near him, the agent never goes near him, and the local bailiff cheats him if he can. How can a man, once he has been taught to agitate, quiet down

under such oppression? Pardon me if I write strongly. I certainly feel strongly, and coming home here to England, and thinking what English landlords spend on their estates, and what reductions they make, I do feel that it is both just and righteous to give some help to the Kerry peasants.[22]

The contrast between Western Ireland and what met him in Devon must have been compelling.

Buller had, in fact, already made his views plain – but in rather more measured terms – to the members of the Cowper Commission on the Irish Land Acts, whose report was to be published the following February. 'You have got a very ignorant poor people,' he told them, 'and the law should look after them, instead of which it has only looked after the rich.' In the subsequent Commons debate, the opposition fastened upon Buller's words with glee and, as the Secretary of State for War put it to the Queen, Mr Gladstone 'relied greatly on the evidence of Sir Redvers Buller, quoting only those passages which supported his view'.[23] The Liberal statesman, John Morley, also quoted Buller's evidence in his biography of Gladstone, and summed the matter up by saying that, when enforcing evictions, the landlords were within their rights, the courts were bound by the law, and the police had no choice but to back the law. 'The legal case was complete. The moral case remained.' The barbarous scenes then revealed, Morley suggested, first brought the realities of the Irish land system to the attention of the British public.[24]

In his letter to Hicks Beach, seeking his approval for this break at Downes, Buller had also asked how much longer he was likely to be remaining in Ireland:

I have about done all I can in Clare and Kerry. A continuance of my arrangements should, in time, and with luck, do the rest. That sounds conceited, but it is not so meant. What I mean is, I have got the police with me; I have started a system for repressing crime by police work, and for discovering crime by detective work. This has been done to the best of my ability and lights. Time must do the rest. The point is, I have made my plan, and if I remain I can carry it out. Is it necessary that I remain to carry it out?[25]

It was not a bad two months' work.

He was not yet to leave Ireland. A further, and even more unexpected job awaited him, that of Permanent Under-Secretary, Hicks Beach's senior civil servant. It was a measure of the latter's confidence in him. Because of the likelihood that the post would shortly be made a political one, to be held by a member of parliament who could help the Chief Secretary in the Commons, its term was to be limited to a mere six months.

At the end of November Buller returned to Ireland to take up this somewhat daunting and quite unwelcome task. Moreover, he was aware that Wolseley had intended appointing him Quartermaster-General, a challenge to which he had been looking forward. So this letter from the Adjutant-General must have been a hard blow:

> In the interests of the State, of course I am bound to be glad that you are to assume these new duties, but I am personally very sorry. I shall miss you beyond measure in carrying out these new arrangements for the amalgamation of the civil departments with the combatant officers of the army. However it can't be helped. I must now look out for a new QMG.

Wolseley went on to say that the Duke of Cambridge had been sounded out and had raised no objection to Buller's appointment; he concluded with the comment, 'HRH is at Sandringham where he is to be for a fortnight. I wish he would stay there for ever.'[26]

Two days earlier, Buller had himself broken the news to the Duke, telling him that, after first refusing the post primarily because he 'did not feel qualified' for it, he had in the end been persuaded to accept 'as an act of duty'. While the situation in Clare had only 'improved slightly', he had been 'lucky in Kerry for I have managed either to arrest or frighten out of the country some of the worst men and I have got on good terms with the Priests . . . very bitter and hostile' when he first arrived.[27]

As before, Buller had extracted an undertaking that he could resign if the prospect of active service came his way, and that he could also leave if Smith were to relinquish the War Office and his successor not make a similar guarantee.[28] Nor was he happy about the financial side. Although the annual salary was £2,500 (plus £200 to maintain the large garden of the Under-Secretary's lodge), life for the occupant of such a post in Dublin was expensive. As he wrote to Hicks Beach, the pay was high but he was obliged to keep up a house in London for his military appointment, the rent and other costs of which amounted to £800 annually. 'I have been badly hit this year, and had been intending economies this winter, instead of which I am living at a higher rate than ever.'[29] The agricultural slump had affected even landlords of Buller's comparative affluence.

One aspect of the appointment the public found especially puzzling: Buller was replacing Sir Robert Hamilton, a senior and able career civil servant, previously Permanent Secretary to the Admiralty, and known as a strong supporter of Home Rule who was said to have been responsible for influencing Gladstone in a similar direction.[30] Lord Salisbury's new government, upon taking office, had removed Hamilton by promoting him to the governorship of Tasmania. But why was it then that an individual of such known liberal views as Buller should be appointed in his place?

Buller himself would seem to have been among those puzzled by the move for on 26 November Hicks Beach was to write:

> If either you or I had known that you were likely to become Under-Secretary, we should doubtless have agreed that it would have been better, whatever your opinions might be, that you should have given no evidence before the [Cowper] Commission. As you did so, however, I know of no reason why I or my colleagues should trust you less, for having said to the Commission what you have said to me.[31]

Buller's evidence was, as might have been expected, outspoken, and aroused the ire of, among others, the 8th Viscount Midleton, a major Cork landowner who depended for three-quarters of his income upon his Irish rents.[32] As Buller remarked to the Duke, Midleton had written 'a singularly injudicious letter about my evidence before the Land Commission was published in the papers'.[33] The career of Midleton's eldest son and successor to the title, St John Brodrick, who had only recently been appointed Financial Secretary at the War Office was, for the next decade and a half, to be linked with Buller's.

By this time Buller had become, as the press often put it, a thorn in the side of the Tory landlords. To the populace, however, he was a hero, an outcome of his appointment hardly anticipated but made good use of by the Nationalists: no longer the brutal militaristic oppressor of the peasantry, it was claimed that the knowledge he had acquired of their poverty-stricken subjection had led to his conversion. From both sides he was now inaccurately and invidiously acclaimed as a 'Home Ruler'.

Another question mark lay over Buller's own replacement. His private secretary and second-in-command, Colonel Turner, whose sympathies towards Home Rule were unquestioned, had moved up to take his place.

What then was the government about? The answer almost certainly lay in a letter from Hicks Beach to Lord Salisbury written the previous month and reporting upon his and Buller's work:

> From all parts of the country I hear reports of a better tone among the people. Landlords are giving considerable reductions of rent; and tenants seem less unwilling to pay, when they can . . . I have been working privately very hard, and I think with success, to make landlords reasonable. I think (and rather hope) that I may have a row with

Clanricarde! You, at any rate, will not suspect me of doing too little in that direction.[34]

The letter also mentions that Nationalist agitation was in places falling flat and that there were signs that the people were becoming sick of what he described as their tyranny. He also describes as 'moderate' certain proposals Buller had made for legislation to help the police, but says that he can see no need for them at the moment. An example of the help Buller was giving Hicks Beach in his efforts to restrain the landlords lies in a letter he wrote to a Colonel O'Callaghan just before he left Downes:

> . . . I go back to Ireland early next week & I hope by then that you will have reconsidered your determination about your tenants. Of course you know your own business better than anyone else, but I cannot help feeling that an evicting 'Army' about Tipperary would do more to help the Nationalists and Home Rulers than it will do to bring money into your pocket and that it will require an Army to carry out your evictions is pretty clearly shown . . .[35]

O'Callaghan failed to take the advice. The result was a major riot the following June.

The Government were, in fact, trying by persuasion to hold the worst of the landlords in check. Individual ministers may not have approved of the way such officials as Buller, Hamilton and Turner tackled the Irish problem – nor the politics of the last two – but their Chief Secretary's approach was taking the bite out of Nationalist agitation and disconcerting the Liberals. This, it should be said, was a time of such political bitterness that Liberal leaders were not invited into Conservative homes.

The surviving correspondence between Buller and Hicks Beach during the former's time in the south-west has illuminated their attitudes and their relationship. Because his move to Dublin brought this exchange of letters almost to an end, far less is known of Buller's work in his new role. Undoubtedly, however, he found it hard going. He was an Englishman, served mainly by junior and sometimes unsympathetic Irish civil servants, working in a rigid bureaucracy less than susceptible to change. His reaction to Ireland's problems, either revealed or misinterpreted by the voluminous press coverage, was often not popular with his subordinates, nor did he always meet with the loyalty and co-operation previously shown him by the police. Moreover, tact was not his strong point; and he tended to take a rather shorter time than the average civil servant to state an opinion, not always with the happiest of results. It is revealing that the Chief Secretary, back in September, had found the need to caution him for an injudicious remark that had found its way on to an official file, warning him of the danger that:

> . . . it is as likely as not to be all over Dublin the next day. I don't at all want to check the expression of your opinion, but if we differ, it is as well that the Dublin clerks should not know it.[36]

Buller apologized, but that indiscretions continued is clear from a subsequent letter written after he had taken up his new duties:

> I note what you say, but I fear I can never make you a silk purse out of a sow's ear! I have all my life got into much of my troubles by an inconvenient habit of saying too much & I fear I am too old to improve but I will try.[37]

Buller's life was to be lightened with the return of his wife on 16 January. She found her new house 'most charming'. Set in the 2,000 acres of Phoenix Park, near the Chief Secretary's Lodge and the vast Georgian porticoed splendour of the Viceroy's, the Under-Secretary's was small by comparison, but older and far more cosy. Redvers himself had supervised the decorations, choosing Chippendale furniture and blue William Morris paper – his aesthetic tastes matched his wife's – for the small 'den' they shared upstairs; there they sat in two 'delightful nooks' each with their papers on separate tables on either side of the fireplace. The servants' rooms, she noted, were also most comfortable. She felt 'very happy' with it all, a subject she often returns to in her diary: 'I have so much happiness – much more real happiness than when I had youth and comparative beauty.'

As a woman of forty-two (she admitted to forty) she was worried about the lines she saw in her looking-glass, describing them as the 'ugliness of advancing years . . . some women got a certain middle-aged peace – & I don't like not being ornamental'. But ornamental she surely was, especially in the peach brocade court dress and train which was made for her at the then enormous price of £42 (the debutante daughter of hard-up parents might afford £5). Even though she declared that she did not like 'society' as such, her daughter Georgiana thought otherwise.[38] She loved the Dublin life, 'new and yet old': the walk with Redvers in the morning to his office in the Castle, where they had another small house and a woman to look after it; the dinner parties, the hunting and the balls; the games and the picnics with her younger children; their pew in the church next to the Chief Secretary's which made her feel 'very official'; her husband looking 'very well and stately' when carrying the Sword of State in an official procession in the State Rooms of Dublin Castle – so 'taken up' was she with him, that she quite failed to notice the Viceroy and the rest of the procession. In the

Under-Secretary's Lodge they were to collect around them people of both religions and all shades of politics, together with a variety of amusing literary and artistic figures.

She enjoyed Dublin, despite 'the grave thought' which always dogged her. For just outside their pretty little house terrorists had stabbed to death her husband's predecessor, together with Lord Henry Cavendish, the then Chief Secretary, in what were known as 'The Phoenix Park murders'. Among all the light-hearted fun, she was well aware of the 'stern realities' of Ireland. Her diary and her daughter's notebooks reveal an intelligent, well-read woman with an inquisitive mind and nice wit who could laugh at her own foibles, one with an avid interest in all the arts and the politics of the day, but who could still delight in social chatter.[39]

In under four months Buller had a new master. Plagued by ill-health and failing eyesight, and worn out by battling with the Irish Nationalists in the House, Hicks Beach was compelled to resign from what was the toughest job in the Government. His departure saddened his colleagues and was regretted by many of his political adversaries, but Buller, despite their productive and happy relationship, admitted to his sister: 'I think on the whole the retirement of Sir Michael was a good thing, owing I suppose to his health. It was impossible latterly to get a decision out of him, and in these times that sort of delay is fatal.' The letter's final sentence probably reveals the writer's frustrations in his role of civil servant: 'Irishmen may have a sense of humour but they have no common sense – and to this or rather to the absence of this I attribute most of the ills of Ireland.'[40]

The new Chief Secretary was to be the yet unproved thirty-nine-year-old Arthur James Balfour, nephew to Lord Salisbury and eventually his political heir, then a willowy and seemingly idle intellectual still disguising brilliance under a cloak of diffident, aristocratic charm. Unlike Hicks Beach, he was to spend little time in Ireland, failing to respond to Buller's many requests to visit the country. His letters to Buller lack warmth, and by June he was rebuking him for suggesting that Turner was receiving inadequate political support.[41] Seldom did Balfour reveal sympathy for the Irish peasantry, even though his estates lay in Scotland, rather than Ireland, unlike many influential Tories. Perhaps he lacked relish for the Celtic fringe as a whole. Political unrest was by no means confined to Ireland: in Wales there was a tithe war and in Scotland many of the crofters were in open rebellion.

Nevertheless, Balfour's long-term ideas for Ireland were not far removed from his Under-Secretary's: coercion for both parties and the reform of land tenure.[42] The month previous to his arrival, Buller had made his views unequivocally, if not brutally, clear:

My deliberate opinion is that unless you can introduce *very shortly* a summary method of procedure for prevention of crime, and also take some power which will enable you to coerce bad landlords . . . you may as well chuck up the sponge.[43]

A few weeks later he went even further. Unless a liberal Land Bill was to be set in train, together with a Criminal Procedure Bill, within eighteen months, he declared, either the landlords would be ruined or there would be civil war.[44] He had his timing wrong. It took twice that number of years for his prophesy to be fulfilled.

Nothing happened, however. Lord Salisbury's Cabinet, although eager to strengthen the arm of the law, was as yet reluctant to bully the landlords or find the parliamentary time needed for reform.

At last, on 15 October, Buller was released and became Quartermaster-General, the post having been kept vacant for him after all. In retrospect, the general verdict was that he had not done well in Dublin. As early as 2 March the Queen had noted that Lord Salisbury, when reporting Hicks Beach's illness and Balfour's appointment, told her that 'Sir R. Buller had not been a success as Under-Secretary and would come away'.[45] From the Prime Minister's point of view, this general officer must have often appeared aggravatingly outspoken and insufficiently subtle. For all that, Lord Salisbury was to retain him for almost five months beyond his original tenure and despite Wolseley's pressure to get him back to Pall Mall.

As the press pointed out, Buller had been prepared to risk his professional prospects by fulfilling the uncongenial task the Government had asked him to undertake. He probably did much better than he himself had anticipated. His correspondence with Balfour makes clear that he had even acquired a mastery of the complicated legislative problems involved.

Formal recognition rested in his enrolment as an Irish Privy Councillor, an unusual honour for a comparatively junior forty-eight-year-old soldier. Nor was his name forgotten in Ireland. At his death, over twenty years later, a Kerry priest and ardent Nationalist sent a telegram of condolence testifying to the respect in which he was held by the Irish peasants.[47] Even in 1922, after Ireland had gained Home Rule, he could still be remembered as the soldier who, by 'strict impartiality, tact and honesty, brought peace to Kerry'.[47] But an early biographer, writing just after his death, suggested that 'his views probably differed a great deal from those of the Government which he was serving and it is possible that his independence of view was remembered to his disadvantage in later days'.[48] It was.

7

DESK-BOUND

By now Buller knew his way around the War Office. It was his fourth time there. Ahead now lay a solid ten-year slog, giving him a total of over fifteen years spent in its labyrinthine Pall Mall buildings, the site of the present Royal Automobile Club. In his young days as a newly appointed DAAG, dining with the Wolseleys after the Ashanti campaign, a fellow guest, that young Arthur Bigge who was to fight alongside him in Zululand, remembered him chaffing his senior, suggesting that if half the staff went on leave, there would hardly be enough work to occupy the rest.[1] The reality was somewhat different. Over-stringent financial control, reluctance to decentralize and hand-written correspondence could demand exacting hours from the conscientous. Punctilious and painstaking, it was Buller's habit to sit in turn at every clerk's desk[2] and go through his year's work with him. But his knowledge of War Office procedure was, as a result, unrivalled.

The constitutional position of the Duke of Cambridge as Commander-in-Chief had been settled with difficulty by Cardwell in 1870 who, despite strong opposition, subordinated him to his own civilian control as Secretary-of-State. To the Duke answered the Adjutant-General, the Quartermaster-General being little more than the latter's senior assistant, his duties ill-defined. When Wolseley first offered Buller that post in September, 1886, he confided that he aimed to broaden its responsibilities to include wide-ranging administrative functions.[3] A Cabinet reshuffle in January, 1887, expedited this, bringing to the War Office Mr Edward Stanhope, a reforming Secretary-of-State in the Cardwell tradition, in place of W.H. Smith. Within the year he had abolished the post of Surveyor-General, so shifting responsibility for the clothing, transport and *matériel* from civilian hands to those of the Commander-in-Chief, and thence to the QMG, whose duties were thus greatly increased in scope, taking on their future shape.

Buller's first – and possibly his greatest – reform as QMG was to create an Army Service Corps, firmly linking supply and transport both in peace and in war. It was done with extraordinary speed. Arriving in the War Office on

15 October, 1887, he minuted his draft plan after only five weeks. Thirteen months later the Corps was in being. So often, a century or so ago, complicated problems could be solved quite rapidly.

His wide experience of war had impressed upon Buller the need for such reform. In every campaign, and especially the Red River, the Ashanti and the Nile, he had observed – as the great General Wavell was later to insist – that administration was the crux of generalship, strategy and tactics being over-emphasized, especially by the amateur critic. Even Socrates, two millennia earlier, had placed first among the qualities of a general the ability to produce for his men their rations and other stores.[4] Except for Marlborough, Wellington and Wolseley, British generals had rarely paid more than lip-service to this simple axiom, and even Wolseley failed to comprehend the need for military control of logistics – to use an anachronistic term. A hundred years or more later, critics were to complain that the study of logistics at the Staff College was still no more than superficial; in the British Army, as in others, there still existed what was to be known as 'G [or operational] snobbery'.

Hitherto, the functions of supply and transport had been largely under civilian control, either War Office or Treasury, exercised through what was in turn known as the Commissary Department, the Control Department or, since 1876, the Commissariat and Transport Staff, no more than a linking of two separate bodies. The Royal Wagon Train had been raised in the Peninsular War but disbanded in 1833; a Land Transport Corps was brought into being in the Crimean War and a Military Train existed for a time during and just after the Indian Mutiny, the last named manned by officers and soldiers transferred from line regiments. The Commissariat, on the other hand, depended upon civilians, together with a number of seconded subalterns, attracted by marginally higher pay. Only in the past six years had civilian entry been abolished, with new appointments to both Commissariat and Transport limited to officers with at least five years' service, and military rank substituted for such cumbersome titles as Assistant Commissary-General.

As yet, however, the Commissariat and Transport Staff was not an integral part of the army, nor did general officers or their staffs consider themselves responsible for its shortcomings. Friction was widespread, prestige low, organizational changes frequent, officers aged and insufficient in number, efficiency problematical.

The title Army Service Corps was not new, having existed from 1869 to 1881 as an other-rank-only corps. Buller's achievement was to link supplies with transport, to put officers and soldiers together under the one cap-badge, and to raise the standard of officers. His thinking behind the latter ran as follows:

I want to officer my new organization with men who have the same position and prestige as officers of the combatant branches. The officers of the new Army Service Corps must be proud of themselves and of their own service, they must be recognised by the Army generally as part – and no unimportant part – of the Army. They must identify themselves with the Army, and the Army must identify itself with them. This can never be the case if their military status is doubtful, or limited, so as to provoke comparison or suggest inferiority. They must have no disabilities, and a full military career must be open to them. I see no reason why Army Service Corps officers should not look forward to the day when it shall be open to them to sit in the chair I now occupy.[5]

Entry for officers into this new combatant corps, in which they, like their soldiers, could make their career, would be by transfer on probation or by five-year secondment of young officers from the infantry or cavalry. Pay, promotion and pensions were to match those of the Royal Engineers, the first some 40% higher than that of an infantry officer.

Of equal, if not greater, importance to the standing and efficiency of the Corps was its removal from civilian control to that of the QMG and his staff. In each command the staff officer responsible to his general for supply and transport matters would be an ASC officer, but one wearing staff uniform and of equal standing with his fellows. All commanders, both in the field and barracks, would be directly responsible for their logistic services, and could no longer blame their failures upon civilian shortcomings or malpractices.

Buller's minute had been dated 17 November, 1887. The new Corps came into being on 11 December, 1888. Its officer establishment numbered 270, forty-six more than before, but Buller had done it without materially increasing costs, a mark of his administrative acumen.

A fine history awaited the new Corps, upon which the title of 'Royal' was bestowed in 1918. But once again, as thinking changed, in 1965 the functions of supply and transport were split. Supply moved to the Royal Army Ordnance Corps; transport to the new Royal Corps of Transport, which inherited and built upon its predecessor's pride and traditions. But recently the slashing of the armed forces has led to the amalgamation of both the RCT and RAOC into the new Royal Logistic Corps, where supply and transport will meet once again. No longer will Buller Barracks, Aldershot, be the home of a Corps which remembers with affection its founder and which, in its early days, was known as 'Buller's Babies'.[6]

There is little doubt that Buller's reputation in the Army as a fighting soldier was instrumental in such a major change being settled so smoothly.

He was helped in this by Stanhope's abolition of the Surveyor-General's branch, and by the support of both Wolseley and Cambridge; with both he was on intimate terms and he could often mitigate their mutual dislike and antagonism. Nevertheless, both had considerable reservations about so-called departmental matters being considered a staff function, one of the mainsprings of the reforms Buller carried through[7]. Wolseley always remained sceptical. As Buller wrote at the outbreak of the second Boer War to the retired Commissary-General W.G.W. Robinson, who had assisted him with the reforms:

> The fact is that Lord Wolseley has never been able to get out of his head that Supply and Transport [are] civil duties, and will always go like clockwork, provided the GOC is prepared occasionally to hang a Commissary.[8]

Wolseley's return from the Sudan had been marked by the uproar he raised about the shoddiness of much of the equipment with which his soldiers had been cursed – bayonets that bent and rifles that jammed. In time he also reopened his attack upon a promotion system that, despite the abolition of purchase, had forced him to leave what should have been first-rate units at the rear: the incompetence of their commanders was such that he dare not risk them in battle. At a time when the extent to which officers might express their views publicly was unclear, in speech and writing Wolseley publicly criticised the Army's defects, conduct that increased both the Queen's and the Duke's animosity towards him.

Cardwell's reforms had been far-reaching but their initial success has been much exaggerated, as has Wolseley's part in advising him. When the latter arrived in the War Office in May, 1871, much of the work had been done or was in hand. As well as the failure to weed out incompetents and introduce a proper staff system similar to that in force in the country's European rivals, the army still lacked an adequate reserve, recruiting having failed to cope with the demands of the short service system. For all that, much had been done to remedy the glaring defects revealed in the Crimea, and Wolseley during his time as Adjutant-General was to force through many vital changes, among them a proper mobilization scheme, the expansion of the intelligence department (where he put Brackenbury in charge), and above all much improved equipment. This egotist and braggart – as Disraeli, his great admirer, described Wolseley[9] – might have accomplished more if he had not alienated both the Monarch and her cousin, the Duke, together with many of the politicians whose support he needed.

When Wolseley's seven-year tour as Adjutant-General ended, Sir Frederick Roberts, who had coveted the post, was offered it, the most powerful in the Army after that of Commander-in-Chief. In the end, however, it proved impossible to find an adequate successor to Roberts as Commander-in-Chief for India. So it was that Buller, a mere major-general, only fifty-one years of age, became Adjutant-General in October, 1890. It was, the Marquess of Lansdowne, Viceroy and Roberts's close friend, complained to the Queen, 'a serious disappointment to him to give up the idea of succeeding the Adjutant-General which had actually been offered to him'. Roberts, who accurately foresaw a long period of unemployment when he eventually left India, in no way concealed his disappointment.[10]

Captain Owen Wheeler, the authoritative historian of the War Office, writing in 1914, summarised Buller's years as Adjutant-General thus:

> He rapidly attained a position different from that held by any occupant of the billet before or since. A man of private means and great independence of character he was able to maintain towards both the Secretary of State for War and the Royal Commander-in-Chief an attitude of far less studied deference than it had been necessary for Lord Wolseley to exhibit in his relations towards officials upon whose favour he was so largely dependent. Moreover, Sir Redvers was also an extremely able office chief, clear-headed, broad-minded, and essentially dominant. The result was that in a few years he lifted the office of Adjutant-General to a plane perceptibly higher than that on which the other War Office Departments stood, and for a considerable period he was, next to the Duke of Cambridge, distinctly the most powerful officer in the Army.[11]

Such a man can, of course, make enemies only too easily. On this subject the views of a War Office clerk carries weight:

> I have served under five Adjutant-Generals at the War Office . . . but there was only one real Adjutant-General amongst them, and he was Sir Redvers Buller. The rest did what was expected of them, but General Buller's idea of duty was different from theirs, and he would not 'let things slide' and 'hush things up' and he stirred up the whole place. He thereby incurred great unpopularity with a certain clique in the Army, and you will find trouble comes from them.[12]

Subordinates can sometimes better judge an individual than his or her superior.

To some extent, and possibly from tact, Wheeler under-estimated Buller's power. As an old man nearing the end of a long tenure, the reins of office were slipping from the Duke's hands[13], but there were limits to what Buller could achieve as the immediate subordinate of his usually amiable but ultra-conservative, if not reactionary, Commander-in-Chief. Yet the old Duke had plenty of sound common sense, and could express himself clearly and often vividly; even Wolseley, so long his bitter enemy, would afterwards pay tribute to the Duke's 'honesty of purpose, loyalty to the Army, devotion to duty, sincere patriotism and deep and real attachment to his Queen and country [which] pervaded all he did'.[14] It helped that Adjutant-General and Commander-in-Chief remained on excellent terms, but the entrenched attitudes of the War Office civilian hierarchy, together with Parliamentary constraints on producing the requisite money, prevented Buller from accomplishing much for which he planned and fought.

On one subject, however, Buller was no reformer. The powerful inter-party commission to investigate both the War Office and the Admiralty, together with their relationship to the Treasury, was headed by Lord Hartington, Secretary of State for War at the time of the Sudan war and later 8th Duke of Devonshire; it included among its members two other former Secretaries of State, W.H. Smith and Henry Campbell-Bannerman, the Liberal statesman. Issuing its final report in February, 1890, its far-reaching recommendations included the formation of a defence committee of soldiers, sailors and ministers to consider such issues as financial estimates and war planning; then, and for many more years, there was a complete absence of any system for regular communication between the two services. The Hartington Commission further recommended that the post of Commander-in-Chief should be abolished, a War Office Council under the presidency of the Secretary of State being substituted instead, its members the Parliamentary and Permanent Under-Secretaries, the Financial Secretary and five senior military officers. However, this last finding was not unanimous, Campbell-Bannerman dissenting.

As might have been expected both the Queen and the Duke of Cambridge objected so strongly to the abolition of the Commander-in-Chief's post that the recommendation was shelved. Others agreed. As the Queen informed Sir Henry Ponsonby, her Private Secretary, 'Lord Wolseley and Sir Redvers Buller (a Radical but a most distinguished officer) are horrified at this report, and say that it is quite impossible to carry out the recommendations.'[15]

To her final days it was an article of faith with the Queen that the Army should remain under Royal command, operated either through the Sovereign or through a close relation. That it should remain under the Queen's ultimate control was also Buller's firm belief. This was to be brought out five years later. By then Arthur Bigge, after fifteen years as Ponsonby's assistant, had succeeded him as Private Secretary to the Queen. Close friend and confidant of Buller, the latter, when the issue was again being argued, queried with the new Private Secretary certain instructions of the Secretary of State:

> which are directed to accomplish the snuffing out of the Commander-in-Chief as the Queen's Commander-in-Chief and the creation of a Parliamentary Army under the Secretary of State. . . . I have the greatest horror of the idea of a Parliamentary Army and so also have I feel sure the vast majority of the Army and also of the inhabitants of this country.[16]

Memories of that earlier army with its 'major-generals' were still fresh even after a lapse of two and a half centuries.

Nevertheless, Buller at the time sought some sort of compromise. The year after the report was published he was stressing the importance of clearing the complicated chain of command, suggesting that the Commander-in-Chief, independent of politics, should promote, reward and administer discipline; at the same time the Secretary of State should decide upon the strength and cost of the Army. In a long conversation with Buller, Hartington was to admit that he saw the latter's objections to the Committee's report, and that his plan for obviating them and, at the same time, meeting the views of the Committee was 'ingenious and would have his most careful consideration'.[17] The only immediate outcome of the matter was further to increase the distaste of Lord Salisbury, the Prime Minister, for the too influential soldier whose objections to one of the Committee's major proposals had been so uninhibited.

One far-reaching reform advocated by Buller during his early years as Adjutant-General was much in advance of its time. Contrasting the enormous financial powers and responsibilities thrust on commanders in war with the severe red tape with which the civil side of the War Office bound their wrists in peace, he was later to suggest that:

> the War Office should hand over to the Army the funds voted by Parliament and allocated by the Secretary of State, and the Officer Commanding the District should be responsible for those funds, and should be accountable for those funds; he should watch their expenditure and account for their expenditure through his staff, and in that way it would be brought down to every man in every rank in the Army that the expenditure of military funds is a matter in which they ought to have a vital interest. . . . I have heard a Commander-in-Chief himself say that he did not consider that he had the slightest responsibility for expenditure, and it is the same with most officers in the Army . . . if you make officers responsible first of all for their finance they will

gradually become responsible for other things, and they will gradually learn to think.[18]

Under this proposal the civil side of the War Office would, in effect, deal only with policy matters, execution being left to the military, whose actions would be controlled by auditors. Nearly ninety years later, and after two major world wars, a financial and budget system on not too dissimilar lines, known in the present-day jargon as New Management Strategy, was introduced into the Army. So far as the writer knows, such ideas were never even discussed in the intervening years.

Such a proposal, pressed with Buller's customary vigour, did little to endear him to the civilian officials, especially Sir Arthur Haliburton, then Under-Secretary of State for War and later the Permanant Under-Secretary. Haliburton's and Buller's mutual dislike persisted throughout the latter's time as Adjutant-General[19], but for all that Haliburton was obliged to admit to a friend that he 'had a regard for Buller, in spite of our differences. He has many good points, though in a rough exterior and an explosive interior'.[20]

As a disciple of his old commanding officer, Colonel Hawley, whose lessons he never forgot, teaching officers and their soldiers 'to think' was fundamental to Buller's military philosophy. As he saw it, to give the man in the ranks a financial allowance for the upkeep of his clothing, the initial outfit being free, would inculcate a sense of responsibility and do a little towards making him consider husbanding his resources, something that would also be of help when he returned to civilian life.

This was just one small measure Buller advocated to help produce individuality and independence of action among all ranks. In 1896 he introduced a new Drill Book, the term 'drill' still covering tactics as well as the parade ground; much of the book was based upon Hawley's elastic teaching, to which the author gave full credit.[21] Later he was also to propose an inspectorate to ensure such training was actually taking place, and the unnecessarily long two-year Staff Course at Camberley cut by half but its output doubled.[22] He anticipated Archie Wavell's ideas on the training of infantry by deploring the absence of what he called the 'hunter instinct' in both officers and their men. This was in part due, as he saw it, to the increasingly high proportion of 'suburban-bred' boys among the officers. This was not mere snobbery. Rather he saw the youngsters as being 'too highly civilized' – brought up in surroundings that failed to instil the ability to take rapid action based upon quick deductions stemming from an understanding of human nature, knowledge of the countryside and accurate observation.[23]

Nonetheless Buller valued mental and moral rather than the physical qualities with which he was so well endowed himself. In giving evidence before the Sandhurst Committee on officer entry, he objected to a physical examination, pointing out that the Army did not require merely 'strong men', but those with the moral courage to overcome any weakness: he had so often seen men who lacked bodily strength last out through a couple of campaigns, whereas well-developed athletes collapsed straight away. He looked for lads educated to fit them for the liberal professions, those who had studied such subjects as Mathematics, Latin and French or German, preferably the latter. He deprecated marks being given for physical accomplishments, including riding and shooting.[24]

Buller remained consistent in fighting for the improvement of the soldier's conditions of service, as did Roberts, Evelyn Wood and Wolseley, his mentor. During his years at the War Office, Aldershot, the only large military centre in the country, was converted from a wilderness of wretched huts into a cantonment of well-built barrack-blocks with separate dining-rooms and decent married quarters. Knowing how the average soldier would spend any money that came his way, in giving evidence to the Wantage Committee of 1892 (yet another of such bodies that studded the 1890s) he advocated giving him better food rather than increasing his meagre stipend of a notional daily shilling; instead, a daily messing allowance of 3d should supplement his basic ration of bread and meat. Haliburton firmly opposed this, as well as a number of other improvements the Committee advocated: it would be another six years before the private's pay and messing were marginally improved.[25] As QMG, Buller had already made his presence felt on messing, introducing improvements to the supervision, equipment and training of the regimental cooks, reforms that led to his later setting up an Army School of Cooking at Aldershot.[26]

Buller was also the driving power behind the disciplinary reforms which were embodied in a revised *Manual of Military Law*. Regimental court-martials, composed of officers belonging to the accused's regiment and over-used by weak commanding officers to shirk the responsibility of sentencing, were in effect abolished, a colonel's powers of punishment being increased from seven to twenty-one days' detention. At the same time District court-martials were made simpler to convene, and the accused were given the right to elect trial before them and have evidence taken on oath. As Buller had anticipated, fears expressed in Parliament that the increased powers would lead to tyranny were to prove unjustified.[27] A legal colleague on the committee which studied the matter had this to say about Buller's qualities:

He struck me as a born leader of men, to be obeyed and followed without hesitation, and as being furthermore endowed with a penetrating and shrewd judgment. . . . In the transaction of business he was admirable; clear-sighted, firm and reasonable; he knew exactly what he wanted, though he was prepared to take less if the House of Commons was not disposed to legislate to the full extent of his views.[28]

On the other hand, this shrewd bluntness was not always appreciated by either politicians or their mandarins. An example was the occasion he was asked at a meeting for his views on the composition of a force to deal with a French encroachment into Nigeria. Well knowing that malaria would deal rapidly with the Frenchmen, he merely suggested that no more than a doctor equipped with a bottle of brandy was needed.[29]

In 1893 Campbell-Bannerman, who had returned to the War Office at the start of Gladstone's fourth and last Administration, offered Buller the post of Commander-in-Chief in India, Roberts' tour there having at last ended.

For the previous year, Buller, in his official capacity, had been in touch with Brackenbury about Roberts' replacement. Now a lieutenant-general – as was Buller, promoted to the same rank some months after becoming Adjutant-General – Brackenbury had, since 1891, been the Military Member of the Viceroy's Council, having returned to India after consolidating his reputation for administrative brilliance when Director of Intelligence in the War Office. In a post that then covered operational matters also, he had succeeded in developing and expanding the organization into something hitherto unknown in Britain.

To judge from their correspondence,[30] Buller was seeking, on the Secretary of State's behalf, information about a possible replacement for Roberts. Brackenbury's views on likely candidates were uninhibited: the abilities of the Duke of Connaught, whom he had instructed as a young man in strategy and tactics, 'were not of a high order'; moreover, he was a martinet under Cambridge's influence, who 'would care more about dress and the details of discipline than about keeping the army a ready instrument for war'. Another candidate suffered from extreme deafness and diffusiveness. Brackenbury admitted to being a runner himself, but felt debarred because he had been away from troops for seven years and was 'a poor horseman'. However, by August, 1892, he was trying to persuade Buller to take the job, setting out his qualities in a memorandum, copies of which he sent both to its subject and to the Viceroy, Lord Lansdowne.

Despite Brackenbury's reiterated attempts at persuasion, Buller declined to accept the appointment. He had likewise been under strong pressure to take it from Campbell-Bannerman (the relationship between minister and soldier was exceptionally close). The future Liberal Prime Minister would describe him as 'My Buller whom I would back to keep his end up above them all',[31] The two made a sound team and had much in common. A genial, kindly man with a pawky Scottish sense of humour, Campbell-Bannerman enjoyed a relaxed attitude towards work; nevertheless, as a departmental administrator he possessed great qualities. As his most recent biographer has written, 'backing his friends' was an obligation which 'C-B' never neglected,[32] a quality that appealed to a soldier.

Buller's reasons for refusing India can be surmised. Friends regretted that he did so, primarily because it would have got him away from what a previous biographer described as 'the slavery of the desk' and given him the chance of training, and possibly commanding, large bodies of troops in the field, something denied to him in England.[33] But years in India would have meant separation from his daughter and his step-children, and possibly from his wife also should she have decided to remain at home with them – a compelling reason indeed. A charming letter to his ten-year-old Georgiana, written about this time, brings out something of the close relationship father and daughter enjoyed. Staying at Windsor Castle, Buller admitted to being 'very comfortable and fancying myself rather'; he had teased a Government Minister who was responsible for 'the Parish Council Act, which is now spreading envy, hatred and malice over England'; and on his way to breakfast he had walked 'all down a gallery more than 100 yards long and full of the most beautiful china, statuary and cabinets, with here and there some of the ugliest and most woodeny pictures.'[34]

And after so long abroad, Buller was also enjoying England – both London life and the countryside. Like Wolseley, his circle of friends was in no way confined to government and the services. Sir Edmund Gosse, man-of-letters, poet and librarian of the House of Lords, has written at length about Buller's wide interests outside his profession.[35] As a fellow member of such clubs as the Savage and Grillon's (of which Buller was for many years joint secretary), Gosse was well placed to enjoy his conversation, incisive yet humorous, qualities unsuspected by acquaintances who found his outward demeanour and lack of small talk forbidding. Around their Bruton Street dinner table, the Bullers gathered artists such as Millais and William Richmond, the sculptor Sir Joseph Boehm and writers, some now forgotten, among them Andrew Lang, Thomas Hardy, Gosse himself, J. R. Green and John Oliver Hobbes, the last in reality Mrs Craigie. Lord Leighton, President of the Royal Academy, who abhorred the social round, was a close personal friend. Such was Buller's reputation for good taste in both art and literature that in 1897 he was to be appointed a member of the Royal Commission for the British Section of the Paris International Exhibition of 1900.

The Bullers were friendly with many of 'The Souls', that group of usually aristocratic men and women – intelligent but not necessarily intellectual – who allied literature to fashionable society and included among its members such figures as Curzon, St John Brodrick, Balfour, Lady Elcho and the Asquiths. But the Bullers belonged neither to it nor any other set. The often thinly disguised country-house affairs in which some 'Souls' indulged would hardly have appealed to them.

One group especially with which Buller would have nothing to do was the Prince of Wales's so-called 'Marlborough House Set', rejected also by 'The Souls' because of the philistinism of their conversation, limited largely to money, racing and sport. Buller went so far as to decline an invitation to shoot at Sandringham – an impolitic act indeed – on the grounds of business at Downes. His real reason was his dislike for the future King's moneyed friends, many of them Jews – often forgotten today is the anti-Semitism normal among all classes of society until after the Second World War. Understandably the Prince was much annoyed,[36] but this was only one of several incidents that offended him. So stubborn was Buller, after he replaced Wolseley as Adjutant-General, in refusing to do 'jobs' for members of the Prince's circle that Princess Alexandra complained to a friend that they found 'the difference between the two very inconvenient'.[37] This disagreement extended also to appointments outside the military sphere, Buller at one point refusing the Prince's attempt to place his clerical protégé in a living adjoining Sandringham, on a part of the Townshend estates which Buller was administering under an Order of the Court.[38]

Buller had aroused the Prince's ire only a few months after taking over. The trouble arose over the Tranby Croft case, the gaming scandal which so offended Victorian middle-class morality after the reluctant Prince had been subpoenaed to appear in Court in June, 1891, as a witness in the slander action brought by a senior Guards officer and fellow-guest accused of cheating at baccarat at a country-house party. HRH's complaint was Buller's refusal, in the absence of the Commander-in-Chief abroad, to prejudice the civil trial by taking military action against the officer,[39] so perhaps avoiding the Prince's appearance in Court. Enraged by Buller's failure to hush the affair up – it may have been inability, for he was acting upon advice from the Judge-Adjutant-General and was supported by his Secretary of State – the Prince exploded to the Duke of Cambridge that:

> The conduct of the A.G. is inexplicable, but he cannot have the interests of the Army at heart, acting in the way he has. I always knew he was a born soldier – and equally imagined he was a gentleman, but from henceforth I can never look upon him in the latter category.[40]

So bitter did the dispute at one point become that Buller is said to have turned the heir to the throne out of his office.[41] Strong-willed, fervently honest and lacking in tact, Buller gave the Prince every reason to dislike him, but the Queen so admired him that the Prince, deprived of all authority by his mother, could do Buller little harm so long as she lived. But Buller had made a powerful and implacable enemy. After her death, the atmosphere of the Court and of a vocal section of Society was to turn markedly hostile. Many slanders about him current in the early years of the century were said to have had their origin in those circles.[42]

Just two years after Buller's rejection of India, Campbell-Bannerman offered him the Duke of Cambridge's post as Commander-in-Chief. Its incumbent, now in his seventy-seventh year and after thirty-nine in office, should have gone long before, but had clung stubbornly and embarrassingly to office. The Queen favoured the Duke of Connaught as her cousin's successor, but both political parties wished to moderate the often negative Royal influence over the Army. But when the new Prime Minister, Lord Rosebery, who had succeeded the eighty-four-year-old Gladstone two years before, told the Queen on 9 May, 1895, that the Cabinet recommended Buller as the Duke's successor, with her favourite son probably following him, she accepted the advice.[43] However, it fell to her, despite her initial reluctance, to persuade Cambridge to go. In a difficult three-hour interview a few days later she told her cousin, who was refusing to surrender to what he termed 'radical clamour', that his decision not to resign 'was inadvisable on every ground'. This Arthur Bigge passed on to his old friend Buller.[44]

A month afterwards, when Bigge told his aggravated monarch that the Duke was still most reluctant to step down, she demanded that 'the matter must be settled,' declaring that 'it is undignified to cling to office'.[45] When at last the Duke succumbed to pressure, the Queen approved Buller as his successor,[46] having learned from Bigge 'that there seems to be a strong majority, including the Duke of Cambridge, favourable to Sir Redvers Buller. But the supercession of Lord Wolseley will create considerable heart-burnings.'[47] Even the Prince of Wales, according to Sir Francis Knollys, his Private Secretary, felt 'sure himself that Sir Redvers Buller would be the best man for the Post'.[48]

From both seniority and experience, Cambridge's obvious successor was, of course, Wolseley, relegated to what amounted to semi-retirement in the Irish command since he left Pall Mall, but the Liberal Government had been deeply offended by his outspoken criticism of Home Rule for Ireland. However, it was to prove fortunate that, when Campbell-Bannerman announced the Duke's departure to the House of Commons, he made no mention of his successor; later in the same debate Lord Rosebery's Government was defeated over the question of ammunition reserves, and the Liberals later resigned. The following month Lord Lansdowne, back from India, replaced Campbell-Bannerman in a new Conservative administration, with Lord Salisbury, as Winston Churchill put it, again reigning 'venerable' and 'august' as Prime Minister.[49] As a result, not Buller but Wolseley was appointed Commander-in-Chief, but with much reduced powers. Buller's prior selection was never made public but became widely known.

Lord Salisbury, to the Queen's extreme displeasure, offered the post to Wolseley without obtaining her prior sanction. But her complaint that Wolseley was 'very imprudent, full of new fancies, and has a clique of his own'.[50] produced from her Prime Minister the response that he distrusted Buller.[51] This annoyed her even more, provoking her crushing rebuke:

> I do not share your distrust of Sir R. Buller, who is most honest and straightforward; I believe him to be a thorough gentleman, with considerable independence of Character; and [he] had held aloof from the press, which perhaps others have not.[52]

The Duke of Connaught, when he heard what had occurred, also sprang to Buller's defence:

> I can't understand Lord Salisbury's statement that *he distrusted Buller*. He is sometimes very contradictory and even hot-tempered, but I have *complete confidence* in him, and look upon him as one of the *most honest* and *straightforward Englishmen* I know. I have had on one or two occasions considerable differences with him, but I have found him thoroughly straight and honourable, and I have the greatest respect for him.

Connaught also hoped that his mother would '*insist* on Lord Wolseley and all his staff *ceasing* for *once* and all to have *any connection with the Press*'.[53] Few indeed of Buller's colleagues or friends failed at one time or another to experience the Duke's 'considerable differences'. Even the steadfast Bigge admitted to Georgiana Buller that 'they did not always agree'.[54]

No firm explanation for Salisbury's distrust has come to light, but the presumption can only be that Buller was paying for his radical approach to the problem of the Irish peasantry and their landlords, among whom were numbered so many Tory politicians, prominent among them Lansdowne. Buller's less than enthusiastic attitude towards some of the proposals of the Hartington Commission, set up under Lord Salisbury's previous Administration, may also have contributed towards his distaste for a too outspoken soldier of liberal sympathies. Nevertheless, Wolseley's views of the Hartington recommendations matched Buller's.

The offer to Wolseley had been a choice between Commander-in-Chief or Ambassador to Berlin, Kaiser Wilhelm II, the Queen's grandson, being anxious that a soldier should fill the post. Buller's name occurred to Salisbury as an alternative after Wolseley made his choice, but the idea seems to have taken no root. As Bigge minuted the Queen, he doubted whether Buller would take the post, nor did he 'think Sir R. would make a good diplomatist and Lady Audrey is not strong'.[55]

Among the calumnies from which Buller has suffered was the accusation that he intrigued to supplant Wolseley as Cambridge's successor. Wolseley was certainly persuaded that he had. As the country's most prominent soldier and also Campbell-Bannerman's personal friend, with whom in their younger days he had collaborated over army reforms, Wolseley assumed that the appointment would automatically be his. When news reached him that Buller was to be appointed, he accused his pupil of being 'a false friend' who owed him everything.[56] Wolseley soon heard also that the sixty-three-year-old Roberts, now Lord Roberts of Kandahar, who since vacating his post in India had been on half-pay writing his memoirs, was with his friends 'moving heaven and earth to get Lansdowne . . . to make him the boss at the War Office'.[57] Roberts, however, was 'absolutely impossible because of ignorance of military affairs outside India,' as the Queen sagaciously reminded Salisbury.[58] Nevertheless support for the ever-popular 'Little Bobs' was strong, especially among the general public. In many ways Buller had been a compromise choice between two mutually jealous field-marshals, as Lady Wolseley revealed to her husband:

I also had a letter from Sir J. M'Neill, which I did not particularly like. He made no offer of services, but declares Sir R.B. is quite to be trusted and most loyal to you. He says that as the country is divided (which I don't believe) as to you or Roberts, the solution is Buller![59]

An unreliable, if not treacherous, horse in their stables was to be named by the Wolseleys 'Sir Redvers'.[60] Suspicious as ever of others' motives, there is small doubt that Wolseley was convinced that Buller had worked behind the scenes to supplant him. But no evidence for such disloyalty has come to light. The opposite seems to be the case. Four years afterwards and incensed that slanders impugning his reputation were still being bandied about, Buller asked Campbell-Bannerman to help clear his name. Relying upon his memory because he was in London and all his correspondence was at Belmont, his place in Scotland, the Liberal statesman replied:

I sounded you as to your ideas and feelings. It was I who opened the subject to you, not you to me, & this was quite preliminary to any decision on the matter. I found you most unwilling to contemplate your own appointment: you dwelt on your own obligations to, and friendship for, Lord W. You deprecated the idea of your promotion, and you did this not by way of a mere . . . affectation of reluctance, but with an evident earnestness which greatly impressed me. One phrase you used remains in my mind – you said you considered yourself a good second man, and that you were by no means sure that you would be a good first man. So far from anything like 'pushing' or 'intriguing' you disclaimed in your communications with me any thought of your own advancement at that time, and advocated the high claims (which indeed were evident) of Lord Wolseley.[61]

An independent witness confirms this. J. A. Spender, the most influential political journalist of his day and Campbell-Bannerman's official biographer, in correspondence with Buller's own biographer, wrote:

He undoubtedly conveyed to Campbell-Bannerman his great reluctance to accept the office, if by so doing he would cause pain or disappointment to Lord Wolseley.[62]

The last word can safely be left to Bigge. He wrote to his friend:

I congratulate you on not being made Commander-in-Chief. The part you are known to have played in the matter is better than any Commander-in-Chiefship in the world, and in the long run will, I hope, give you infinitely more satisfaction.[63]

As Adjutant-General to Wolseley until his seven-year tour ended in 1897, Buller was ably and loyally to support his old master.

8

A RELUCTANT COMMANDER

Buller's eventual departure from the War Office was followed by twelve months on half pay. It was a year put to sound and pleasurable use during which he could attend to the many problems of Downes and his other estates. Then, in October, 1898, now a full general, he succeeded the Duke of Connaught at Aldershot. It was the only worthwhile command in England. With some semblance of an organization for war, Aldershot District housed in up-to-date barracks an infantry division, a cavalry brigade and attached gunners and sappers; moreover there was enough land to exercise – albeit with some difficulty – a brigade at a time. Until 1898, when 41,000 acres of Salisbury Plain were bought for the purpose, the Army owned no area where larger formations could manoeuvre. Before that, large-scale training depended upon the agreement of landowners, whose goodwill was often baulked by the objections of shooting tenants worried for their pheasants.[1]

The opportunities for senior officers and their staffs to practise their trade were, therefore, limited. The alternative were 'staff tours' or 'staff rides', during which imaginary bodies of troops were exercised in battle against one another. Although such a cheap and worthwhile method had long been current in Germany, not until 1895 was the first held in England, an exhausting six-day marathon conducted by Buller. A number of future World War leaders, including French, Haig and Rawlinson, were among those who took part;[2] others such as Plumer, Wilson and Byng were at the time serving under him as staff officers at Aldershot.

Soon after taking over at Aldershot, Buller encountered a serious challenge. Given charge of one of two army corps, each more than 20,000 strong, matched against each other over Salisbury Plain and Dorset, his opponent was Connaught. The manoeuvres were a success, in so far as they exposed many deficiencies both tactical and administrative, but it was generally agreed that Buller did not handle his force especially skilfully. To the openly expressed astonishment of many, including Lord Roberts, who was staying at Aldershot with St John Brodrick – now Under-Secretary at the War Office – the Duke was said to have had the better of it all.[3] Brodrick remembered Wolseley's indirect criticism of Buller at the summing-up for ordering a frontal attack with insufficient and weary troops, short of artillery support; to this, Buller was heard to ejaculate, 'I have been making a fool of myself all day'.[4] So surprising was the outcome that it was rumoured that he purposely gave victory to the Queen's favourite son to avoid upsetting her.[5]

As even Buller's greatest admirers have confessed, there was no doubt that more than ten years at an office desk had sapped the powers of a fifty-eight-year-old man rather too fond of good living. Jowls had blurred his previously clean-cut features, giving his countenance a sulky, if not ill-tempered, look when in repose. As the daughter of a general is said to have remarked, 'He should have taken out a libel action against his face'.[6] For all that, as a hard rider to hounds he was still in sound physical shape. This he was soon to prove. Nevertheless, sedentary work is not conducive to mental agility or rapid decision making, and, like many generals before and since, Buller lacked experience of commanding large formations in the field, either in war or on training. It was perhaps a pity that he had refused to accept the command in India, an active and operational theatre where the countryside lent itself to handling sizeable bodies of troops.

Although Buller was to remain in Aldershot for no more than a year, he made his mark there in a number of ways, not least in his refreshing ideas on training. These he showered upon his subordinates in a succession of pithy and practical memoranda on such subjects as field-firing, the duties of commanders, tactical manoeuvres, the study of ground and fire power[7] – all seemingly elementary, but hitherto largely neglected. However, he was given little time to correct the widespread faults existing in what should have been the Army's best-trained formations and units. In mid-June Lord Lansdowne summoned him to the War Office to tell him that the Government had reason to fear that war in South Africa was in certain circumstances probable, and that he had been selected to command there.[8]

The likelihood of war between Britain and the South African Republic of the Transvaal had long been clear. The peace Buller had helped Evelyn Wood patch up under Gladstone's instructions in 1881 to end the previous war there might, but for one unseen chance, have held indefinitely: in 1886 gold was discovered on the Witwatersrand, just south of the capital, Pretoria. The result was an influx of prospectors and their camp-followers, individuals drawn from everywhere, but especially Britain; despite the unexpected wealth mining brought to the Transvaal, their presence was resented and feared by the God-fearing descendants of the *voortrekkers*, whose aim had been to escape just such influences. To control their own political integrity, the Boers denied these so-called 'Uitlanders' all political rights. But Uitlanders were soon to match Boers in their numbers. It was a situation ripe for exploitation.

In 1895 Cecil Rhodes, as Prime Minister of the Cape, was at the summit of his power and influence. In the twenty-five years since he arrived in South Africa as a sickly and penniless youth, he and his associates had gained control of the Kimberley diamonds and had acquired vast stakes in the Rand gold-mines. But he amassed money primarily to further his vision of a federated South Africa firmly under British control, one linked as far as Egypt by a carpet of British colonies and protectorates. Extensive areas north of the Transvaal were already his, run by his Chartered Company and named Rhodesia after him. To Rhodes and to his fellow financiers, prominent among whom were the principals of Wernher-Beit, the firm which controlled much of the rest of the Rand gold, the backveld Boers of the Transvaal seemed set to counter their ambitions, both political and financial.

The outcome was the ill-conceived and worse-managed raid into the Transvaal by a handful of Rhodesian policemen and volunteers led by Dr Leander Starr Jameson. Starting from Mafeking, their arrival in Johannesburg was to have been the signal for a general Uitlander uprising. But the mining community had too much sense. The Boer commandos rounded up Jameson's men; Rhodes, who, with the financial help of Wernher-Beit, was shown to have planned and paid for the entire sorry business, had his reputation irreparably harmed and was obliged to resign his premiership.

It was fortunate for Salisbury's Government that Joseph Chamberlain, the Colonial Secretary, succeeded in disguising his prior knowledge of the Jameson Raid. A self-made Birmingham businessman, Chamberlain was both radical and imperialist. As leader of the Liberal Unionists with Lord Hartington, he had sacrificed office under Gladstone in 1886 in protest against Irish Home Rule and crossed to the benches opposite. His ruthless cover-up of the Raid succeeded in concealing his complicity from the public, the Opposition and most of his Cabinet colleagues alike. To this Joe Chamberlain brought the qualities of determination and machine-like precision for which he was famous.

Determined to avoid any similar scandal, Chamberlain despatched to the Cape as Governor and High Commissioner Sir Alfred Milner, a man whose record suggested that he was the cautious and conciliatory diplomat South Africa needed. His background was unusual. A quarter German and schooled in his grandmother's country, he lacked both money and social position. But he was a member of a brilliant generation of Balliol graduates. Already, at the age of forty-two his career had encompassed journalism, private secretary to a Chancellor of the Exchequer, financial secretary in Egypt to Evelyn Baring and Chairman of the Inland Revenue. And hidden under his mandarin's opaque exterior was a romantic and near reckless nature.

Moreover, he was a determined imperialist, not in the acquisition of fresh black colonies, but in the consolidation of the white Empire into a supreme world power. In South Africa he visualized a major step forward; unification under British control with the Transvaal's riches the basis for its prosperity.

In this Milner faced the implacable enmity of Paul Kruger, elected for a fourth term as President of the Transvaal, the hero not just of his own people, but his fellow Afrikaners in the Orange Free State and the Cape Colony also. Now over eighty but still active, Kruger was a part of Boer history: as a ten year-old he had taken part in the Great Trek. A 'flat-earther', he lived by the Bible and had proved himself repeatedly both in battle and politics. In contrast to Kruger – a massive, puffy-faced old backveld Boer – was General Joubert, the second most powerful man in the Republic, whom Buller had so distrusted in the aftermath of Majuba. A generation younger than Kruger, the latter had thrice beaten him for the Presidency. But as Buller was later to tell his wife:

> I liked Kruger much more than I did Joubert. The latter was Slim Piet and . . . I saw nothing else. The former has always the idea of a Boer Empire, and as far as his lights went was an astute honest peasant. He is as the French peasants were in the Revolution capable of cruelty but it would only be incidental cruelty and due to his thinking it either necessary or unavoidable. Joubert on the other hand always strikes me as a cold schemer.[9]

This 'Boer Empire', as Buller put it, referred to Kruger's ambition, one that matched that of Rhodes and Milner, to found a united – but Afrikaner – South Africa. Such a nation would embrace not just the two Boer Republics of the Transvaal and the Orange Free State, but the British colonies of Natal and the largely Boer Cape, together with Rhodesia and the several black protectorates.

Convinced that Kruger was unlikely to agree to any reform that would endanger the integrity of his Afrikaner homeland, and that an armed struggle was inevitable, Milner based his policy on 'working up to a crisis', as he put it to Chamberlain,[10] one that would drive Kruger into aggression. Chamberlain, on the other hand, advocated a waiting game until such time as Kruger faded out. Nevertheless, and despite the risks previously run over the Jameson Raid, Chamberlain still – and possibly deliberately – gave Milner the freedom of action which allowed him to lure his country into war. In so doing, Milner had few allies, but those were powerful. Rhodes's influence had been destroyed by the Raid, but the Uitlander leaders, prominent among them the so-called 'gold bugs' of the Rand, the Wernher-Beits and others, gave him their full support. Meanwhile the Salisbury Government did not itself seek war, nor was the British public especially concerned about the fate of the Uitlanders.

Even Milner's senior soldier, who was to act as High Commissioner when the former went home in November, 1898 – ostensibly on leave but primarily to enlist support in his own influential circles – openly sympathized with Boer aspirations and opposed the Uitlanders. This was no other than William Butler, now a lieutenant-general and as brash as ever. Like Buller, he had fought alongside Boers and liked and admired 'a sober, steady, peaceable people . . . utterly destitute of swagger or pretension, yet having plenty of resolution'.[11] He agreed with the philosophy that Johannesburg was akin to 'Monte Carlo superimposed upon Sodom and Gomorrah'.[12] He protested also to Wolseley at the War Office that the Uitlander problem was capable of being settled and that a failure to do so was likely to result in 'deeper national discredit at home, and a certainty of misery and misfortune to this country greater than it has heretofore known in its history'.[13] Such a Cassandra-like and open opponent was not to be tolerated, and in July Milner forced Butler to resign.

After months of ceaseless pressure, culminating in an emotive despatch from Milner in which he described the plight of 'thousands of British subjects kept permanently in the position of helots . . . calling vainly to Her Majesty's Government for redress',[14] the Cabinet decided to intervene – but peacefully. This coincided with a proposal by the leaders of the Cape Afrikaners that Milner and Kruger should meet. The outcome was the conference at Bloemfontein, the capital of the Orange Free State at which, after days of stonewalling, Kruger at last offered a concession upon the franchise, one that Milner brushed aside, bringing the proceedings to an abrupt end with Kruger wistfully complaining, 'It is our country you want'. He was right. Milner could have saved the conference but he had taken a further step towards the war he sought. He now asked the Cabinet for an 'overwhelming' force of 10,000 troops as reinforcements to help defend the frontiers of the Cape and Natal. Tension rose throughout South Africa.

Buller's summons to see Lord Lansdowne stemmed from the failure of the Bloemfontein Conference. It was an unhappy meeting between two men who could not stand one another. As Buller confessed to his brother some months later, 'We did not agree; he found it difficult to work with me, and I with him, though I certainly say that I have never worked harder for anyone. In the end he told me what he had said before that I was disagreeable to work with.'[15]

That being so, it was perhaps surprising that the Secretary of State, knowing Buller well and disliking him intensely, should have chosen him to command in the coming war. As his country's most prominent fighting general other than Wolseley, and in charge at Aldershot of what could be described as the Army's strategic reserve, he was, of course, the near inevitable choice. Buller, however, came to the conclusion that Lansdowne did not want any serious preparations for war put in hand and that his appointment was merely a 'party move in the political game'.[16]

According to Buller, Lansdowne received him at that June meeting 'in a most ungracious manner'.[17] Aloof, severe and unbending in official life, his previous quasi-regal posts of Viceroy of India and Governor-General of Canada hardly fitted the Secretary of State for the hurly-burly of political life. Criticism from anyone, let alone an over-outspoken soldier, was hardly welcome to this great patrician of mixed English, Irish, Scottish and French blood, over-conscientious but of modest intellectual ability. As Campbell-Bannerman, his possibly prejudiced – albeit easy-going – political opponent put it, 'Lansdowne is weak and pleasant, but exceedingly secretive and anxious to get the credit for everything'.[18] Not that the Liberal statesman held Brodrick in high regard either: writing at the same time about the two men, he dwelt upon their 'vanity and self-confidence . . . their jealousy of others and each other.'[19] And, of course, of Lansdowne's several houses the one he loved best was Dereen in County Kerry, a place he had extended and made beautiful, but which became something of a millstone when his Irish tenants withheld their rents. As a frequently absentee landlord, Lansdowne would hardly have forgotten Buller's activities in south-west Ireland.

His innate honesty led Buller straight away to remind Lansdowne that he had never held an independent command, and that he had always considered himself as a better second-in-command than commander in anything complex. Any war in South Africa, he suggested, would be a complicated affair and a better arrangement would be for Wolseley to be in charge, with him as his Adjutant-General; it was the arrangement, so Buller told the Secretary of State, that he had previously recommended to Campbell-Bannerman when the question was being discussed. He could, he claimed, hold his own with anyone as a commander in the field, but he had never had the responsibility of commanding such an expedition 6,000 miles from home; he feared also that 'because he was combatant by nature' he would, if difficulties arose, be likely to 'plunge into the actual struggle'.[20] Yet again Buller had felt in no way inhibited from confessing to his lack of self-confidence. And this to someone he thoroughly disliked at the moment when command in a major war – a soldier's greatest prize – was in his grasp.

An alternative could well have been Evelyn Wood, who had replaced Buller as Adjutant-General, having previously enhanced his reputation as an able trainer of troops. That Buller had twice served under him in South Africa added to Wood's bitter disappointment at not being chosen.[21] Buller himself, on the eve of sailing, was to reveal to a friend that, 'I have always

12. The Battle of Abu Klea as depicted by R. Caton Woodville for the *Illustrated London News*. (see p75)

13. General Buller in Ireland. (see chapter 6) *Illustrated London News*.

14. Spy cartoon of Bull
from *Vanity Fair*, Janua
1900.

15. General Piet Kronje.
(see p171)

16. 'Louis Botha, the future Imperial statesman.' (p136)

17. 'The flat-topped and commanding Spion Kop on his right.' (p167)

18. An engraving of Buller from the painting by Henry Tanworth Wells. (*Mrs Peter Parker*)

19. 'In September, 1905, Buller watched the unveiling of the superb bronze thirteen-foot-high equestrian statue of himself that stands at the end of Queen's Street, Exeter.' (p207) (*Royal Albert Memorial Museum, Exeter City Museums and Art Gallery*)

looked upon this as Evelyn's journey, and had been wondering whether when it came off I should have a look in. . . . I think he would have done it better than I shall, but I shall try my best.'[22]

In what Buller described as 'a desultory conversation', he and Lansdowne discussed possible plans of campaign. An advance by way of Delagoa Bay would require the co-operation of Portugal; that by Durban was objectionable because of the rugged country and the danger of a flank attack from the Orange Free Staters, if they came in on the Transvaal's side, as was thought probable. For the same reason the railway route through Kimberley was equally difficult. Such considerations had already led Buller to the conclusion that the only way of attacking Pretoria was by way of the Central Railway through Bloemfontein, one that postulated either the Free State's neutrality or war against her as well. When told by Lansdowne that the Bloemfontein route was out of the question, Buller insisted that before undertaking a war against the Transvaal, the Free State must be obliged to declare itself one way or another: the proposed force of two infantry and one cavalry divisions, with seven extra battalions for the Lines of Communication, was enough to tackle the Transvaal alone, but it was impossible to leave the Free State out of account.[23]

Buller went straight from Lansdowne's office to see Wolseley, whom he found equally perturbed that their political master seemed unable to understand that serious preliminary preparations would need to be put in hand. Also present was Colonel Neville Lyttelton, a War Office staff officer who had also served there under Buller and who knew both his seniors well. Before him, Buller repeated to Wolseley the doubts he had expressed to Lansdowne. As Lyttelton (who early in the next century became the first and a most ineffective Chief of the General Staff of the Army) remembered the conversation, 'He expressed very strong objections to accepting the command, said he was sick of South Africa, and if he was forced to go out would come away as soon as he could.'[24] Seldom can a general have approached his greatest challenge with less enthusiasm.

Another matter Buller put to Wolseley, as he had done to Lansdowne, was the difficulty he faced in retaining the command at Aldershot while attempting to plan a major campaign. That Wolseley failed to press Lansdowne over-hard on either this or the preliminary preparations was, perhaps, symptomatic. Since a serious illness in 1897, his memory and capacity for work had been failing, the onset of premature senile decay and a sad old age.[25] Nor did it help that Wolseley and Lansdowne thoroughly distrusted one another. As a friend of Roberts, the latter had little use for the now senior officers of Wolseley's old 'Ring' who filled many important posts in the War Office; the Commander-in-Chief, on the other hand, viewed his political superior, whom he detested personally, as the epitome of cost-cutting and red-tape, and for his failure, as Wolseley saw it, to stand up for the Army.[26]

For a month Buller heard nothing further. Then, at a second meeting on 6 July, Lansdowne informed him that the despatch of 10,000 troops to the Cape was being considered but that no plans for their use had been made; Buller could, however, dismiss from his mind any question of using the Free State route to invade the Transvaal. Buller's response to this second vague conversation was to send Wolseley a closely argued minute setting out the sequence any preparations should follow. Its recommendations read:

1. Strengthen the Cape Colony and Natal garrisons to the extent that local authority there now think sufficient to protect those colonies.
2. Make up your mind as to the route, and definitely as to the attitude to be adopted towards the Orange Free State.
3. Commence the formation of Magazines on the intended route, and the Mobilization of the active force.
4. Send out this fighting force.[27]

When Buller wrote this minute, the British garrison in South Africa numbered less than 9,000 men, with three batteries of field artillery, some sappers, and a handful of special service and ASC officers either on their way or recently arrived. Against this small force the Transvaal Boers alone could field no less than 25,000 mounted burghers. To these might be added 15,000 Free Staters, if they threw in their lot with their fellows, helped possibly by an unknown number of Cape Colony Afrikaners. Accustomed to the saddle and the rifle, the Transvaalers were armed with brand-new Mausers and plentiful ammunition, supplies of which were still being freely imported through the Cape. Nor was modern artillery lacking. Manned by professional blue-uniformed artillerymen, Transvaal's only regular troops, six 75-mm field guns and four 155-mm heavies (the 'Long Toms') had recently been supplied by Creusot in France, together with eight 75-mm and four 120-mm howitzers from Krupps in Germany. Twenty of the experimental Maxim-Nordenfeld 1-pounder 'Pom-Poms' had even been bought from Britain, a weapon not yet available to her own Army. More artillery pieces were on order.

A near accurate measure of the Boer forces and their armament had been made by the War Office's small Intelligence Department, but its officers mistakenly forecast that the Boers would confine themselves to sending raiding parties, some 2,000 or 3,000 strong, across their borders. Despite Majuba, it was not thought that such unmilitary farmers would constitute a serious threat, the reasoning being that their leaders lacked knowledge of handling and supplying large bodies of men whose discipline, in any case, was likely to be poor. From the intelligence standpoint, however, the British were at a disadvantage: in 1898 the Transvaal spent £3250 monthly upon espionage, twenty times the sum available to British intelligence.[28]

Buller's critics have made much of Wolseley's statement before the subsequent Royal Commission on the War in South Africa that, at a meeting on 17 July between himself, Lansdowne and Buller, the last-named declared 'that as long as clever men like Butler and Symons [commanding the brigade in Natal] on the spot did not say that there was a danger, he saw no necessity for sending out any troops in advance of the Army Corps'.[29] Lansdowne, giving evidence subsequently, admitted to not recollecting the conversation, but did not 'question the substantial accuracy'.[30] As Buller pressed continually for the garrison to be strengthened, it was a most unlikely comment for him to have made; if he did say something on these lines, it was more likely to have been an expression of his reluctance to send out any part of his own Army Corps ahead of the rest. What is more likely is that Wolseley's failing memory was to blame after a lapse for four years; he was, as he admitted, speaking from memory alone.

Kruger, under pressure both from his more cautious advisers and his compatriots in the Cape, on 19 July offered the franchise to the Uitlanders after seven years' residence. It was a generous improvement upon his Bloemfontein terms but one that in no way stilled the ever-rising tension with Boer extremists near surpassing the Uitlanders in provocation. The relief of the British Cabinet at Kruger's concession matched Milner's annoyance, who suggested that it was a sham and pressed again for the extra troops. Their arrival, he visualized, would cause either Kruger's complete climb-down or force him into war. The latter, as he cabled Chamberlain, 'however deplorable in itself, would at least enable us to put things on a sound basis'.[31] But Chamberlain over-optimistically assumed that the crisis was over and the Cabinet decided against despatching the extra 10,000 men, a figure estimated as sufficient to safeguard the British colonies from attack, despite the Boer preponderance in numbers.

As the summer passed, War Office staff officers, denied the money needed to make any significant preparations for the coming conflict, planned as best they could in the absence of a proper General Staff organized for such a task. Buller, alarmed by the chaos arising from the conflicting instructions being issued by the various branches, suggested behind the scenes that regular co-ordinating meetings of departmental heads be held. This was a system he had himself instituted as Adjutant-General, but which Lansdowne had abolished on taking office, substituting in its place an Army Board which could assemble only to consider papers referred to it by himself. The result had been that co-operation between branches had become fitful. Anxious to avoid giving Lansdowne grounds for further offence, Buller failed to insist that he should himself be present at these revived meetings, a decision he admitted afterwards was mistaken.[32] Lansdowne, in attempting to refute Buller's subsequent complaints, denied to the Royal Commission that the War Office had in any way 'boycotted' him, commenting, with some justification, that 'it had never occurred to me that he was a particularly diffident person, or very easily intimidated, particularly by civilians'.[33] It was perhaps a measure of the ill-will existing between minister and soldier that the latter felt unable to put his problems fairly before his political master.

Faced with the command of the largest expeditionary force Britain had sent overseas since the Crimea, Buller had no direct responsibility for its preparation. Furthermore, because he was never made aware of the exchanges taking place between Milner and Chamberlain,[34] he depended for political intelligence upon what he could glean from personal contacts and the press. A proposal by Wolseley to collect Buller's troops together for training on Salisbury Plain was rejected for fear that it would be seen as provocation, and the sending of Buller himself out to the Cape as Butler's replacement, but with wider powers, does not seem to have been seriously considered.[35]

By early September Buller was so alarmed by the failure to prepare for a war, by then clearly near inevitable, that he took it upon himself to approach the Prime Minister direct, without telling Lansdowne. He had been spurred to such an aberrant, if not defiant, measure through learning that Chamberlain was meditating the immediate despatch of more troops to South Africa. His informant was the talented and attractive Miss Flora Shaw; anthropologist, *Times* correspondent, historian and writer, she was later wife to Lord Lugard, the distinguished African pro-consul.[36]

Buller's go-between with the Prime Minister was the latter's Principal Private Secretary, Schomberg K. McDonnell, a close personal friend whose views on Lansdowne matched his own, and who was astounded to discover not only the near absence of contact between the War and the Colonial Offices, but the lack of preparations for immediate military action to back any ultimatum that the Government might despatch to the Transvaal. McDonnell went as far as to encourage Buller to 'put it strongly' and 'not to be too susceptible to Lansdowne's feelings'. A document was needed, McDonnell urged, that would 'startle the Cabinet', the fact that both Wolseley and Buller had been pressing their views upon Lansdowne being 'quite unknown to Ministers'.

This document Buller produced, with McDonnell's assistance. At the same time, after making the initial approach, he ensured that Wolseley knew what he was about.[37] On 8 September two papers were presented to a startled Cabinet, the first a copy of a detailed minute addressed from Buller to the

Commander-in-Chief, setting out his views, the second this memorandum from Buller to Lord Salisbury, dated 5 September:

As you ask for my ideas, I give them to you privately. I am not happy as to the way things are going. There must be some period at which the military and the diplomatic or political forces are brought together, and in my view, this ought to be before action is determined upon. In other words, before the diplomat proceeds to an ultimatum, the military should be in a position to enforce it.

This is not the case with regards to affairs in South Africa. So far as I am aware, the War Office has no idea of how matters are proceeding and has not been consulted. I mean they do not know how fast diplomacy is moving.

From the military point of view, a campaign in the Transvaal is one which demands careful organization. A large transport establishment is absolutely necessary, and it will be, when obtained, a *strange* transport; so it wants very careful organization.

We have, say, 13,000 men in South Africa, who are all well equipped. We have both the Cape Colony and Natal to defend, and we have some 10,000 men in Natal and 3,000 in Cape Colony. *These figures are conjectural; I have no certain facts by me.* [author's italics].

I estimate that to reinforce them we could get –

5,000 men from *India* in *five* weeks from the date of the date of the order;

10,000 men from England in eleven weeks from date of order;

An army corps from England in sixteen to twenty weeks from date of order.

Before we operate against the Boers we should know the line on which we are to advance, i.e., whether by the Orange Free State or by Natal. (These are, for military reasons, the only two possible routes; I am informed that Delagoa Bay is out of the question.)

I have never had yet had the route fixed, but I have gathered from Lord Lansdowne that he thinks the Natal route will prove the only possible one. Natal is a wedge 240 miles deep, and for 100 miles of that depth the point of the wedge is bounded by a hostile country, the Orange Free State to the west, the South African Republic to the east. The commander of any force invading the Transvaal by that route would have –

(a) To take an army of 20,000 men into the Transvaal.

(b) To hold his communications with, say, 10,000 men.

(c) To have a free force in Natal of, say, 10,000 men, to resist invasion.

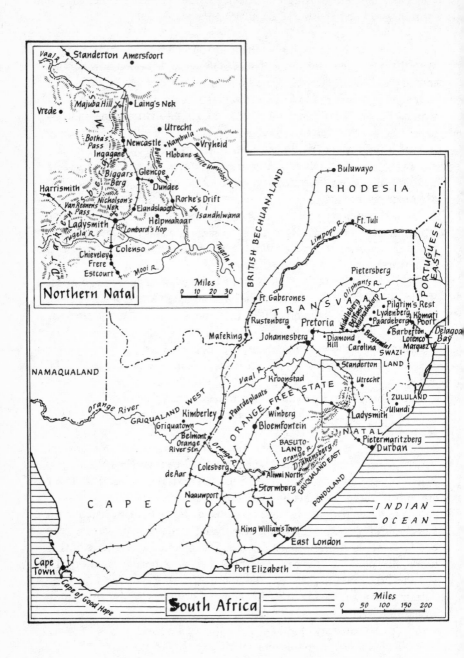

Northern Natal

Vaal R.
Standerton   Amersfoort
Vrede
Majuba Hill
Laing's Nek
Utrecht
Botha's Pass
Newcastle
Kambula
Vryheid
Ingagane
Hlobane
Biggars Berg
Glencoe
Harrismith
Dundee
Van Reenen's Pass
Nicholson's Nek
Rorke's Drift
Elandslaagte
Isandhlwana
Helpmakaar
Ladysmith
Lombard's Kop
Tugela R.
Colenso
Chieveley
Frere
Estcourt
Mooi R.

Miles
0 10 20 30

South Africa

RHODESIA
Buluwayo
Ft. Tuli
BRITISH BECHUANALAND
Limpopo R.
Pietersberg
Oliphants R.
Ft. Gaberones
TRANSVAAL
Pilgrim's Rest
Lydenberg
Komati Poort
Rustenberg
Paardeberg
Barberton
Pretoria
Diamond Hill
Lorenço Marquez
Delagoa Bay
Mafeking
Johannesberg
Carolina
SWAZI-LAND
PORTUGUESE EAST
NAMAQUALAND
Standerton
Utrecht
Kroonstad
Paardeplaats
ORANGE FREE STATE
ZULULAND
Ulundi
Orange River
Vaal R.
Winberg
Ladysmith
GRIQUALAND WEST
Kimberley
Griquatown
Bloemfontein
Belmont
Orange River Stn.
BASUTO-LAND
NATAL
Pietermaritzberg
Durban
Orange R.
Drakensberg
de Aar
Colesberg
Aliwal North
GRIQUALAND EAST
CAPE   COLONY
Naauwport
Stormberg
PONDOLAND
INDIAN OCEAN
King William's Town
East London
Cape Town
Cape of Good Hope
Port Elizabeth

Miles
0 50 100 150 200

(d) To have a free force of 10,000 men in Cape Colony to resist invasion.

The forces (a), (c), (d) would require transport and *must be mobile* [author's italics].

Until they are mobile the army could not advance, and consequently no ultimatum could be enforced; on the other hand, if an ultimatum is sent before they are mobile and can advance, the Colonies will be liable to invasion by the Boers, if they can mobilize in, say, three weeks.

Conclusions

The situation is one in which the diplomatic authorities should consult with the military authorities.

(signed) REDVERS BULLER,

General.[38]

From that Cabinet meeting came the decision to despatch as soon as possible 10,000 men, drawn from India and the Mediterranean garrisons, to reinforce Natal. The pressure for this came primarily from Chamberlain, who at last had succumbed to Milner's arguments – arguments that had been reinforced by the jingoistic cries of the larger part of the British press, many of whose editors had been influenced by Milner's widespread network of contacts. The Cabinet decision was just what Milner had intended, another step in provoking the Boers towards war.

Although all references that might have hurt Lansdowne's feelings were omitted from Buller's final draft to Lord Salisbury,[39] it was hardly surprising that his most irregular approach to the Prime Minister, together with the criticisms implicit both in that approach and the contents of the draft, enraged Lansdowne. At a stormy interview after the Cabinet meeting, Lansdowne bitterly reproached this general, who in any case he considered to be 'pro-Boer', for 'going behind his back'.[40] The mutual dislike of the two men had been even further intensified. Salisbury, judging by past history, was hardly one of Buller's admirers; the old statesman's readiness to connive at his behaviour suggests a deep concern at Lansdowne's slipshod methods.

To command in Natal, Lansdowne sent another personal friend, the sixty-four-year-old Lieutenant-General Sir George White, VC, who, despite being a member of the Roberts 'Ring', was serving under Wolseley as QMG at the War Office. Before recommending White, whom he believed to be 'Clear-headed and of sound judgment', Wolseley had checked with Buller that the latter approved of his choice, both as a subordinate and his replacement 'in the event of some "Dopper" putting a bullet into you'.[41] Asked for his opinion by Lansdowne, Buller, who knew White only from his short time as QMG, could say no more than his background suggested that 'he must possess the sort of experience a Commander now in Natal should have'.[42]

125

Although, as we shall see, both Wolseley and Buller would strongly criticize White's subsequent actions, Brodrick's comment, made after the passage of years, that 'Sir Redvers Buller had little opinion of Indian soldiers and none of Sir George White; hence the Ladysmith imbroglio',[43] seems quite unjustified. Buller was still close enough to Wolseley to have refused White should he have so wished.

Buller did not let matters rest after Lansdowne's rebuke. The day after his return to Aldershot, in the same letter in which he agreed to White's appointment, he urged the Secretary of State to send to Natal a further force, in addition to the planned 10,000 men, providing there were no political objections. He feared that 'if the Boers are bold and have really good military advisers, they have now the chance of easily inflicting a serious reverse upon us in Natal'. It is revealing that he also found it necessary to remind Lansdowne that he hoped 'care will be taken that full medical arrangements are made for the troops now ordered to the Cape and Natal, these are sometimes forgotten'.[44] Lansdowne's reply was negative.

While Milner and, to a lesser extent Chamberlain, were trying to push the Boers towards war, the British Government was still trying to avoid provoking them. Buller's concern at the risks he saw the politicians taking is evident from the tone of a yet further appeal to Lansdowne: two months had been lost and our troops were 'now face to face with an enemy in vastly superior force' and 'reinforcements should be at sea and arriving in a continuous stream, ready to retrieve any disaster, which may, though God forbid, have happened to our arms'.[45] At the same time he urged that White should not push his force too far forward but remain on the defensive behind the Tugela River. To garrison Ladysmith, Buller warned Bigge, the Queen's Private Secretary, was to invite disaster.[46]

Seldom can a commander designate have been more frustrated. Denied political intelligence and provided with inadequate military and topographical information, he had no executive control over the composition of the force, his role being little more than that of an unofficial adviser. Because no single War Office branch was yet responsible for war planning, confusion was endemic. The influence and powers of his Commander-in-Chief, to whom he looked for support, were rapidly waning – so far was Wolseley removed from reality that he was predicting a walk-over with Pretoria possibly occupied by Christmas.[47] The Secretary of State, to whom he was directly responsible, loathed and distrusted him. Nor was he given a say as to how his future subordinates should set about defending Natal, or even the opportunity of discussing their plans with them.[48] It was all a far cry, as Buller afterwards complained, from the responsibility and freedom given Wolseley in 1882.[49]

Meanwhile Kruger had also concluded that war was now unavoidable. On

9 September the news of the despatch of the first British reinforcements reached him. With just a month in which to strike a blow against Natal before the 10,000 extra troops arrived, speed was now vital for the Boers. But President Steyn of the Free State procrastinated, still hoping to avoid the tragedy he feared. Then, on 25 September, the Boers learned that Major-General Penn Symons, the British commander, another gallant, elderly but ineffective officer from the Indian Army, was moving troops to Dundee, close to the Transvaal border and seventy miles north of Ladysmith, thus dangerously isolating a large part of his force. For Kruger it was both a challenge and an opportunity. On 28 September the Transvaal officially mobilized, followed four days later by the Free State. However, bodies of Transvaalers, including their regular State Artillery and various parties of volunteer Hollanders, Germans and American/Irish, had for several weeks been concentrating under General Joubert on the Natal frontier.

The Boers had wasted September, but so had the British. Far from speeding up preparations, an order for the purchase of 1,000 mules in South Africa was even cancelled. Then at last, on 23 September, Lansdowne asked Buller for his detailed written views on an invasion force taking the Orange Free State route. This was produced the next day in a lengthy, well argued memorandum. Five days later the Cabinet decided to adopt Buller's recommendations and to go ahead with all preparations except the actual troop mobilization. It was a further week before this was put in hand.[50]

Counsels within the government were divided. Lansdowne was still not prepared to accept that the Boers might go so far as to invade Natal. Hicks Beach, still in the Cabinet, remembered too well the outcome of the previous war against the Boers; now Chancellor of the Exchequer, he was appalled at the prospective cost. What is more Hicks Beach disliked the way Chamberlain had handled the Boers, as did Balfour, who, until the end of September, regarded war with the Orange Free State as no more likely than war with Switzerland.[51] As for Lord Salisbury, that conservative traditionalist, a statesman whose every action stemmed from his strong moral principles and his obligations to his country, he was at sixty-nine becoming lethargic, corpulent and absent-minded. Moreover, he was preoccupied by his grief for a wife dying of cancer. Antipathetic towards the profession of arms and bored by matters military, he was suspicious of its practitioners. But the leader of this broken-backed administration did not believe that Kruger would pull back. War for Lord Salisbury was an unpleasant necessity, one to be faced if Britain's position in South Africa were not to be destroyed.

To return to South Africa. White – who was to describe himself none too accurately as 'Buller's John the Baptist'[52] – arrived there as the Boers were starting to mobilize. He had never seen South Africa before and his knowledge of the country was as meagre as his understanding of modern warfare. A conscientious officer and an Indian Mutiny veteran, it was White who had in the end succeeded Roberts as Commander-in-Chief in India.

White had, however, brought with him two outstanding staff officers, Colonel Ian Hamilton and Lieutenant-Colonel Henry Rawlinson. Previously one of Roberts's ADCs, the name of the future General Lord Rawlinson of Trent was to be forever and sadly linked with the carnage of the Somme. Hamilton, now the Army's acknowledged musketry expert, had developed a liking for White, whom he had served as Military Secretary, that almost matched his near adulation of Roberts. Against Buller, Hamilton's rancour had been in no way tempered by the generous treatment he had received in the Sudan. His biographer has claimed that in 1899 he did not dislike Buller personally. The facts hardly bear this out. Buller was that 'evil genius', whom Hamilton held responsible for his acting promotion on Roberts's staff not being confirmed; moreover, Hamilton and others of Roberts's officers thought the previous Adjutant-General had prevented them from receiving the accelerated promotion they saw as their due.[53]

Two days after White's arrival, the Transvaal issued its ultimatum in which Britain was accused both of interfering in the country's internal affairs and of massing troops against her. Demands included the withdrawal of these troops from her borders, together with the return of any recently landed and those still at sea. Non-compliance within forty-eight hours would be regarded as declaration of war. The terms were deliberately framed so as to be unacceptable to a world power. Milner had triumphed. The Boers had been provoked into starting the war.

In splitting his force by moving one of his infantry brigades north to Dundee, Symons had acted without reference to his superiors. While White's contempt for the fighting powers of the Boers matched that of too many other senior British officers, his few days' experience of South Africa had awakened him to some of the problems confronting him. Nevertheless, Sir Walter Hely-Hutchinson, Natal's Governor, persuaded him that any withdrawal of Symons's force might provoke a rising not only of Natal's many Afrikaners but its Zulus as well. Although White was aware of Buller's repeated warning that nothing should be stationed north of the Tugela River, he still thought him unduly alarmist.[54] So it was that White did not withdraw the troops from Dundee, and he himself joined the balance of his 10,000 strong force at Ladysmith, his intention to hold a position on the Biggarsberg range of hills immediately to the north.

Only Rawlinson would seem to have been concerned by his commander's over-confidence, recording in his diary that the sole military option was to withdraw from Dundee and Ladysmith and hold the line of the Tugela, some ten to twenty miles south of Ladysmith. Without flanks, White's positions courted disaster. The 15,000 to 20,000 mobile Boers on the frontier

– their strength either known to Rawlinson or estimated accurately by him – could either press forward, avoiding both places, or surround and annihilate each in turn.[55]

Rawlinson's dismal forecast proved correct, matching that of Buller who less than two weeks before had again warned Lansdowne of that 'disaster, which may, though God forbid, have happened to our arms'.[56] On 12 October Joubert's Boers struck camp and rode south past Majuba Hill. A week later their leading commando occupied the undefended Talana Hill, overlooking Dundee and its garrison. Symons's subsequent attack was in line with the tactics then common to all European armies – artillery preparation preceding a close order infantry advance, after which the cavalry would cut off the retreating enemy. But it was the first time that European troops had been at the receiving end of modern magazine rifles firing smokeless powder. The British regulars seized Talana's summit, but only after heavy losses, including Symons, hit when urging on his faltering troops.

Talana was a barren and pointless victory. The next day a further commando occupied Mount Impati, four miles to the north, from which one of the 6-inch Creusot guns, surprisingly dragged all the way down from the north, threw its 40-pound shells into the British camp. Almost surrounded by some 10,000 Boers, Symons's equally elderly successor decided to retreat to Ladysmith, abandoning all his supplies, stores, wounded, medical staff as well as the townspeople. Because Elandslaagte, between Ladysmith and Dundee, had been occupied by yet another Boer column, a lengthy round-about route had to be taken by already weary troops. Fortunately Joubert failed to pursue them. On 26 October the exhausted and starving survivors of Symons's force staggered into Ladysmith.

This near disastrous business was partly offset by the recapture of Elandslaagte by a force under Major-General John French, that cavalry officer last encountered in the Sudan. In charge of French's three infantry battalions was Ian Hamilton, whose men tackled the Boers in open order, two or three yards between each man, making sound use of their commander's revolutionary and effective tactical ideas. In the subsequent savage fighting Hamilton's men in the end overwhelmed the Boers, who in retreating were slaughtered by the British dragoons and lancers. It was the first and last old-fashioned copybook massed cavalry action of the war. French's name was made.

With the Free Staters approaching Ladysmith from the east through the defiles of the Drakensberg Mountains, White's 13,000 men were outnumbered by almost two to one. He had, however, no intention of just sitting in Ladysmith: the Boers had to be beaten in the open field. So it was that on 30 October he launched the larger part of his force against the nearby Boers.

The result was a decisive defeat just outside the town which ended in a near rout and the subsequent surrender of almost 1,000 British troops at Nicholson's Nek – another Majuba but on a larger scale.

White, his spirit completely broken, as was that of many of his beaten troops, was cut off in Ladysmith, the railway to the south severed. Southern Natal lay defenceless and open to invasion. And White's own force needed to be rescued before it starved.

9

THE TIGHTEST PLACE

News, albeit largely inaccurate, of this disastrous start reached Buller on 29 October on the deck of the *Dunottar Castle* in which he and his staff had left Southampton fifteen days before. On a large blackboard, hung over the side of a passing tramp-ship, was chalked: BOERS DEFEATED – THREE BATTLES – PENN SYMONS KILLED.

They had learned already that the war had started when their ship coaled at Madeira. Waiting for Buller was a telegram from Sir George White, dated 15 October:

Transvaal and Orange Free State are converging towards Dundee and Ladysmith, and are in strength inside Natal border. Hunter's [Buller's chief-of-staff designate] loss here would be heavily felt. I propose keeping him for the present.

Another, sent two days later from Lieutenant-General F.W. Forestier-Walker, Butler's replacement at the Cape, reported that Mafeking and Kimberley were isolated and set out the steps he was taking to protect a 400-mile long border with just four regular battalions of infantry.[1]

For a general approaching his theatre of operations a week ahead of his leading units, it had been a disquieting time. Although a brigade of cavalry and two of infantry, seasoned troops all, had by then reinforced Natal, Buller had known before leaving England that against his reiterated advice troops were to be pushed too far forward into the trap formed by that exposed northern apex of Natal. As he had feared, during his two-week voyage thousands of well-armed Boer horsemen were driving south towards the two British colonies, bypassing the few troops opposing them. And the reinforcements would take time to arrive. When he had learned from Lansdowne on 29 September that all military preparations were to go ahead, the subsequent news that the Reserve would not be called out until 7 October had elicited his response that 'The Government would be incurring a very grave responsibility in so delaying the despatch of the troops'.[2] The Government's further postponement of mobilization was never explained, nor was its delay in despatching Buller to South Africa: although he had urged that he should start on 7 October, he was not allowed to sail for a further week.[3] Why a fast warship was not made available is even harder to understand.

A few days before he left, the Queen had summoned her uninhibited old friend to Balmoral. 'He had,' she recorded, 'much that was interesting to say in his blunt, straight-forward way. . . . There had been delays & waste of time, which was to be regretted, & he said the War Office left much to be desired & needed entirely remodelling.' Outspoken though he was about the preparations for war, he seems to have tried to spare the feelings of his elderly and now infirm Queen about its outcome, reassuring her with the hope 'that it would not be a long business' and that there would not 'be much hard fighting'. She begged him to write to her as often as he could and recommended to him her soldier grandson, 'Christle'[4]: Major Prince Christian Victor, a not especially able officer, was a burden with which Buller could well have dispensed, remembering as he did another royal prince's tragic end in that same country.

According to a magazine gossip column, Buller stayed at the Beefsteak Club until 1.30 a.m. on the night before he embarked. Commenting that he was 'in love with books as well as the table', the journalist added that he had taken a small library of old favourites to South Africa as well as £5 worth of new books. This may have been surmise. But the revelation that among his entourage was a 'shorthand-writing clerk and Remington' was correct.[5] Handwritten official communications were on their way out. Even the Royal Household had acquired one of the machines.

Although Buller had been widely known to the general public fifteen or twenty years before, the crowd which gathered to see him off from Waterloo Station failed to recognize the burly mufti-clad figure. Among those in the official party, *The Times* reported, were the Prince of Wales, Lansdowne and Wolseley; and all along the route country people, who somehow had learned what was afoot, waved their handkerchiefs. The writer reminded his readers that Buller had 'experience in dealing with disturbances and disaffection in Ireland, experience to which he is by no means fond of referring'. At Southampton his reception was rapturous, the assembled multitude bellowing out 'Rule Britannia' and 'God Save the Queen'. His emotion was manifest as he said goodbye to his wife and daughter.[6] This was hardly surprising: in July the family had learned that one of his two step-sons had died of enteric in South Africa.

As well as the Commander-in-Chief and his staff, the passenger list included Tory politicians and war correspondents, among them the young Winston Churchill. Author of a succession of 'instant' but superbly crafted war books, based on his newspaper reportage, he had been commissioned by *The Morning Post* at the vast fee of £250 monthly – some £10,000 in today's currency – and all expenses paid.

During the voyage Buller was to be criticized for aloofness and arrogance towards his fellow passengers. Most of them had good reason to try to pump him, but even a member of his staff, Lieutenant-Colonel Charles à Court (later the celebrated war correspondent and historian, who was to change his name to à Court Repington) condemned his reserve and lack of communication.[7] It aggravated some of the passengers that his manners towards the ship's crew and such people as the operator of the biograph – the first cine-camera to be taken to war – were informally easy. There is small doubt that Buller's normal shyness among strangers, contrasting as it did with his relaxed manner among his friends and among ordinary men and women, especially his soldiers, was aggravated during the voyage by worry about the challenges that lay ahead. And he had to avoid being questioned.

Suppressed excitement, not jubilation, was the response of the *Dunottar Castle*'s passengers to that chalked message. The death of Penn Symons, a well-known and popular officer, was saddening but the news of three British victories created the fear that the war might be won before they arrived. The suggestion to Buller by one of his staff that it could well be all over evoked the dry response, 'I dare say there will be enough left to give us a fight outside Pretoria,'[8] a remark that heartened the officers but likely had its roots in his doubts about what lay ahead for them. To a friend on board he had already confided that the business was too great for one man and that Lord Roberts would be sent out after him.[9]

Late on the night of 30 October the *Dunottar Castle* at last moored alongside the quay at Table Bay. The following morning Buller drove in state in an open landau through Cape Town streets gay with flags, cheered by dense crowds that had waited for hours to see him. Vague rumours of failure in Natal and of invasion into the Cape had cast gloom over the civilian population, many of them Uitlander refugees from the Transvaal who had lost everything they owned. To them and to others, Buller's calm, impassive countenance – a personification of John Bull – was a reassurance: help was now at hand, even though he came alone. To many he was a legend and behind him was massed the full force of the Empire.

Buller's first visit was to Government House where Milner handed him the cables from White that revealed full details of the defeats in Natal. The High Commissioner was despondent. To Ian Hamilton, who had lunched with him on his arrival four weeks earlier, he had posed the rhetorical question, 'Surely these mere farmers cannot stand for a moment against regular troops?'[10] Now the war he had recklessly provoked had gone disastrously awry. Nearly every entry in his diary dwells upon the bad news.

'Very sleepless nights' were frequent. On 2 November 'matters look extremely black all round'; two days later was the 'blackest of black days'.[11] Colonel Frederick Stopford, Buller's Military Secretary, hardly overstated it all when he wrote to Lady Audrey:

> When we arrived in Cape Town we found everybody, including Sir A. Milner, in a rather demoralized condition and it was wonderful to see the way in which Sir Redvers restored confidence all round . . . really by the time we left the Cape for Natal he had induced all the authorities to take quite a cheerful view of the situation.[12]

Calming though Buller's influence was and optimistic his outward demeanour, his true state of mind comes out in what amounted to a testamentary letter of some 1,500 words to his brother, Tremayne, written only three days after he landed:

> I am in the tightest place I have ever been in, and the worst of it is I think none of my own creating – I don't know if I can[?] get out of it alright, and I think if I fail it is fair my family should know afterwards what at any rate I had to say on my own defence.

He went on to describe his relationship with Lansdowne, the manner of his appointment as Commander-in-Chief and the errors made in the launching of the expedition; to the letter he attached copies of his correspondence with Lansdowne, Wolseley, Lord Salisbury and the latter's Private Secretary.[13]

On 7 November, in his first private letter to Lansdowne, Buller set out the doubts that beset him: 'The general fear seems to be that we are in measurable distance of a Dutch rising. In our unprotected state that would mean almost a walk-over, I fear. I hope and believe we shall tide over that danger.'[14] On the same day he sent his first – and a long – letter to the Queen in which he expressed his regrets that he had nothing but bad news for her.[15]

During this first week in the Cape, Buller had also despatched a series of official telegrams to Lansdowne, in which he pointed out the circumstances that made it possible for both Ladysmith and Kimberley to fall before he could launch his main offensive towards Bloemfontein. Because of this, he told the Secretary of State, he now considered that he must reinforce Natal with a division and despatch his other to relieve Kimberley, so delaying his main thrust until January.[16] To the Queen this did 'not sound very cheering'.[17]

With the white population of the Cape only two-thirds British, the fear of a rising was real. On 1 November Free State commandos, enthusiastically welcomed by their fellow Boers, had crossed the Orange River and appeared to be driving deep into the Colony. The threat led Buller to withdraw the two small and isolated British detachments holding the railway junctions at Naauwpoort and Stormberg, a decision made against the advice of the civil authorities and Milner's wishes; prestige was at stake and likely rebels might receive further encouragement. But three garrisons, all by then beleaguered but not surrounded – Mafeking, Kimberley and Ladysmith – were quite enough: Buller had no wish to offer further hostages to fortune. With only 4,000 troops to guard the long Cape Colony frontier, open to attack at almost any point, there was little else a general without an army could do. As yet he lacked a single battalion in reserve.

The Mafeking garrison of irregulars, commanded by Colonel Baden-Powell, soon to become even more famous as the founder of the Boy Scout movement, had already repulsed a Boer attack. What is more, its commander had refrained from appealing for help. Kimberley, the diamond boom-town, was another matter. There, among the mines in which his fortune had been founded, Cecil Rhodes had deliberately incarceratd himself on the outbreak of war. The town's defences consisted of a half battalion of British regulars, 300 policemen and some 4,000 hastily raised local volunteers, most of them employees of De Beers. Its commander was a regular officer, a Lieutenant-Colonel Kekewich, with whom Rhodes's relationship soon became less than friendly. Still the arrogant 'Colossus', politically influential and financially powerful despite his loss of prestige after Jameson's Raid, Rhodes was not accustomed to dealing with a mere lieutenant-colonel on an equal footing. Repeated demands for assistance soon arrived on Milner's desk, not from Kekewich but from Rhodes and other Kimberley civilians; neither the military commander nor the local government officials had been shown them.

The crux came with a telegram from the De Beers directors, dated 31 October and complaining:

> In our opinion we could have already been relieved without risks by the present forces in Cape Colony . . . now that the General has arrived we respectfully request to be informed as to the policy to be adopted regarding relief, *so as to enable us to take our own steps in case relief refused.* [author's italics]. We are sending this by special messenger to Orange River and await your reply.[18]

Kekewich had neither sanctioned nor seen the message, which both Buller and Milner read as a threat to surrender. Signalled by Buller for his views, Kekewich replied that it depended upon whether the Town Guard would stand the strain of the trench work, a reminder that the first loyalty of the men in question was likely to be to their employers.[19] As Fortescue put it, Kekewich held command only under sufferance from Rhodes.[20]

The news from Ladysmith was equally unsettling. The first of the series of telegrams from White, seen by Buller the day he arrived, had appealed for immediate reinforcements, while the last, dated 30 October, had revealed the full horror of the surrender of 1,000 British regulars at Nicholson's Nek. In a further signal, despatched the following day, White confessed that he was no longer able to withdraw from Ladysmith, but had sent back a battalion of Dublin Fusiliers to hold the bridge spanning the Tugela at Colenso, all he could spare to defend southern Natal.[21] Until then White had not so much as hinted that he was in danger of losing freedom of movement.

Help to save southern Natal was vital. After establishing themselves at Colenso, the Dublin Fusiliers had come under attack from Boer artillery firing from the hills north of the river and completely outranging the few British guns supporting the battalion. Their colonel had little choice but to vacate his untenable position and pull his small force twenty-five miles back to Estcourt. Other than one at Durban, this was as yet the sole regular battalion south of the Tugela. Most of Natal's mounted volunteers were needlessly locked up in Ladysmith, with them the regular cavalry brigade, wasted because White insisted upon keeping it.[22] Buller was afterwards to be criticized for failing to order him to send the brigade south, but from 700 miles away he could hardly query his experienced subordinate's views on the local tactical situation.

The Boers were now within eighty miles of Pietermaritzburg, Natal's second city and its capital. Even Durban had only its single battalion, together with some contingents of townspeople, among them the Durban High School Officer Training Corps, issued with live ammunition to the delight of the boys.[23] To make that major seaport just a little less insecure, Buller arranged for the Royal Navy to take charge of its defences; as a result the Fleet landed some 450 sailors and twenty-eight guns of various calibres.[24]

It was fortunate for Natal that the Boer generals were hesitant and lacking in boldness. Not until 15 October did Joubert with 2,000 well-mounted burghers start to move south from Colenso; as his second-in-command rode the young Louis Botha, the future Imperial statesman.

That decision to divert the extra troops to Natal had been a difficult one for Buller, and one strongly opposed by Milner, whose priority was the defence of the Cape Colony. To ensure its safety a major internal Afrikaner rising had to be avoided and Kimberley relieved; the loss of the latter would not only give great encouragement to the dissident Cape Boers, but damage still further Britain's dwindling prestige within and outside Europe. And it seemed clear to both Milner and Buller that unless the place were succoured, Rhodes and his fellow De Beers directors might well make terms with their besiegers. In the High Commissioner's opinion all Buller's resources should be devoted to freeing Kimberley and defending the Cape Colony as a preliminary to undertaking the planned invasion of the Transvaal.[25] As he admitted to Chamberlain, 'I write this quaking; I fear every hour for Kimberley.' His 'gloomy view' of Boer power, as he admitted to the Colonial Secretary, 'had been surpassed by reality'.[26]

In the meantime Milner was ready to abandon White to look after himself in Ladysmith, with its sixty days of supplies. The rest of Natal, Milner decided, could fall into Boer hands if need be, minuting Buller that 'I think the time has come to be ruthless and sacrifice everything to military necessity'.[27] This 'sacrifice' was, of course, 12,000 British soldiers and the integrity of a colony, nine-tenths of whose white inhabitants were of British stock, one made in order to rescue the financiers who had conspired with him to bring about the war.

Buller saw the problems in Natal as twofold. If the Boers captured Durban they would hold a port through which assistance could reach them from their many European sympathizers, particularly Germany.[28] Secondly, there was the presence in Natal of the major part of the Boer armies, a force he would need to defeat in the field before the war could be won. In Natal, as he later declared, 'lay my true objective – the principal force of the enemy'.[29] To lose the British colony would also be a blow to prestige far more severe than the loss of Kimberley.

This then was Buller's dilemma. Natal south of the Tugela must be saved and the wasted troops in Ladysmith relieved. At the same time Kimberley could not be ignored: it also must be relieved, its civilians evacuated, and its garrison increased to about a couple of regular battalions, enough to hold it against any subsequent attack. But to do all this would mean postponing the invasion; it would also force him to split his force and break up the organization of his Army Corps. It was a decision he took with the greatest reluctance and one for which he was to be much abused. Even Leo Amery, author of *The Times History of the War in South Africa* and Buller's most savage contemporary critic, admitted that he had no other choice.[30] If the advice he had tendered to Lansdowne in July had been taken to put the two Colonies into a proper state of defence, none of this would have been necessary.

To Milner's intense relief, the first of the vast armada bringing Buller's 50,000 strong Army Corps arrived on 9 November. Soon Table Bay was crowded with vessels carrying the largest expeditionary force ever to leave England, double the size of that shipped to the Crimea. But it was rather more effectively organized. For this even Chamberlain, a hard taskmaster,, gave credit to those responsible. 'The War Office,' he wrote to Milner, 'has done what has never been done before in the history of this country & has placed an enormous force safely at the seat of war six thousand miles from base.'[31]

The first arrivals diverted to reinforce Durban were a brigade of the 2nd

Infantry Division under Major-General – brigade commanders still held that rank – Henry Hildyard, lately an effective Commandant of the Staff College. These troops were straightaway followed by a brigade of Sir William Gatacre's 3rd Division under Major-General Hart, together with the 1st Division's artillery. After them came another brigade of the 2nd Division, its commander Lyttelton who had taken charge of it during the summer, together with his divisional commander, Lieutenant-General Sir Francis Clery, who for the time being commanded the 14,000 troops south of the Tugela. Clery was another ex-Staff College Commandant, nicknamed 'Old Blue Whiskers' and far inferior to Hildyard, an ineffective old eccentric who spurned wearing khaki in battle and a sufferer from varicose veins.

On 18 November, when about one-third of his troops had arrived, Buller decided that he could send the rest of Gatacre's division to Naaupoort, so recently evacuated. Lieutenant-General Lord Methuen, a pleasant and gallant Scots Guardsman, who like so many senior officers had seen much action in a variety of small wars, commanded the 1st Division; Buller now directed him along the Western Railway with a couple of brigades, his task to relieve Kimberley.

For the time being Buller kept the Cavalry Division in hand near the Cape, but to command it he signalled White to send him back French, the victor of Elaandslaagte, the only direct order he took upon himself to issue to the besieged garrison. French, accompanied by his brigade major, a Major Douglas Haig, escaped under heavy fire by one of the last trains to steam out of Ladysmith before the Boers cut the line. During the next two years the initiative and dash displayed by these two cavalrymen set them on the path to supreme command in the First World War. The news they now brought was discouraging, a tale of indecision mixed with rashness, poor morale and shortage of shells. It further convinced Buller that White's force was powerless to protect Natal, and it also helped implant in his mind the conviction that he might well have to go there himself to take charge.[32]

Because of the need to rush troops to Natal as soon as they arrived, the original organization of Buller's Corps had been almost destroyed. But it scarcely mattered. Only Hildyard's Brigade, which had been stationed under Buller at Aldershot, had trained properly as such; elsewhere both cash and training areas had been hard to come by.

Buller's first three weeks in South Africa were a time of intense pressure. Units had to be disembarked and moved inland, not as planned but to meet the fresh demands now placed upon them. A vast administrative complex had to be set up from scratch – the supply, transport and medical back-up for formations as far removed from one another as Paris is from Venice. It was another of the few feats for which Amery managed to give Buller due credit.[33]

A shortage of mounted troops to counter the very mobile Boers was one of Buller's main problems. The day he landed he set in hand the raising of two more regiments of mounted infantry. He was to be criticized for not straightway recruiting more, but for the present weapons and equipment were in short supply,[34] as well as the special service regulars needed to officer them.

A legend was to grow over the years that Buller, before he left England, had refused the offer of the white colonies, all of them agog with enthusiasm, to lend a helping hand to the 'old country' by providing mounted men for the war;[35] instead he had signalled them that 'infantry most, cavalry least serviceable'. It was an absurd charge. No one was more aware than Buller of the value of horsemen in such a war; after all he had made his name as a commander of mounted irregulars in South Africa. What happened was this. Lansdowne had told him of such an offer during the course of a casual conversation, in which Buller neither saw the telegram nor knew which colony had originated it. According to Buller, their talk had centred largely on the question of the colonials' pay. Small bodies of their cavalry (initially only small bodies were on offer) would be difficult to integrate and use. Moreover, Buller assumed that they would be paid as British troops and not the five shillings daily that South African irregulars cost, of whom he intended upon arrival to raise between 8,000 and 10,000. Such disparity would inevitably cause trouble. To quote his evidence before the subsequent Royal Commission, 'My idea was that all colonials could ride [he was wrong on this point], and that I could count upon them and turn them into Mounted Infantry and pay them all [South Africans and others] alike, 5s. a day.'[36] In no way was Buller responsible for that 'unfortunately worded' reply – to use Lansdowne's words.

The shortage of special service officers had caused Buller to send off two of his best staff officers, Repington and Major Julian Byng (yet another future field-marshal) to raise and command the new irregulars, although the former did return to Buller's staff in due course. This was just the start. During the next few weeks he was obliged to detach nearly all the senior members of his staff, his sole source of able officers, either to help organize the lines of communication or to command isolated detachments. To compound the problem, White had insisted upon retaining Major-General Archibald Hunter, Buller's Chief-of-Staff designate, until it was too late for him to get away from Ladysmith, a serious loss indeed to the Commander-in-Chief. In due course Hunter was to earn the reputation of being 'the life and soul' of Ladysmith's defence and was to show equal ability later on in the war. Also immured with Hunter were three exceptionally capable and knowledgeable intelligence officers, all of them due to join Buller's staff.

Parallel with Buller's conclusion that his operational plans would have to be changed was his decision that he must himself take personal charge in Natal. Of this possibility he had warned Lansdowne as early as 4 November in a signal outlining his likely new deployment and asking for an additional division to be made ready but not for the time being despatched.[37] Subsequent events in Natal, and especially Joubert's raid, finally convinced him that his presence there was essential. Not only had Clery, Lyttelton and Hildyard all urged him, from the moment they arrived, to take personal command;[38] Hely-Hutchinson from Pietermaritzburg had also been pressing for him since the day he landed.[39]

White's considerable seniority was also a matter of concern. In any joint action between a relief force and the Ladysmith garrison, he would automatically take charge, but Buller's confidence in him had been destroyed by what he had learned of his handling of the fighting on 30 October. Wolseley had already decided that White must be removed, and when Lansdowne signalled Buller for his approval, the reply was, 'French is here, conversation confirms doubts I have of White's ability. . . . White seems to have been weak and vacillating, and much influenced by Hamilton, a dangerous adviser'.[40] White was, however, to be spared. Although Buller had the authority to sack him, it was unfortunately not in his nature to leave a man so distinguished to rot in disgrace in a beleaguered town. A younger general might have been brought out, slipping through the encircling Boers, but White was far too old and unfit for such a venture.

Not until 22 November did Buller see his way to leave Cape Town. In charge there he left Forestier-Walker, together with written instructions that made it clear beyond doubt that once Methuen had relieved Kimberley, the northern districts of the colony were to be cleared of Boers as a preliminary to advancing, as previously planned, upon Bloemfontein. Lightness touched this formal document: the first paragraph read, 'Ever since I have been here we have been like the man, who, with a long day's work before him, overslept himself and so was late for everything all day.'[41] That was certainly so, but as was generally acknowledged, Buller had achieved much in a short time, performing wonders of improvisation.

Buller's departure evoked widespread surprise. Even senior members of his staff, Repington among them, did not learn he was leaving.[42] Security had been well kept and there was need for it. Cape Town was full of spies against whom little or nothing could be done because of Milner's understandable caution against taking what might be seen as harsh measures, so offending the Cape Dutch; when Buller arranged for the police to shadow the principal Boer spies preparatory to putting them on a slow-moving ship to Lourenço Marques, Milner abandoned the project at the last moment.[43]

Amery was to accuse Buller of deciding to leave Cape Town on the spur of the moment, and, 'In accordance with his wont, he neither took counsel nor informed others of his intention'. This was a palpable absurdity. Written in 1902, it is just possible but unlikely that Amery was then still ignorant of the facts; he had the ear of everyone, including Milner, with whom at this time he dined at least twice.[44] Those few who needed to know did, among them Forestier-Walker, Hely-Hutchinson and, of course, Milner.

Amery's accusation was to gain further credence when the future Lady Milner published her memoirs. Daughter-in-law to the Prime Minister, the attractive and intelligent then Lady Edward Cecil, whose husband was locked up in Mafeking, was staying at Groote Schuur, Rhodes's superb Dutch-Colonial mansion, and working for the Uitlander refugees. She went everywhere and knew everyone, especially Milner, her future second husband, whose close companion and confidante she quickly became. A lady utterly lacking in false modesty, in writing of her first acquaintance with Lord Salisbury, she confessed to feeling immediately his great mental and moral stature, 'used as I was to first-class minds, accustomed as I was to greatness'.[45] On one Cape Town evening, she found it:

> interesting dining with Buller in the little house he had taken for himself. The servants waited on us in their khaki uniforms, and everything was very picnic-y. He, himself, was in excellent form and spirits, and he is always good company.[46]

Then, on the day Buller vanished, an agitated junior member of his staff, according to Lady Edward, called upon her to ask her to break to Milner the news of his general's secret departure. This she did, arousing Milner's apparent disbelief; but, when she told him her source, he enjoined her to say nothing.[47] After keeping his gossipy lady-friend so in the dark about his plans, it seems that he was a little reluctant to admit to her that he had done so.

This slander that Buller had kept the High Commissioner in ignorance lived on, even the editor of Milner's carefully censored private papers giving it credence, as he did the accusation that Buller had 'abandoned' the invasion of the Orange Free State when he moved to Natal.[48] Although Milner wrote freely about his association with Buller, nothing has surfaced to suggest that he was not fully aware of Buller's intention. After all, Lansdowne had known about it for three weeks; Hely-Hutchinson was to signal on 24 November that 'Buller will be here tomorrow',[49] Milner's private diary merely mentions on 23 November 'Buller having left for Natal'; an unannounced departure would have warranted something more to the point.[50]

When Milner discussed the move with Buller, he had objected strongly to his going, as he had done to Buller diverting troops to Natal. But although the two disparate individuals disagreed upon these and other matters, as Milner told Chamberlain:

> Personally, I have absolutely no dislike for Buller, &, as long as he was here, we got on perfectly well and I did my best to prevent his going to Natal.[51]

Get on well together they might, but Milner suffered from an underlying distrust of what he assumed was Buller's attitude towards the Boers. Even before the latter's arrival, his outlook had been poisoned by a letter from a friend, marked 'Personal and Secret' and warning him that 'Buller has, during the last few days been (to me) alarmingly influenced by Butler'[52]; Butler was, in Milner's opinion, 'an astute traitor' engaged in 'concocting' Boer propaganda.[53]

When Buller reached Durban on 25 November, he straightaway inspired much confidence in the Governor of Natal.[54] He also found the worst over. Ten days before, when the Boers began to move south from Colenso, they had ambushed an armoured train which had been rather pointlessly despatched north from Estcourt; British killed and wounded numbered seventy, and among the prisoners taken by the Boers was the impetuously gallant war correspondent Winston Churchill. After the ambush the Boers had made a leisurely progress southwards, looting and stock-rustling as they rode, to surround Estcourt. By then, however, the first British reinforcements were landing at Durban and being rushed up-country by train. After some skirmishing and a single inconclusive engagement on 23 November, the elderly Joubert, whose health had collapsed, decided to pull back across the Tugela. Three days after Buller's arrival the Boer rearguard crossed the river, destroying the railway bridge after doing so; it suggested that they no longer cherished any intention of laying hands on southern Natal.

Joubert's advance had, after all, been no more than a half-hearted raid. Kruger's strategy was inherently defensive, his political object Transvaal's complete independence – best secured by holding positions, attacks upon which would cause crucial losses to the British attacking infantry. To occupy Natal, that very British colony, would inevitably bring the full force of the Empire against him.

Buller brought with him to Natal only Stopford and his ADCs, leaving at the Cape what was left of his staff to help Forestier-Walker cope with his manifold problems. Equally short of officers, the latter had been sent out by the War Office with a grossly inadequate staff and so had been obliged to purloin special service officers in their place. On arrival, Buller was, as a result, obliged to issue his orders through Clery's divisional staff, a thoroughly unsatisfactory arrangement. In effect, Clery then became little more than a second-in-command to Buller who assumed full and direct control of the 20,000 troops then assembled in Natal. Well-equipped they were, but only one in eight of them was mounted.

The Tugela was an immensely strong natural position. From Potgeiter's Drift, at the foot of a spur of the Drakensberg Mountains, to Colenso, fifteen miles downstream as the crow flies, a ridge of broken and rocky hills lines the northern bank of the river, completely commanding it. Moreover, it could be crossed by wheeled vehicles at only five drifts (or fords), all but Potgeiter's being difficult for loaded ox-wagons. East of Colenso the country was so broken that a flank march by troops still unfit after their sea-voyage and hampered by slow-moving wagons, was deemed impossible. To defend this forbidding position, something between 5,000 and 8,000 Boers were now available (unofficial leave continually thinned their ranks), but all were mounted and led by the young and energetic Louis Botha, who had replaced Joubert. There was no way the movements of Buller's lumbering infantry force could be concealed from the Boer defenders, who could switch their mounted men to any threatened point; moreover, the Boer artillery out-ranged the British guns and the northern approaches to the river were as gentle and easily accessible as the southern were precipitous.

Buller's original intention had been to use his few colonial horsemen to threaten the Boers besieging Ladysmith from the east, while his infantry forced the Tugela, but due to rinderpest he found it impossible to obtain the ox-wagons needed for such a wide encirclement.[55] He then had two choices. He could make a direct assault at Colenso or carry out a flank march to Potgeiter's. The latter would mean abandoning the railway and supplying his force by wagon, but this he chose because an attack at Colenso would involve assaulting across a flat and near featureless plain. What is more, from Potgeiter's he could strike at the Boer communications – just as he did, his enemies depended upon the railway to move supplies and large bodies of troops over long distances. To relieve Ladysmith was vital, but this could best be done by destroying the Boer forces encircling the town after first cutting their supply route.

In this respect, Buller's strategic vision matched Kruger's. The enemy had to be defeated in the field. When the war was over, he outlined his thinking – possibly but by no means necessarily with hindsight. As in the American War of Independence, a civilized war was being fought in an uncivilized country. Because the Boers were a nation of independent individuals not dependent upon a central seat of government, the 'mere occupation of provincial capitals . . . is of little furtherance to the work of conquest'. It was plain to him that:

> the war could only be carried to a successful conclusion by the actual conquest of every armed man in the field; and this task promised to be

doubly difficult owing to the extreme mobility of the enemy. It seemed to me, therefore, that the best chance of success, until our troops could have been trained in a novel style of warfare, was to allow the Boers, if possible, to take up some tactical position, and strive to crush them by sheer weight of numbers. But in any case I was convinced that my true objective was the enemy's force in the field, wherever it might be, and that any strategical movement undertaken, except in obedience to this guiding principle, would be a mere flourish in the air.[56]

The destruction of the enemy, that basic principle of war, is so often forgotten by those who write about it.

10

BLACK WEEK

Incarcerated within Ladysmith, during the night of 29 November Lieutenant-Colonel Henry Rawlinson spotted a light flashing on the clouds. This he rightly concluded was a signal, a searchlight beam laboriously spelling out the morse code. Deciphered with difficulty, the message was from Buller enquiring how long White could hold out.[1] This makeshift arrangement sufficed after a fashion until regular heliograph contact was set up between the two forces a week later.

But fears of the Boers reading the cipher and of spies operating within Ladysmith inhibited the two commanders from properly co-ordinating their plans. Added to this, the effect of White's confinement, allied to his age, illness and defeat, had all but destroyed his self-confidence; his lack of initiative and vigour were reflected in the vagueness of several of his signals to Buller.[2] There was a further problem. If the Boer forces were to be destroyed, White's force would need to sally out of Ladysmith to cut off their retreat once Buller had broken through the Tugela defences, but so difficult were all the circumstances that Buller concluded that White could not be given directions for such a complicated operation until he had established himself firmly north of the river.

With Clery organizing the arrival of the field force units around Frere, a dozen miles down the railway from Colenso, Buller made use of his first ten days at Pietermaritzburg to ensure that the transport, supply and medical arrangements were sound. The latter especially was one of the administrative functions from which British generals had often held aloof, even though losses from disease regularly outnumbered battle casualties; Buller was one of the first to perceive that in the long term the efficiency of his medical services was almost as vital to his eventual success as that of his other arms.[3]

Those troops who gathered at Frere, some half of them reservists called up only a couple of months earlier, many from sedentary jobs and sometimes ill-fed, were far from fit after their long voyage in packed troopships. Nor were they yet properly welded into their units nor all their units into homogeneous brigades and divisions. Pitched out from trains into the flies and dust of the near-waterless African veldt at high summer, their poor morale was to be restored by Buller's arrival. A number of his soldiers have testified to his extraordinary popularity, a combination of his personal magnetism and ease of manner, his fighting reputation and care for every detail of their well-being, all this allied to that massive John Bull-like appearance.[4]

Buller was still, of course, responsible for that other war beyond the Drakensberg, over which, as he admitted to his wife, he could exercise no more than 'a sort of benevolent control'.[5] But if he had remained in Cape Colony he would not have been able to assume personal charge of the various bodies of troops scattered along its vast border in the way he did in Natal; control could be exercised only by telegram and this he could do almost as well from Pietermaritzburg or Frere as from Cape Town. Lost, however, was his personal contact with Milner, something the latter badly missed. Yet another of the latter's letters to Chamberlain emphasizes:

> It was a great mistake Buller going to Natal. I always thought so. The military situation there is no doubt difficult, and bad. But it is comparatively simple. Here it is intensely complicated. All his directions show it. While he was here he showed grasp. For those 3 weeks I certainly did feel in one important respect a sense of relief which I never had before or since.[6]

That Buller continued to take a close interest in events in the Cape is clear from his response to a further argument with Rhodes about the number of white civilians to remain in Kimberley after Methuen had relieved the place. His telegram to Forestier-Walker, dated 10 December, read:

> In dealing with Kimberley we must put De Beers out of the question. Tell Methuen that he and Kekewich are to decide on the minimum garrison required on the assumption that we shall occupy Bloemfontein on the 30th January at latest. All we have to do is to keep the Union Jack flying over South Africa, and I trust Methuen and Kekewich to help me to do that without fear or favour to any particular set of capitalists . . . do not be misled by sympathy for De Beers directors, and get out all the non-combatants you can.[7]

Buller was not alone in his belief that the war had been brought on largely by the financiers, and that the Governments both in London and the Cape were too subservient to their interests. It was an attitude not calculated to increase his popularity among the politicians, especially when expressed in his usual blunt terminology.

This further row with Rhodes was to prove pointless. Kimberley was not to be relieved for another two months, the delay due to the decisive repulse of Methuen's relief force on 11 December with the loss of 1,000 men. It happened at Magersfontein, ten miles beyond the Modder River, over which Methuen had forced a crossing two weeks before. The Boers, who had by then learned that they were less vulnerable to the British artillery when they were dug in on the flat veldt rather than on steep kopjes, had slaughtered the Highland Brigade in a muddled dawn attack that ended in its panic and rout. Officer casualties, severe as they were, would have been heavier still if Buller had not, soon after his arrival, ordered them all to dress like their soldiers.[8] For all that, fifteen years later officers were still wearing swords at the Battle of Mons.

The day before Magersfontein, Gatacre had lost 700 men in an equally ill-organized attempt to recapture the railway junction at Stormberg, even though Buller had ordered him to avoid taking risks for the time being. These two defeats were serious enough in themselves, but Buller now foresaw the danger that the Boers, mobile as they were, might cut off both Methuen and Gatacre from their bases, so incarcerating two further British columns.

Until these two defeats Buller had felt justified in risking tackling the Tugela by means of that forty-five-mile flank march to Potgeiter's Drift, even though he would be encumbered with a nine-mile-long wagon-train, open to attack at almost any point. With the Boers buoyed up by their successes, such boldness now no longer seemed warranted. Moreover it would involve cutting himself off at a time of crisis from direct telegraphic touch both with the Cape and Europe. So he switched his plan to one of tackling Ladysmith by the direct route through Colenso, even though the Boer defences were concentrated there and the rugged country further north, between the river and Ladysmith, was perfect for the defence.

Reporting this decision to Lansdowne, Buller emphasized both his problem of attacking a strongly entrenched enemy with inferior forces and his belief that he would succeed, but at heavy cost. He added also that whether he failed or succeeded, he now felt it necessary to stand on the defensive both in Natal and the Cape until the South African winter arrived; in the meantime the much-needed mobile troops could be organized and trained for the subsequent offensive into the Transvaal.[9]

In planning all his operations, Buller was to be hampered by a lack of topographical information. The maps he first obtained were rudimentary: funds had been sparse and large-scale survey work had been inhibited by fear of alarming the Boers.[10] Because the intelligence staff, together with most of its scouts and guides had been locked up in Ladysmith, Buller had been obliged to assemble from scratch a completely fresh organization; after just two weeks it had garnered little more than some limited intelligence on

Boer strengths at the various drifts over the Tugela.[11] Reconnaissance patrols amplified this information, but it was dangerous work approaching the river across the flat veldt that led down to its banks. On two occasions Buller himself accompanied mounted patrols in their attempts to pinpoint the enemy defences and obtain a sight of the stone walls built or being built by the Boers.[12]

These patrols were provided by Buller's mounted brigade, a mixed bag of regular infantrymen, local volunteers and newly raised irregulars, later augmented by a mobile machine-gun company. Their commander was Lord Dundonald, who had served Buller so well in the Sudan; despite being a Lifeguardsman, he was a forward-looking officer who deprecated the cavalry's devotion to shock-action. Hoping that work would turn up, he had made his own way to South Africa. It did. Dundonald was just the man Buller needed to take charge of the mounted forces south of the Tugela, and there Buller had sent him. It was not an easy command. Many of the irregulars were virtually untrained, a problem eased by Buller's readiness to support Dundonald by sacking inefficient officers out of hand.

In the end the Gunners produced a large-scale sketch-map and the intelligence put together a smaller-scale blue-print; although lacking in detail the latter provided a reasonable but far from complete outline of the main features, especially the river and the kopjes.

Because of Joubert's illness, Piet Botha was now in charge of the defence of the Tugela and had put to sound use the three weeks that had elapsed since his commandos pulled back to the north of the river. Helped by huge forces of conscripted African labour, he had built fifteen miles of rifle pits and gun emplacements, cleverly backed by both alternative and dummy positions. Except for the tiers of entrenchments on the lower slopes of the Colenso kopjes, most were invisible from the south bank. To man them, the mounted commandos, operating on interior lines, could be shifted from area to area in a matter of hours.

By 14 December Buller was ready. During the previous days his troops had moved forward to fresh camps five miles south of Colenso. That afternoon, having spent the day studying what he could see of the enemy positions, he gathered his senior officers for their orders, the outline of which was confirmed in writing at 10 p.m. There was to be little sleep for anyone that night. Six hours later his units were on the move.

Among the first to leave camp was Major-General Hart's 5th Brigade, three of its four battalions Irish. Before moving off in close order, the men had endured in the dark – of all things – a thirty-minute spell of drill, presumably to sharpen them up. A very old-fashioned officer, Hart was even less well-equipped than most of his generation for this new-style warfare.

The task of this Irish Brigade was to cross the Tugela at the Bridle Drift to the west of Colenso and then make its way down the left bank of the river to take the Boers opposite Colenso in the flank. In front rode cavalry patrols, and, as guides, Hart took with him a white civilian and an African, the latter a local man.

Ahead of them, as the sun came up, were outlined row upon row of high kopjes, the closest a couple of miles north of the river. Except for a single ill-concealed Boer gun, the Irishmen could neither see nor hear anything of the enemy. Not until 5.30 a.m. was the silence at last broken when the 4.7-inch guns of the Naval Brigade began bombarding the hills opposite and overlooking Colenso, over and beyond a loop in the Tugela to the right of the drift which the Irish were due to cross. When he neared the western corner of this loop, Hart had his first glimpse of the river, some 360 feet wide and lined on either side by high tree-lined banks.

At this point Hart committed what was to prove a fatal error. Instead of bearing off towards the Bridle Drift on his left, the guide veered right, straight towards the bend, indicating at the same time to Hart that the drift lay there. Ignoring the evidence of the map he was carrying, and too impatient to send forward patrols to discover the truth, Hart followed the guide, leading his four battlions into the re-entrant made by the river's loop – a near-island, a mile long and a third of that across.

A massacre followed. A storm of Mauser bullets and shrapnel from the well-concealed Boers on the opposite bank swept the packed mass of Irishmen, still in their close formation, their losses aggravated by their gallantry. Time and again small parties braved the fire to rush towards the river, unaware that even if they reached it there was no way of crossing the recently swollen waters. As Hart urged his men on, units became intermingled. Soon all control was lost. And no one could pinpoint the enemy riflemen or the guns, both firing the smokeless propellant that heralded 'the empty battlefield' of the future. This smokeless powder was nothing new, the consequences of its use having been debated during the 1890s; Afridi tribesmen in the recent Tirah War had even used stolen British weapons firing the ammunition against their previous owners.[13] It was, however, the first time its effects had been experienced in modern war. Also revealed that day was the near impossibility of issuing orders in a mobile battle against an enemy using long-range, accurate and quick-firing weapons: the era of commanders and their ADCs – or gallopers as they were known – riding about the battlefield had ended, but not until the advent many decades later of mobile wireless-telegraphy was a solution found.

From his headquarters on Gun Hill, close to the Naval guns and three miles from Colenso, an outwardly impassive Buller watched and heard the tragedy of the Irish Brigade: Hart's blunder into that deadly loop, his failure to use his supporting twelve guns, the steady drumming of the Boer Mausers.

Twice Buller sent off ADCs; the first, with orders to stop Hart entering the loop, never arrived; the second ordered him to halt his futile advance.

Meanwhile, two miles downstream, a matching catastrophe loomed. Here at Colenso itself, a settlement of a dozen brick and tin houses, Hildyard's 2nd Brigade was to cross the river using two further drifts and the still intact iron wagon bridge. The Brigade was from Aldershot, well-trained under Buller's own eye by a commander in whom he had full confidence. To support it were a further twelve 15-pounder field guns, together with half a dozen Naval Brigade 12-pounders, all under the direct command of the senior gunner, Colonel C. J. Long, the officer who had ordered Churchill's armoured train into that ambush. The previous evening Buller had personally pin-pointed on Long's map the place for the gun positions, one well out of range of the Boer rifles.

At about 7 a.m. Buller's attention was distracted from Hart's misfortunes by the sound of heavy artillery fire ahead and seemingly close to the river. Scenting trouble for Long, he despatched Stopford to pull Hart's brigade back and himself rode forward towards the firing to discover what was happening.

Afterwards Long was to admit that 'the light was deceptive, and I got a bit closer than I intended'.[14] But on the ship to South Africa he had confided to J.B. Atkins, the *Manchester Guardian's* correspondent, the importance of getting guns close to the enemy because 'the only way to smash these beggars is to rush in on them'.[15] In propounding such tactics, he would have drawn on his experiences in command of Kitchener's artillery against the Sudanese 'fuzzy-wuzzies' at the recent victory at Omdurman.

Ridiculing the protests of Lieutenant F. C. A. Ogilvy, the sailor in charge of the ox-drawn 12-pounders – he was Buller's second cousin – which were lagging behind the field-guns, Long now insisted that the Boers had deserted their position[16] and brought his 15-pounders into action 1,000 yards short of the river bank. But the Boers were still there, holding their fire. Although the gunners for a time fought their weapons superbly, upon them was concentrated the long-range fire of some 1,000 Boer riflemen. Only when a third of the Royal Artillerymen, including Long himself, were dead or wounded, did the senior surviving officer order the rest back to take shelter in a near-by donga. Meanwhile, Ogilvy's weapons, coming into action 400 yards further back, were virtually unscathed.

Learning the worst from a couple of officers who grossly exaggerated the losses, a not unusual occurrence in such circumstances, Buller straightaway rode off to halt Hildyard and tell him to deploy two battalions to cover the rescue of the guns. To proceed with the attack was, he had decided, now out of the question. Inwardly raging but showing his usual imperturbable face to those around him, Buller again recaptured his taste for the excitement of battle.[17] Of those who saw him in action, Dundonald was among those who recorded the confidence his quiet self-control instilled in those around him.[18] French, who saw much of him, both in the field and on manoeuvres, remembered how he never raised his voice on training but left people to get on with the job.[19] Understanding its value, this outward calmness was almost certainly deliberate, as it so often can be: Evelyn Wood, never one to belittle his own qualities, was to record that outside Colenso Buller had recounted the story of his old commander's gallantry at Hlobane as an example of the encouragement a senior officer's composure could be to those under him.[20]

Buller now rode forward across the bullet- and shell-torn veldt to direct in person the rescue of the guns. With him were his staff and his personal doctor, the latter soon to be killed alongside him. Shortly before this happened, Buller himself was hit in the side by an almost spent shell-fragment; although obviously badly shaken, he refused to admit that he was more than winded. First he arranged for horses to recover Ogilvy's weapons, nearly all the oxen having stampeded together with their African drivers, but out on the flat plain still lay the abandoned field-guns of the Royal Artillery. Encouraged by their general, standing there in the open, a number of volunteers galloped out gun-teams from their sheltering donga in successive attempts to recover the weapons. Two were brought back among a hail of bullets and shrapnel fire, but several of the volunteers were hit, including the mortally wounded Lieutenant Freddy Roberts, the Field-Marshal's only son who was attached to Clery's staff. Before Buller in the end halted this near-hopeless gallantry, Roberts and six others had won the Victoria Cross.

To Gunners, especially their officers, their weapons are near sacred emblems, and among the several criticisms afterwards levied against Buller, with one of which his great admirer Dundonald agreed,[21] was his failure to stay and recover the 15-pounders after dark. Immured in Ladysmith was Major (later Major-General) May, a thinking artilleryman and author, a previous recipient of Buller's esteem, who wrote in 1925, 'To this day every Gunner is indignant at what evolved.'[22] But Buller's infantrymen could do no more. The searing heat, and above all the lack of water, had proved too much for the still unfit and not yet acclimatized reservists. Lyttelton, whose brigade had been deployed to support the two attacking formations, described the 'dead-beat' and parched Irishmen staggering that five miles back from the river.[23] Even worse, the damage the men had taken from the unseen enemy had shattered morale. When Buller finally broke off the action, he and his staff had to ride up and down the dongas to help force Hildyard's men and Barton's, the latter also in reserve, to leave their temporary shelter and pull back.[24] There was no question, as Buller saw it, of leaving them there in the searing sun, waterless until nightfall, and so risking a major catastrophe merely to recover the easily replaceable pieces of hardware.

Dundonald's mounted men had also suffered badly in covering the right flank from the area of the dominant Hlangwane Hill, on whose lower slopes he had attempted to bring a battery of guns into action to help support Hildyard's attack. When withdrawn to camp, unhappy at having to do so, he was straightaway sent out again to help round up the 'hot, tired and thirsty' stragglers.[25] Those who had previously suffered a summer on the torrid Indian plains found at Colenso an equal torment.

British losses that day numbered 1,139 from some 19,000 engaged, about half of them from the Irish Brigade. By comparison with the coming major world conflicts, the proportion was small, but the nation was not yet accustomed to facing such a bill; battle losses in small wars against uncivilized enemies were rarely large. Casualties would have been far higher if Buller had not abandoned the guns because he judged that lives expended in further rescue attempts would be disproportionate to their value.[26] To Lansdowne he described his failure as a 'reverse'. So perhaps it was, rather than a defeat: having lost a high proportion of the guns needed to force a passage over the river, he had pulled back rather than lose more men to little purpose. But neither the soldiers nor their commander saw it as such.

Atkins, who had been present at the battle, saw 'an old, old man' clambering limply off his horse at the end of the day.[27] That evening Buller asked Stopford, rather than his servant, to help undress him. The shrapnel blow had left him black and blue from shoulder to loins, and he wanted no one else to know.[28] Sixty-one years old, he had been on the go for thirty-six hours without a break, fourteen of them in the saddle. Exhausted and in great pain, he straightaway wrote two lengthy telegrams to Lansdowne, the first official and the second personal, reporting the day's events. He also despatched another to Forestier-Walker, as well as a letter to an old friend telling him that his son, although wounded, was safe and recommended for the Victoria Cross.

Aggravating Buller was a telegram from Lansdowne sent on 14 December, telling him that Lieutenant-General Sir Charles Warren of the 5th Division would take command of Methuen's force on arrival; furthermore, contrary to Buller's advice, the Secretary of State proposed that both Methuen and Gatacre should be relegated to the lines of communication. Assuming that the order applied to Warren's division, as well as to its commander, it seemed to Buller that the authorities in Pall Mall, advised by Milner, had decided to handle strategy themselves by giving priority to Kimberley's relief, so ignoring his own views.[29] With fatigue and pain compounding this intense annoyance, he was in a raging temper, as he later admitted,[30] when he drafted this personal signal to Lansdowne:

My failure today raises a serious question. I do not think I am strong enough to relieve White. Colenso is a fortress which I think if not taken in a rush could only be taken by a siege. There is no water within eight miles of the point of attack, and in this weather that exhausts [sic]. The place is fully entrenched. I do not think either a Boer or a gun was seen by us all day, yet the fire brought to bear was very heavy. Our infantry was quite ready to fight, but were exhausted by the intense heat. My view is that I ought to let Ladysmith go, and occupy good positions for the defence of South Natal. . . . I now feel that I cannot say I can relieve Ladysmith with my available force.[31]

Ill-conceived and ill-worded, it had been hurriedly composed prior to the start of yet another long day in the saddle. It was to be the culmination of Buller's long conflict with Lansdowne. He was, as he later told the Royal Commission, 'In the position of a man who had never been consulted at all, whose advice had never been taken, and whose advice had usually been rather curtly, not very politely, refused'. In England, he complained, the Government ignored him; in South Africa they interfered. To advise Lansdowne was useless: his only alternative was 'to present to him strongly the situation created by his interference'.[32]

Those words 'let Ladysmith go' created consternation in Pall Mall. Moreover, the news was the culmination of what was immediately dubbed 'Black Week', the three successive defeats at Stormberg, Magersfontein and now Colenso. Buller's words were interpreted by Lansdowne and others as an intention to abandon the place to the Boers, and the reaction to them was swift. On the very evening of Colenso and in response to Buller's first telegram, Lansdowne advised Balfour, as deputy Prime Minister in Salisbury's absence from London, that Roberts should be sent out to supersede him, and that the forty-nine-year-old Lord Kitchener, ennobled for his victory at Omdurman and the Army's rising star, should go with him as his Chief-of-Staff. The problem of obtaining the approval of Lord Wolseley and the Queen was solved by consulting neither. The latter, who had written that very day to Buller, expressing her 'great confidence' in him, thought it 'quite extraordinary' that her Commander-in-Chief had not been consulted and 'very wrong' that she had not been told first.[33] Wolseley was choleric.

'Let Ladysmith go' was, as Buller later insisted and the military member of the future Royal Commission confirmed, no more than the then current military technicality to describe the suspension of military operations; the expression was, in effect, the Army's equivalent of the Royal Navy's 'part company with'.[34] In the Intelligence department of the War Office an unknown young captain found himself unavailingly explaining matters to his betters. On duty that evening was 'Wullie' Robertson, a rather unusual officer – a working man who had begun his career as a cavalry trooper and was to end it as Field-Marshal Sir William Robertson. Brought the fateful telegram, he found himself advising the Government why the relief of Ladysmith should present difficulties: after all, the combined strength of White's and Buller's forces greatly outnumbered the Boers; as the nutcracker with the enemy within its jaws, surely the Boers could be crushed. His explanation that fighting a battle involved more than a mere head-count failed, he thought, to convince the unnamed minister he briefed.[35]

So it was that the first response Buller received was:

Her Majesty's government [?considers] abandonment and consequent loss of White's force as a national disaster of the greatest magnitude. We should advise you to devise another attempt to relieve it, not necessarily by way of Colenso, making use, if you think well, of additional troops now arriving in South Africa.[36]

To this his brief reply was dryly pointed:

Much obliged for your No 53 cipher. Exactly what I wanted. I was in doubt as to what weight I should attach to financial considerations at Kimberley.[37]

That further attempt against Ladysmith he had already started planning.

Hard behind the government's initial reply followed a further telegram, its contents anticipated by its recipient. Roberts was to supersede him. The grounds given were that the operations in Natal were quite distinct from those in the Cape and required his undivided attention.[38] Later there arrived a personal message from Lansdowne:

Decision communicated to you in telegram No 57 may, I fear, be distasteful to you, but we have arrived at it from a strong sense that the step is inevitable. I have seen Lord Roberts, and I am quite sure you need have no misgivings as to your relations with him.[39]

It read, Buller was to remark, like one to a girl who was being put in charge of a strict governess; nevertheless his civil reply expressing his agreement with HMG's decision revealed no rancour.[40]

Wolseley, who feared that Buller would assume that he had been involved, wrote straight away to Lady Audrey, saying that he had told Lansdowne that 'he thought it a most unwise arrangement, superseding by far the best general in the Army by an indifferent one'; on the other hand it would bring him home to her sooner, for he was sure her husband would resign.[41] Wolseley's many surviving letters, both to Buller and his wife, demonstrate his strong support and affection for his old comrade, that unjustified rancour over the background to his appointment as Commander-in-Chief apparently forgiven or forgotten.

But Buller was not the resigning type. His attitude towards it all is summarized in this hurried conclusion to a letter to his wife:

Just as I was writing to you an unpleasant surprise has supervened. A telegram has come to say that Lord Roberts is appointed C-in-C, and I am relegated to the command in Natal. I have expected this [?]. Two days after I arrived here they ordered me to supersede Sir George White, and I would not, they then later ordered me to supersede Gatacre and I would not, and then Methuen and I would not, so now they have superseded me. I honestly confess I am not sorry, though I fear you will be disappointed. Personally I think they are right, this show is too big for one man, it is impossible for me to run this place and look after the Cape, which is a thousand miles away. Whether I was right to come on here or not is another matter, as I think I told you at the time when Sir A. Milner wanted me to stay in Cape Town, I said that I regarded the attempt to relieve White as a forlorn hope, and did not want anyone to take the risk of a failure that I ought to be responsible for. So I came but I felt at the time that as the thing got bigger I left by leaving the front door open. However, I can truly say I did what I thought was right.[42]

The forebodings that had dogged him from the first, that lack of confidence in himself he had expressed when first appointed, had been proved correct. He also anticipated that still worse might happen. Two days later he wrote to the Skinners' Company in the City of London rejecting for the time being the offer of their Honorary Freedom because 'I consider my present position is most peculiar' and because 'scapegoats' might have to be found, he should not accept before he was sure that he would 'not be one of those who are held to come out as failures'.[43]

For Roberts, bitterly disappointed at his relegation to Ireland, this was the chance he had long sought. During his forty-one years in India, he had shown himself as the most political of generals. He possessed the only too common attribute of denying that he would ever seek a favour for himself while doing just that. He cultivated influential newspapermen – Spencer Wilkinson, leader writer to the *Morning Post*, Amery, Rudyard Kipling and many others – with the same assiduity as he did politicians. His natural charm captivated everyone, regardless of class, creed or colour; his staff, able men like Ian Hamilton and Henry Rawlinson, all adored him. To the British public he was 'Little Bobs' or 'Bobs Bahadur', the subject of Kipling's famous rhyme, and successor to his rival, Wolseley, as their current military idol. Wolseley, within his own circle, made little secret of his loathing; Roberts was outwardly more circumspect.

The relationship then existing between Buller and Roberts is rather harder to unravel. They had long corresponded on official matters, especially when Buller was at the War Office and Roberts held India. The former's surviving letters are unfailingly civil and informative, at times friendly and humorous. In a happily informal way, Buller could confide that, 'The Duke of Cambridge is disporting himself in Egypt and I pray he will be in no hurry to come home as this Gordon Cumming scandal is a little troublesome'. In another letter, he emphasizes that he has no wish to succeed his correspondent in India, and that in White, who had just turned up in London, 'India has the best available C-in-C', although he feels that Evelyn Wood may have been badly treated.[44] It has been mistakenly said that Roberts had never met Buller until the Boer War, but during that irritating and anxious two-year wait before the former obtained Ireland, he had written almost weekly to his close friend, Ian Hamilton, by then White's Military Secretary. In one letter, sent soon after his return, he reflects:

> My impression is that Buller can't [sic] so much for or against me. I don't suppose he likes me, but he is civil enough when we meet, which is very seldom. . . . Wolseley I met, also Lady W, the other day at the [?] who kindly asked them to lunch with us. They were so very nice.[45]

Still convinced that Buller was his 'deadly enemy',[46] an accusation for which little or no evidence has surfaced – and Buller rarely bore malice, and then only against journalists and perhaps Tory politicians – Hamilton did much to influence Roberts against him.

For someone who prided himself upon never seeking an appointment, Roberts's letter to Lansdowne, his old friend and supporter, written just a week before Colenso was fought, might be said to be revealing:

> I am concerned at the very gloomy view Buller takes of the situation . . . As, I think, I have often remarked to you, it is impossible to gauge a general's qualities until he has been tried, and it is a remarkable fact that not a single commander in South Africa has ever held an independent command in the field. It is the feeling of responsibility that weighs down most men, and it seems clear, unless I am very much mistaken, it is having too frequent an effect on Buller. He seems to be overwhelmed by the magnitude of the task imposed upon him, and I confess that the tone of some of his telegrams causes me considerable alarm. From the day he landed in South Africa he seemed to take a pessimistic view of our position, and when a Commander-in-Chief allows himself to enter-

tain evil forebodings, the effect is inevitably felt within the army. I feel
the greatest hesitation and dislike in expressing my opinion thus plainly,
and nothing but the gravity of the situation and the strongest sense of
duty would induce me to do so, or to offer – as I do now – to place my
services at the disposal of the Government.

Over several further paragraphs Roberts continues both to justify his conduct
and to entreat Lansdowne not to divulge the letter's contents.[47] Lord
Salisbury was the only person to be allowed to see it, but the Prime Minister,
only too conscious of the effects of age on his own dwindling powers, was
emphatic that Roberts, at sixty-seven, was too old to command in the field.[48]

Evelyn Wood, equally frustrated at being pinned to his Adjutant-General's
desk, intrigued in much the same way to get to South Africa, but he did at
least offer to serve under Buller, junior to him. Anticipating as early as 31
October that Buller would go to Natal, he suggested to Lansdowne he should
hold the fort in the Cape until such time as Natal was safe.[49]

Roberts had written his letter before Buller had even fought a battle.
Except to the equally worried Milner, Buller is not known to have communicated his doubts to those around him. The opposite was the case. There is
evidence in plenty that his arrival heartened everyone. And Roberts's
pleading was special indeed: while emphasizing that no one in South Africa
had held an independent command, he failed to mention that, except for
Wolseley and Kitchener, he alone of the Army's senior officers had done so.

While agreeing with Roberts's strictures, Lansdowne was forced to point
out to him that it was hardly possible to supersede Buller 'merely on account
of the gloominess of his views'.[50] But Colenso was the excuse he sought to
replace him with the man he afterwards felt justified in describing as 'the
most absolutely genuine and sincere' person he had ever met, one whom he
loved as 'I have loved few people in the world'.[51]

So it happened that, the morning after Colenso, two telegrams arrived in
Dublin for Roberts. One was from Lansdowne, summoning him to London
and warning him to make ready to leave for South Africa; this crossed with
a cable from its recipient, yet again pressing his services upon the Government. The second was from Buller, telling him that Freddy, his only son,
had been dangerously wounded and was recommended for the Victoria
Cross. Another was on its way. It read, 'Your gallant son died today.
Condolences, Buller'.[52] A week later a stricken old man sailed from
Southampton to take up his new command.

Not for many months did the Government learn of a further carelessly
phrased signal despatched from Buller's headquarters in the aftermath of the
battle. The morning after – heliographs had, of course, to await sunrise –
Buller sent White the following:

I tried Colenso yesterday, but failed. The enemy is too strong for my force, except with siege operations, which will take one full month to prepare. Can you last so long? If not, how many days can you give me to take up defensive position, after which I suggest your firing away as much ammunition as you can, and making the best terms you can. I can remain here if you have alternative suggestions, but unaided I cannot break in. I find my infantry cannot fight more than ten miles from camp, and then only if water can be got and it is scarce here.[53]

This in itself was bad enough, its wording the outcome of Buller's rage with White, first for incarcerating himself in Ladysmith, second for doing nothing to extricate himself despite his more powerful and battle-hardened force. But worse was to come. As Buller was mounting his horse, stiff and in even greater pain than the previous afternoon, he dictated to his cipher clerk some changes to the message which included, 'whatever happens recollect to burn your cipher and decipher and code books and any deciphered messages,' this the result of his learning that the Boers had laid hands upon Penn Symons's code books.[54]

Stupid was the word Buller used to describe the signal, and stupid it was. But 'the most effective lever I could employ to move him,' as he later justified his action to the Royal Commission, 'would be the warning that unless he could offer me active assistance he might possibly have to surrender'.[55] The wording of a subsequent signal, transmitted on 17 December, makes it clear that in no way was Buller contemplating White's immediate surrender,[56] something inconceivable either to White, to Buller or any other commander of that era.

Today such a casual way of despatching messages seems strange. But this was the British Army of the 19th Century. Staff work in battle was not properly codified, nor did commanders know how to get the best out of their staffs.[57] Kitchener and Roberts were noteworthy culprits. These were among the many lessons learned from the Boer War which improved instruction at the Staff College, together with the long-awaited introduction of a Continental Europe-style General Staff did much to correct before 1914.

The widespread criticism of Buller's performance in the fighting south of Ladysmith was in many ways justified. Nor can it be argued that those telegrams to Lansdowne and White were anything but carelessly worded and open to misinterpretation.

His awareness of his own limitations and his reluctance to accept the command in South Africa have already been emphasized. He well knew that he was past his best after so many years spent at a desk, but the task was forced upon him against his wish. Nevertheless his physical unfitness has been grossly exaggerated by a succession of writers. Most of his spare time from London had, after all, been spent at Downes, where country sports and the care of his estates had kept him active. Otherwise he could hardly have survived fourteen hours in the saddle at Colenso – few people today appreciate what this means – in the course of a thirty-six-hour waking spell under continuous pressure, mental as well as physical, during which he suffered a near-shattering blow. To withstand such rigours at sixty-one denotes a high degree of fitness. Too old he may have been to command an army in the field, but not more so than most of his contemporaries.

Buller also stands accused that the physical degeneration with which he is reproached was largely due to over-indulgence. T.E. Lawrence of Arabian fame went so far as to repeat gossip that he drank 'terribly' and that this was the cause of his failure at Colenso.[58] Certainly he enjoyed both his food and his drink, as was the custom at the time among those who could afford it. Arthur Balfour, no friend of Buller, years later had this to say about him:

Buller was a fine brain in a way – he drank too much though, I don't mean he got drunk, but he would sit on all night like they did in Ireland in those days. He got through an enormous quantity of drink.[59]

References to the quantity and quality of champagne consumed by his guests in the field are also frequent. But a century ago champagne was seen rather differently. It was provided as a medical comfort for use in hospitals, and even taken by Jameson on his raid. Guests at Buller's headquarters, and these included both important civilians and foreign military attachés, would have expected to find champagne there, often served in a tankard. That he was overweight, like most men in their sixties, is emphasized by his detractors, one of whom found it necessary to describe his snatching a bite in the saddle at Colenso as 'gobbling sandwiches'.[60]

Rarely mentioned is the way Buller shared in part the discomforts of his soldiers when supplies were short, as had always been his habit. As one of them put it, 'Now, no one loves his dinner better than Buller, but if the canteen is not up, Buller won't eat his dinner, and when they 'ears that Buller can't eat his dinner they hurries up the canteen, and then Buller eats his dinner.'[61] When transport was available, much was needed to move his mess, but when he left so secretly from the Cape, he left behind most of his heavy kit, not bothering about it.[62] When tents had later to be abandoned, Buller, like his troops, slept in the rain.

Of all Buller's contemporary critics, none matched the twenty-eight-year-old Amery in both virulence and influence. Reporters had poured into South Africa, among them a large *Times* team, headed by him. From a 'double-first' at Oxford and a fellowship of All Souls, he was afterwards to progress by way of journalism to a Conservative seat in the Commons and a succession of Cabinet posts, culminating in 1940 in Churchill's wartime Government. His finest hour was in May, 1940, when he declaimed to the Prime Minister, Neville Chamberlain, Cromwell's famous words, 'You have sat too long here for any good you have been doing. Depart, I say, and let us have done with you. In the name of God, go.' His politics were throughout his life well to the right.

As editor of the whole work and the principal author of two-thirds of the six-volume, 3,500-page *Times History of the War in South Africa*, Amery created a forum from which he savaged the political and military system responsible for the manifold shortcomings displayed in the army his country had despatched to South Africa. Meticulously prepared and superbly written, his concept of his task was, as he frankly admitted, 'in essence propagandist – to secure the reform of the Army in preparation for coming dangers'.[63] In this he succeeded, although as an eminent historian has recently suggested, he often overstated his case.[64] Among the many influential officers he consulted were Roberts, White, Hamilton and Kitchener, all but the last-named 'Indians' and none of them well-disposed towards Buller. Amery was also one of Milner's fervent admirers.

With good reason, Amery condemned British generalship. But it was at Buller that he levied the greater weight of his invective. Writing in 1905, while his target still lived, he named him as 'the embodiment of the qualities and defects which the British military system tended to produce',[65] describing him in terms such as baffled, bewildered, distracted, disheartened and unnerved.[66] He wrote of Colenso that Buller had failed both his men and his country.[67] In his 152-page index, no fewer than seventeen entries point the reader to specific criticisms of Buller.

Did Amery have a personal reason for so stigmatizing Buller? A contemporary anecdote relates how, before the Colenso battle, he asked him where he could best view the battle from a place of safety, an unwise question to put to someone whose gallantry was proverbial and who loathed the press. A contemptuous 'Go anywhere, to New Zealand, if you like'[68] was the response. But there is a snag. Amery was not at Colenso. The incident could have happened to him elsewhere, or even to another *Times* writer – unlikely as one of the paper's representatives at Colenso was 'Bron' Herbert, a very gallant man and the model for John Buchan's 'Greenmantle'. (Herbert was also Buller's second cousin, but never managed to obtain an interview from him.) It could, of course, have been a slander spread by one of Buller's many and sometimes uncritical supporters. The truth is not known, but if there was anything in the story, Amery, a proud man, would have had good reason for personal dislike.

Another journalist and historian to be whom Buller managed to offend was the brash young Winston Churchill, recently back from Pretoria after his dramatic escape from his Boer prison. A fellow guest with Buller at Government House in Pietermaritzburg, Churchill erred at dinner by laying down the law to Buller on the best method of conducting the campaign, only to be told not to be a young ass.[69] It has also been said that Buller once described him as a scoundrel,[70] unlikely indeed as he granted Churchill a commission in an irregular regiment after his escape, despite his continued journalism. In his *London to Ladysmith*, published in 1900 and based largely upon his *Morning Post* despatches, Churchill was generous in his praise of Buller. Thirty years later, when any need to be circumspect had long passed, his sneers matched Amery's[71]; by then Buller's incompetence had been accepted as the revealed truth, unfashionable to query.

The *Official History*, the first two volumes of which were edited by the now Sir Frederick Maurice, was emasculated both by politicians fearful of impeding reconciliation with the Boers and soldiers anxious to avoid scarifying old wounds. Subsequent historians and others have, therefore, tended to quarry Amery's lively volumes, rather than Maurice's dull but factual pages. In this way Buller became the bogeyman of the Boer War, the epitome of all that was wrong with British generalship. That name 'Buller' helped, as did his appearance, his visage jowled and heavy in repose. Douglas Haig was to occupy a similar place in the demonology of the First World War.

11

LADYSMITH

Before he left for South Africa on 23 December Roberts had signalled Buller that he intended, when he arrived, to advance in force through the Orange Free State; as for Buller, after he had turned the Boer position on the Tugela and so relieved Ladysmith, he was to hold the line of that river, and thus release troops to reinforce Roberts's own thrust.[1]

Buller's response to these instructions was contained in a long and percipient letter which awaited Roberts when he reached Cape Town on 10 January. In it the writer recapitulated the lessons of the campaign to date and gave Roberts his views on the future. He expressed optimism about the disaffection among the Cape Dutch; this he thought would be contained by the arrival of further troops. Also emphasized was his hope that the Boers would in time lose much of their mobility as they used up their limited supply of horses. Moreover, the Tugela, as he pointed out, could not be turned: 'the only open question is whether one part of it is easier to get through than another'. This he would now attempt by forcing a passage at Potgeiter's.[2]

The misconception that positions could always be turned and expensive frontal attacks avoided was common not just among the uninformed critic but also among many who should have known better – not just in that war but everywhere and in every era. It sprang from the craving for a cheap and quick solution, a reluctance to accept the inevitability of losses. It led to Buller complaining of 'all the rot they have been writing in the papers about frontal attacks and now half our officers have an idea that you can break a position without fighting,' a comment contained in a letter to his wife in which he grieved for the killed and wounded, both men he knew and numbers he did not – a sorrowful recurring theme in his correspondence.[3] To cross the Tugela in the face of long-range, accurate and concealed weapons was as much a siege operation – the capture of a well-fortified position – as was Passchendaele, Alamein or Normandy. This often led to attrition, an ugly word describing an ugly reality.

Grimly though the Boers would fight to protect their country, their numbers were sparse, each man precious to the *volk*. Because of this, offensive operations, expensive in lives, were disliked by their generals and often avoided by individuals. Consequently, Ladysmith, like Kimberley and Mafeking, had to date been encircled and bombarded but its fourteen-mile perimeter never seriously assaulted. Now, so as to win a resounding victory, Kruger decided to tackle Ladysmith, despite its 14,000-strong garrison. Without denuding the Tugela line, only 4,000 men could be spared for the task, but on the night of 6 January a full-scale attack developed against the Platrand, a 300-foot-high feature dominating the town from the south-east. Holding the Platrand was a force commanded by Ian Hamilton, whose organization and construction of the defences belied his high reputation; caught off balance, his handling of the subsequent battle was equally faulty, despite his personal gallantry. During the confused and savage sixteen-hour struggle, much at bayonet-point, virtually all White's reserves were drawn in to prevent the breaching of this vital sector of the defences. It was a near thing, provoking White to appeal for help in terms that verged on the desperate[4] and which persuaded Buller to create an immediate diversion at Colenso.

After such a demonstration by the Boers, the need to relieve Ladysmith was unquestionable. Moreover, the morale of the garrison was poor. The ration of biscuit and stringy trek-ox had been pared; next to be eaten were the cavalry horses. One-fifth of the force was sick, and deaths from enteric, jaundice and dysentery were multiplying. The Boer 155 mm 'Long Toms' could bombard the town with near impunity, and only rarely did White's troops mount raids against their lines. The garrison, as Major May wrote, was 'gradually becoming weak and feeble, individually and collectively'.[5] The comparative comfort enjoyed by the staff contrasted with the squalor suffered by the regimental officers and soldiers manning the perimeter. Inevitably it caused friction.

Not that White's staff were happy. Old Indian hands and close friends such as Hamilton and Rawlinson were unflinchingly loyal, but despairing comments in the latter's diary reveal the garrison's despondency. A sound soldier and decent man, Rawlinson understood Buller's problems, doubting whether he was strong enough to force a passage at Potgeiter's, even when reinforced by a further division. He appreciated also that at Colenso, 'Buller had found his troops unequal to the task', knowing that in South Africa 'when men have done 10 miles in hot weather they are beat'.[6] Nevertheless, Rawlinson's diary reveals the innate prejudices of a member of the 'Indian Ring': White is always 'Sir George', while Buller is never 'Sir Redvers' but either plain 'Buller' or the oddly snide 'Sir Buller'.

Nor had it helped that Buller's ill-formulated signal after Colenso had

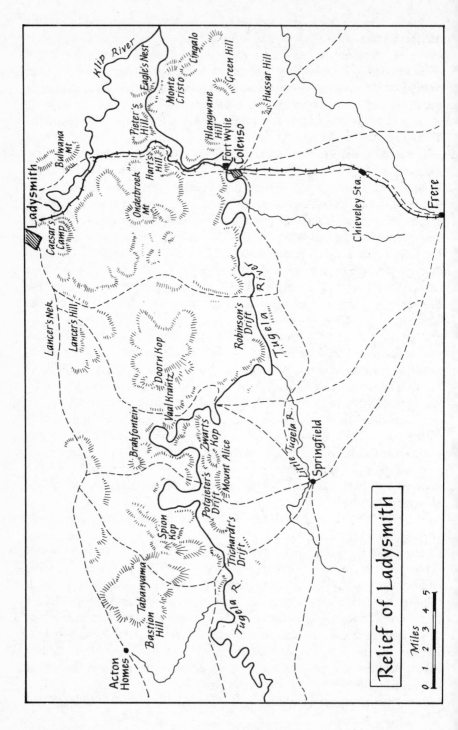

Relief of Ladysmith

been misread by the staff as an encouragement to surrender. Rarely do the besieged give proper credit to the efforts being made by those outside the walls, but Buller had his defenders in the garrison, among them young Marling of Sudan days, very ill with dysentery, who wrote that although most people were a bit sceptical about Buller's speedy arrival, 'Personally I have every confidence in him. He saved us at Suakin and also in the Khartoum expedition in 1885. . . . He had the toughest job and fewest men to do it with.'[7]

Marling's confidence was to be justified, but not as yet. On 9 January, the day before Roberts's arrival, Buller's leading units set out to march towards Potgeiter's by way of Springfield, eighteen miles north-west of Frere, where a 15-day supply depot was being set up. His force was now augmented by the newly arrived 5th Division, its commander the sixty-year-old Lieutenant-General Sir Charles Warren, late of the Royal Engineers, a prominent archaeologist who had spent most of his service on survey work but never commanded more than the equivalent of a brigade. Inexplicably, he had been brought back from retirement for the task. Although Buller had rejected the suggestion that Warren should replace Methuen, the War Office had specified that he should take Buller's place should anything happen to him. Afterwards Buller insisted that Lansdowne had also specified that Warren should hold the position to which his rank entitled him – something that the Secretary of State was to deny.[8] Not only had Warren been forced upon him, Buller claimed, but he found it hard to establish a sound relationship with his new subordinate.

For the attack on Potgeiter's Buller decided to use both Warren's and Clery's divisions, leaving a single brigade to cover Colenso. The move went slowly, the coming of the rains having temporarily solved the shortage of water, converting the Tugela into a torrent which soddened the veldt and filled the spruits. Warren's troops who had left England just four weeks before, 'waded, sliding, sucking, pumping, gurgling through the mud; the horses floundered and tobogganed with all four feet together; the wagons lurched axle-deep into heavy sloughs and had to be dragged out with trebled teams of oxen. And it was cold too . . . men . . . shivered with grey, wet faces'.[9] The speed of the columns was reduced to about a mile in the hour.

Overlooking Potgeiter's Drift from the southern bank was Mount Alice whose northern flank fell precipitously towards the river. Seized by Dundonald's horsemen on 11 January, it commanded a panoramic view of the Boer-held hills north of the Tugela, which here doubled and redoubled upon itself in vast loops. Beyond and to the north-east could be caught a tantalizing glimpse of Ladysmith, twelve miles distant. Unlike the more southerly approach from Colenso, where a succession of broken ridges had to be surmounted after the river line had been forced, at Potgeiter's only a single but steep range barred Buller's subsequent progress. Its centre was the flat-topped Spion Kop, rising some 1,500 feet above the river; to the west the Tabanyama Hills ended in the Bastion Hill escarpment; to the east lay the rather lower Brakfontein and Vaal Krantz. From Potgeiter's a track curved between Spion Kop and Brakfontein towards Ladysmith; four miles to its west another led from Trickhardt's Drift across a spur of Tabanyama in the same direction.

From his headquarters, set up on Mount Alice, it was clear to Buller that the track leading from Potgeiters ran through a dangerous re-entrant overlooked both from Spion Kop and Brakfontein. As a result he decided to seize and hold Potgeiter's Drift with a force of 9,000 men and twenty-two guns, commanded by Lyttelton; meanwhile Warren would cross at Trick-hardt's with 15,000 men and thirty-six guns, his task to swing around or over Tabanyama to take the Boer positions in the rear. Lyttelton could then drive through the hills once Warren had drawn off the bulk of the defenders.

Shocking were the conditions, but even worse was Warren's inertia. Each day the Boers could be observed improving their positions on the hills overlooking the river as more and more commandos rode in from the east. Not until 17 January did his force start to cross the Tugela; by that evening two brigades had established a bridgehead among the foothills of the main range, while Dundonald's 1,500 horsemen had swung around to a lateral track that ran to Acton Homes, north-west and beyond Tabanyama. On the same day Lyttelton seized a crossing at Potgeiter's.

All seemed at last to be going well, but indecision and further delays were to follow. Dundonald had assumed that infantry would follow his horsemen, but none did; nor did Warren push on to the still almost undefended Tabanyama. Instead, he withdrew Dundonald from Acton Homes, which had been reached with little trouble, much to the latter's unrestrained and undisguised aggravation.[10] For Warren had decided that this wide flank approach was altogether too risky and that a way must be forced up that track leading across Tabanyama. Not until 20 January did he tackle it and there his infantry stuck in exposed positions for four days, suffering casualties in a series of ill-coordinated attacks.

Buller watched all this with increasing impatience. As early as 19 January he had been debating whether to remove Warren, but decided against it. Two questions must be answered. Why did he delegate such a task to Warren instead of doing it himself? Why, having seen his aimless and irresolute – to use Buller's adjectives – behaviour, did not he straightaway relieve him?

The second question has already been partly answered. The circumstances of Warren's appointment by the Secretary-of-State as second-in-command were such that Buller considered that after so short a time in charge, his shortcomings did not justify his removal.[11] Rather more difficult to answer is the first charge. With this his critics, foremost among them Amery, have reproached him on the grounds that he should never have put Warren in charge in the first place and was avoiding his responsibilities by doing so. Was this accusation justified? It is possible that Colenso had aggravated Buller's lack of confidence in himself, but he was a man whose moral courage equalled his physical; his life bears witness to this. It would have been out of character for him to avoid responsibility. More acceptable is the explanation that, having divided his force to mount with poor communications and in rugged country an inevitably complicated operation, his place was near Lyttelton. By not having to exercise detailed control of the operations on his flank, he would be best placed to decide the right moment to commit Lyttelton's units, and so trap and perhaps destroy the Boers.[12] Only recently at Colenso had he experienced the dangers of becoming too involved in the immediate battle.

When Buller rode over to see Warren on 23 January, his ADC, Lieutenant Algy Trotter, noticed that Warren did not 'like being advised by Sir R'.[13] By then Warren had all but decided that his only way forward was to attack the commanding and flat-topped Spion Kop on his right, on which he could then position his artillery so as to overwhelm the Boers below. Given by Buller two alternatives, either attack or withdraw, he tackled Spion Kop that same night. By dawn, after a stiff scramble over boulder-strewn slopes by two battalions of already exhausted men, the summit was reached and a Boer picquet brushed aside.

When the early mist lifted, the 1,700 men, crammed on to one end of a plateau no more than 400 yards wide, became targets not only for the Boer riflemen but the concentrated fire of their unseen artillery as well. The inactivity of Major-General Woodgate, their commander, matched Warren's, failing as he did to push forward patrols while the mist lasted to discover the extent of the plateau. It was an error of which Botha, from below, took full and sound advantage, pushing men up the hill to seize positions from which they could fire down into the shallow British trenches and sangars. A savage fight ensued which lasted most of the day. Out of proportion were casualties among the British officers, visible as they rallied their men, although by now they carried rifles and had discarded their badges of rank as well as their swords to make themselves that less conspicuous. With all their officers gone, about 170 men in one of the exposed trenches surrendered. Men of three further units (one from Lyttelton's brigade, despatched by its commander on his own initiative to render help) arrived on top, replacing losses but reinforcing what was fast becoming failure. In Atkins's memorable words, the summit had become 'an acre of massacre'.[14] Overcrowded behind their stone sangars among the dead and wounded, the troops crouched, exhausted and parched with thirst. Many began to help wounded comrades down the hill; others slipped away without even that excuse. Repington, who was with the force, had forecast another Majuba and so it was.[15]

With Woodgate dying, that evening the senior surviving officer, out of touch with Warren for most of the day because his heliograph had been smashed by a shell, decided to pull his men down from what he saw as an untenable and tactically useless summit. His decision to do so almost coincided with the departure of the almost equally shattered Boers; their numbers had been fewer, but their losses had been comparable to those of their enemies – 1,750 in eighteen days of battle. It was judged to have been a year before the Spion Kop commandos were again in action.[16]

That night Buller at last took over the direction of the battle from Warren, who throughout that long day had made little effort to discover what was happening hardly a mile away. Unaware that the Boers in the Spion Kop area were all but finished, Buller decided to break off the battle and try elsewhere. Churchill, who had been caught up in the fighting himself, watched the subsequent withdrawal over the river:

> Buller took personal command. He arrived on the field cheerful, inscrutable as ever, rode hither and thither with a weary staff and a huge notebook, gripped the whole business in his strong hands, and so shook it into shape that we crossed the river in safety, comfort and good order, with a most remarkable mechanical precision, and without the loss of a single man or a pound of stores.[17]

If he had 'gripped' it all a few days earlier, the outcome of the campaign might have been different.

This second failure gave rise over the next few days to an interchange of signals and letters between Buller, Roberts, the War Office and White. Roberts, now fully in charge, counselled Buller against a further attempt on the Tugela defences; White dwelt on the weaknesses of his force, while the War Office urged White to try to break out and join Buller. By 28 February he hoped to be in Bloemfontein, Roberts confidently informed Buller, thus relieving pressure on Natal.[18]

However, Buller did not accept Roberts's forecast of so rapid an advance to Bloemfontein; nor did he judge that the threat to the Orange Free State capital would draw off many of the Boers opposing him, most of whom were now Transvaalers.[19] Having learned that a fifth of White's force was in hospital, Buller, insistent that Ladysmith should be relieved, decided that the plans he had already formulated for a further attempt on the Tugela should go ahead. This was to be at a kopje called Vaal Krantz, past which another track led to Ladysmith; once that flat-topped hill was taken, the way to Ladysmith seemed to lie open.

But the failure at Spion Kop was to be repeated. Once again detailed topographical information was lacking, but once again the objective was to be taken, this time by Lyttelton's 4th Brigade. By midday on 5 February it was crossing, under fire but with small loss, newly built pontoon bridges; a couple of hours later his leading battalions had driven the Boer defenders off the hill at the bayonets' point. To distract the enemy, Buller had previously mounted a feint towards Brakfontein by another brigade, and at the same time he had deployed Hildyard's and Hart's brigades ready to back Lyttelton.

So far all had gone as planned. The artillery had been well handled, a part of it to support the feint and the whole massed to cover Lyttelton's main attack. But continued success depended upon dragging some of the guns up to the summit of Vaal Krantz to support the onward movement to Lady-smith. This was not to happen. Instead of being an isolated hill which the infantry could clear to make room for the artillery, Vaal Krantz was found to be joined to a spur of Brakfontein by a narrow saddle covered by fire from all the surrounding hills. Again the well hidden Boer guns could hammer at will the frantically entrenching British. Next day Lyttelton reported that he could not get forward, and that even if he could he would still be exposed to the encircling Boer fire; that evening Hildyard's brigade relieved his exhausted troops on the summit.

Already, however, Buller had taken stock of the situation. To push on by way of Vaal Krantz would be expensive in lives and he had promised Roberts that he would not compromise his force.[20] His thoughts were set out in this telegram to the Field-Marshal:

After fighting all day yesterday, but with small loss, I have pierced the enemy's line, and hold a hill which divides their position, and will, if I can advance, give me access to the Ladysmith plain, when I should be ten miles from White, with but one place for the enemy to stand between us. But to get my artillery and supplies on to the plain, I must drive back the enemy either on my right or on my left. It is an operation which will cost from 2,000 to 3,000 men, *and I am not confident, though hopeful, I can do it. The question is how would such a loss affect your plans* [author's italics], and do you think the chance of the relief of Ladysmith worth the risk? It is the only possible way to relieve White; if I give up this chance I know no other.[21]

Reluctant as Roberts had hitherto been to permit Buller to press on, his reply was an astounding volte-face. Ladysmith, he insisted, must be relieved at any cost and his signal ended with the unnecessary, if not insulting, peroration, 'Tell your troops that the honour of the Empire is in their hands, I have no possible doubt of their being successful'.[22]

Buller's enemies were to read what they saw as 'Machiavellian schemes' into that telegram. Amery, whose history was to be used by most of Buller's subsequent detractors as their major source, accused him both of avoiding responsibility for coming to a decision and ensuring that, if Ladysmith fell, Roberts and not he would bear the blame.[23] This suggestion of pusillanimous behaviour on Buller's part was to be reinforced by the omission of the italicized portion of the message in Roberts's published despatch – an omission that could hardly have been accidental.

A personal inspection on horseback early on 7 February further convinced Buller that it was useless to attempt to press on from Vaal Krantz, a decision with which all his general officers – other than the fire-eating Hart – agreed that afternoon at a council of war, during which he read them Roberts's message. Instead, he told them, they would break off the attack and fall back to Chieveley so as to tackle the Tugela from Hlangwane, east of Colenso.

This second withdrawal across the river inevitably disheartened everyone – staff, commanders and soldiers alike. But although expressions such as 'Sir Reverse Buller' and 'The Ferryman of the Tugela' began to be heard, Buller's troops never seemed to lose that personal confidence in their General with which few are blessed. They were now a battle-hardened bunch, fit and tough, coping with fatigue, thirst and hunger when need be.

Lack of success had, however, led to in-fighting among the generals, something Buller failed to control. Among them, Lyttelton, a man in whom he often confided, was actively disloyal, writing to his wife that he had 'lost all confidence in Buller as a General and am sure he has himself'. What was reprehensible is that he said the same to the young *Times* reporter, Bron Herbert.[24] Of these elderly officers with whom Buller had been saddled (as in all wars a younger generation would soon supplant them), Lyttelton was among the least unsatisfactory. Picked by Buller at this juncture to take over the 2nd Division, commanded by Clery who had fortunately fallen sick, he climbed rapidly upwards to become, in 1904, the first Chief of the Imperial General Staff. It was a disastrous appointment: his Secretary of State wrote of him as having an empty head which 'simply rattled'.[25]

Major Henry Wilson, Lyttelton's Brigade Major, was among those who comprehended Buller's problem. An amusing, cheerful and highly intelligent officer, as indiscreet in conversation as he was on paper, he was in later years a successor to Lyttelton (for whom he had little use[26]) as CIGS and was subsequently murdered by the IRA. To have pushed on at Vaal Krantz, in Wilson's opinion, could well have ended in disaster; to drive a hole in the enemy's defences was always possible, but there was small hope of rapidly exploiting such an initial success and, with less than double the number, breaking through a force between 8,000 and 12,000 strong, well-entrenched in natural fortresses.[27] It was a foretaste of the challenges that those bright young men of the Boer War – Wilson, Rawlinson, Haig, French, Hamilton, Byng and others – would afterwards have to face.

The withdrawal from Vaal Krantz coincided with the start of Roberts's major thrust with five divisions, including the newly arrived 6th and 7th. On 11 February his vanguard crossed the Orange River, aiming at Bloemfontein by way of Kimberley; after this he planned to leave the railway line and strike due east across the veldt, supplying his 34,000 men by animal transport. Four days later, French's Cavalry Division, bypassing General Piet Cronje's commandos which were still facing Methuen's troops at Magersfontein, galloped into Kimberley.

Speed had been the essence of French's dash, but speed to relieve Kimberley had not been quite so necessary. Life there was not too uncomfortable – for the white population, of course, not the starving black labourers. But, as with Buller, Roberts had been subjected to Rhodes's blackmailing threats to surrender. For the cavalry, however, the consequences of this lightning strike were serious: most of the horses were unfit after their voyage, while their officers, odd to relate, proved inept at animal-management. That dash to Kimberley almost wrecked Roberts's sole horsed division. What is more, the urgency had led to Christiaan de Wet ambushing and scattering Roberts's unguarded oxen-train at Waterval Drift.

Roberts's subsequent transport problems were to be compounded by the ignorance and arrogance of Kitchener, his Chief-of-Staff. As already touched upon, Buller was to be criticized for his failure to use his staff to the best advantage. But Kitchener knew nothing at all about staff work and lacked any talent for organization. Like Roberts, he had seen little and knew less about the British Army and, in any case, was to be used by Roberts, not as a chief-of-staff but a second-in-command. This forty-nine-year-old general had abundant drive, determination and energy. On the other hand, he was reluctant to accept advice or to use existing systems. Failing to understand the flexibility of the transport, based as it was upon Buller's recent and effective reorganization, as soon as he arrived he scrapped the lot, removing regimental transport from units and setting up a cumbersome and over-centralized system in its place. The result was often chaos.[28] Half-rations soon became the rule among Roberts's men. Losses from disease multiplied.

The capture of Kimberley had been the signal for Cronje to begin his retreat northwards, encumbered by his wagons, which he refused to abandon. On 17 February Kitchener, temporarily in command with Roberts sick, overtook him on the Modder River, near the Paardeberg Drift. Well entrenched in a natural defensive position, Cronje turned at bay. The next morning Kitchener mounted an ill-coordinated and unsuccessful attack across the open veldt which cost him over 1,200 casualties. The hungry and thirsty men, who had slept for a week in the pouring rain, marched through the night to be thrown into the battle as their units arrived. The many tactical lessons learned by Buller at such cost in Natal were all ignored.

Taking over command the following day from Kitchener, Roberts vacillated. His first impulse was to renew the attacks, then he planned to retreat.[29] But in the end he made the obvious decision, one urged upon him by his senior commanders, to invest and bombard the Boers until death and lack of ammunition did the work for him. Trapped among the stinking carcasses of men, horses and oxen, Cronje surrendered on 27 February, despite a gallant rescue attempt by Christiaan de Wet; he, with Louis Botha, was outstanding among the new generation of Boer commanders. Paardeberg, the first British victory of the war, had been won – and on Majuba Day. But the cost had been high, unnecessarily so. Despite superb marching at times by his infantry in the grinding summer heat, it then took Roberts a further fourteen days to cover the 100 miles to Bloemfontein against sporadic Boer resistance.

Meanwhile Buller had once again turned to the Colenso area. To Roberts he reported his difficulties in dealing with an enemy operating on interior lines who could switch his forces from one part of the Tugela to another in hours as against the days it took him. Reinforcements, he insisted, were needed if he were to break through to Ladysmith, but he was also ready to relinquish his command if Roberts thought that anyone else could do the job better. It was an offer which his superior refrained from accepting, but he did order Buller to remain on the defensive. This latter instruction evoked the protest that it was wrong to 'rest supine' and leave Ladysmith to its fate. As the argument between them continued, Roberts in the end asked Buller to send him Warren's views on the subject; these he was told on 12 February 'closely coincided' with Buller's.[30] A week later, however, at the height of the Paardeberg crisis, Roberts was urging Buller 'to push on to Ladysmith' so as to take pressure off him, and to do everything possible to effect White's relief.[31]

Despite Roberts's earlier and inhibiting instructions, Buller's preparations for his fourth attempt on the Tugela line had gone steadily ahead. Overlooking Colenso itself and the Boer-held kopjes north and across the Tugela was the dominant Hlangwane. Upon that hill's flank Dundonald had attempted to place his guns to support the first Colenso battle; so rugged was it and so thick its thorn-bush that Buller had at the time decided to bypass it, deeming it too much for his then raw and unfit troops. And in a great horse-shoe east of Hlangwane lay a ring of hills and ridges, all now occupied by the enemy and ending in Monte Cristo, twice Hlangwane's height. This time Buller planned to deal with these outlying defences before pushing his troops across the river to tackle the even more serious opposition on the other side. The coming battle was to be fought across a tangled area of broken hilly country, some ten miles by six.

Buller's plan marked a major change in tactics, the outcome of six weeks' hard and often bitter experience. In the battalions and batteries, the troops had been learning from their enemies the skills of concealment, dispersion and the proper use of ground. And to their commander it had become clear that a single hard thrust would not succeed in penetrating the successive layers of well-concealed Boer defences; instead a step-by-step siege-type operation was required in which over a period of days chunks would be bitten out of the Boer positions. Above all, the attacking infantry had to be supported by artillery barrages fired close in front of them, crushing the enemy positions and lifting as they advanced. It was revolutionary stuff, a small-scale dress rehearsal for a far grimmer future when battles would last for weeks or months instead of a murderous couple of days or so.

For this fresh attack Buller mustered 25,000 troops, double or treble the Boer strength, but only a thousand of them mounted. However, his advantage lay in his preponderance of artillery. Against Botha's mere eight guns, he mustered seventy, including two newly arrived 5-inch pieces, as well as twenty-two machine guns. But no more than six were howitzers, the only weapons capable of lobbing their projectiles over intervening hills; for gun positions, the summits of the flat-topped hills had to be captured, and the weapons somehow hauled to the top.

Without, so far as can be established, waiting for Roberts's final approval, on 16 February Buller began to pick off in turn the ring of features – Hussar Hill, Green Hill, Cingalo and Monte Cristo, leap-frogging his guns forward from one feature to the next. Progress was steady but slow, mainly because Buller, knowing what lay ahead, refused to push his infantry on too fast in the grinding summer heat of 100° in the shade, if there had been any. A limiting but vital factor, hardly understood by those who have never known thirst, was that water had to be brought forward from Frere on ox-wagons in 200 gallon metal tanks, each just about enough to fill a single battalion's two-pint water-bottles.

On 18 February Monte Cristo was secured. Its capture coincided with Cronje's surrender at Paardeberg. From its summit Ladysmith could again be seen. The next day Hlangwane was taken; then Colenso village was again occupied. Each hill had involved hard fighting, but British casualties numbered only 300. The preliminaries were now over.

Buller has been castigated for swinging left in this way towards Colenso instead of driving due north across the river from Hlangwane or making a wide easterly sweep from Monte Cristo. Superficially these alternatives had their attractions. To attack from Colenso involved battering into the heart of the Boer prepared defences. Repington, whose advice Buller sought, strongly advised the alternatives, although he admitted he did not know the country. Later, Repington was to accuse Buller of having accepted the slipshod report of a young engineer officer that the favoured routes were impracticable, voicing his criticisms to junior officers, Churchill among them, just as they were about to face Boer fire once again. Buller had, in fact, carefully examined the country himself, and Repington's 'young officer' was no less than Lieutenant-Colonel A. E. Sandbach, Buller's very able senior intelligence officer. From his detailed reconnaissance Sandbach had reported that the wide swing right was as impracticable as the direct assault northwards from Monte Cristo, the latter involving clambering in and out of the deep gorge through which the Tugela curved.[32] That right flank was the route Buller had originally intended to take. Cavalry might have made it, but this he lacked; for his guns it was impossible. And, in any case, Roberts had just informed him that the Free Staters were leaving Natal, information confirmed by his own intelligence staff; he would have, it seemed, to cope with no more than a rearguard.[33]

Crossing the Tugela by a pontoon bridge floated into position on 21 February two miles north of Colenso, Buller's leading brigade the next day began the assault on the tangle of hills north of the river. It was the start of five days of bitter and continuous fighting which was to cost his units 2,000 casualties, some 10% of his force and most from the infantry. As always, losses among officers were disproportionate, one Irish battalion losing all but five. Buller's estimate of casualties prior to the battle had been 3,000, that 'long list of killed and wounded, which I cannot bear', as he told his wife.[34]

The Free Staters, many of them shattered by Spion Kop, were certainly pulling out, but fresh Transvaalers were arriving from north Natal, as White signalled Buller just after the news about the Free State burghers was confirmed.[35] With grim determination, Buller's troops struggled forward, fighting for one summit after another, pounding into the hills like bloodied battering rams. Worst was Hart's Hill, named after the brigade which suffered there. It was another Spion Kop: a false crest leading into a killing ground no more than 250 yards across, quickly covered with dead and wounded Irishmen, an eventual rout that left the injured screaming there in their agony for two days and nights.

It was brought to an end on 27 February, after Sandbach had spotted from the north of the river a just possible route into the gorge. Sappers and fatigue parties improved what was the roughest of tracks, and the 100 yard long pontoon bridge was shifted secretly three miles downstream. Three brigades were then passed over it, their task to roll up the Boer positions from north to south, Pieter's Hill on the right flank first, then Railway Hill and finally Hart's Hill. Each attack was supported by the full force of the British guns, firing from the captured hills opposite. Against still tough Boer resistance, the British battalions moved steadily from crest to crest, observed by Buller from his grandstand near the guns. 'Never was an attack better timed,' Atkins accurately judged.[36] It was too much for Botha's men. The next morning British observers in Ladysmith watched a five-mile ribbon of Boer wagons, accompanied by large groups of mounted men, wending its way northwards.

Now was the time for pursuit, but White's infantry were too weak to march and his cavalry's horses had mostly been eaten. On Buller's side a regular cavalry brigade had augmented Dundonald's horsemen, but he was still short of mounted men. Moreover, they were on the wrong side of a flooded river spanned only by a now damaged pontoon bridge; repaired after a fashion, the next morning no more than a single gun or wagon could be passed over it each forty-five minutes. Three teams and 100 men were then needed to drag each one out of the steep ravine. And Buller, from his long experience of fighting with Boers instead of against them, had learned that attempts to force their rearguards merely wasted men. So he decided to use his 'leaky, crazy and worn-out' bridge for supplies for Ladysmith rather than guns to support his cavalry.

His decision was to be reviled by his usual critics, among them Lyttelton.[37] As for Amery, after at least giving him credit for his final breakthrough,[38] he relapsed, a few pages later, into a libel that was breathtaking in its inaccuracy and arrogance:

Buller had not the slightest intention of pursuing. The necessity of getting to Ladysmith somehow at last forced him into the attack at Pieter's. With the success of the attack he immediately relapsed . . . into a settled determination to have as little to do with the enemy as possible.[39]

For Buller, as he told his wife, 'It has all seemed to me like a dream'.[40] Late in the afternoon of 28 February 300 of Dundonald's fit and ragged horsemen had ridden into Ladysmith through an emaciated throng of cheering soldiers and townsfolk. The next day 75 wagon-loads of food and medical stores lumbered into the battered place. Two days later Buller led a ceremonial march-past through the town, watched by that gaunt garrison wilting in the glaring sun. It was a somewhat flat occasion,[41] despite the way Buller's troops broke discipline to cheer White as they passed the saluting base. 'Dirty and ill-clothed, begrimed with dirt and often with beards flowing,' they were a magnificent sight, admired by Rawlinson whose idea the parade had been, one accepted by White despite Buller's reluctance. The saying, Rawlinson wrote, that 'once more the British infantry has saved the reputations of their generals is one that has been eminently true in this case.'[42] But Buller's infantrymen did not see it like that. Careful of their lives and their stomachs, so far as could be, Buller, always to be seen, had inspired them to do what he had told them could be done.

Seventeen weeks of semi-starvation, disease, defeat, boredom and inadequate leadership had destroyed the garrison's morale and, as usually happens, Ladysmith's defenders sought someone to blame for it all. Buller was the obvious target. In Rawlinson's diary further evidence of an ambitious soldier's frustration comes out in such assertations as 'Buller's fancy schemes which do not come off'.[43] Contact with those of Buller's officers who were prepared to malign their commander now fuelled Rawlinson's prejudices. Lyttelton, whom Buller trusted and had promoted to command a division, was, with Repington, another detractor. The latter, whose career was to be marked by a series of breached confidences and indiscretions, one of which was soon to cost him his commission and propel him through the divorce courts into journalism, had probably taken offence at Buller's rejection of his advice before Pieter's Hill. But there may have been others, whom we do not know. Some of his staff officers – unlike his devoted Stopford and ADCs – saw only the brusque exterior of a general who sometimes failed to take them into his confidence. That he lived apart from the main body of his staff may not have helped.[44] 'Buller is universally crabbed by everyone, including his own staff; Lyttelton who lunched here today was full of abuse of Buller,' wrote Rawlinson[45], who with Hamilton, his close friend, would seem to have been the recipients for such indiscretions. However, Rawlinson, a thoroughly decent man, on his way to join Roberts, his old commander, was able to examine the wilderness through which Buller had fought his way. It was, Rawlinson recorded, 'marvellous they got through at all'.[46]

Hamilton's attitude failed to match that of his friends. One of his contacts was the influential Spencer Wilkinson of the *Morning Post*. Another of Roberts's protégés, he was to end his career as the first Chichele Professor of Military History at Oxford; arrogant and conceited, during his years in journalism Wilkinson never travelled to a theatre of war. Before leaving Ladysmith, Hamilton sent him a long letter:

On the day Buller came in I succumbed to a rattling go of Peshawar fever [enteric] which still has me in its clutches. I cannot write much therefore and must concentrate my poor brain on the one essential I want you to know sharp. *Buller is no use*. He is indeed far, *far* worse than useless. You know that ever since the big manoeuvres when Buller funked fighting, I have thought him a duffer. . . . Now, however, it is a question of life or death of our own selves here as well as the empire in general and I write to beg you to use all your influence to get the man recalled before he does more mischief. Supposing anything happened to Roberts he would be in supreme command and the idea is appalling.

A lengthy catalogue of Buller's further alleged ineptitudes followed.[47]

A similar letter to his wife was despatched at the same time, containing much the same accusations and suggesting that she might pass on his opinions to George Wyndham, Lansdowne's junior minister.[48] Later, when convalescing at Groote Schuur, he saw much of both Rhodes and Lady Edward Cecil and wrote a further letter to his wife, in which he told her that he had no objection to St John Brodrick also seeing the previous one.[49] Yet another went to Roberts, containing the additional accusation that 'Buller was very rude to Sir George and spoke to him in the vilest way of you and Kitchener, whom he appears to dislike and to attribute dishonest motives to, almost as much as he does to you.'[50] It was an astounding statement, Buller's alleged behaviour being utterly out of character; in any case, Hamilton was so ill at the time that he was unlikely to have been present at White's welcoming dinner.

Fever can partly explain Hamilton's extraordinary virulence. He may even have intrigued in the way he did because he genuinely saw Buller as a threat to British arms. But his behaviour did tie in with his long-lasting dislike, something his biographer has denied.[51] In that letter home from Groote Schuur, he had observed:

It is lucky I have got away from Buller as I now realise that he hates me even worse than I thought he did. He told Sir George that when he heard of Elandslaagte he said at the War Office, 'I told you so, that fellow Hamilton has forced Sir George's hand and let him in for this fight.' . . . He told Lady Ned Cecil something of the same kind.[52]

Hamilton also blamed Buller for delaying his promotion to major-general and holding up his recommendation for a Victoria Cross.[53] Certainly Buller did have reservations about Hamilton's judgment, especially after Elandslaagte.[54] As for the VC, among the criteria for its award was the presence of witnesses senior to the individual recommended: at both Elandslaagte and on the Platrand there was none.

12

FINAL SUCCESS

Buller's entry into Ladysmith on 28 February was matched just two weeks later by Roberts's triumphal arrival at Bloemfontein, a national capital of a mere 4,000 white inhabitants living in a few blocks of tin-roofed bungalows surrounded by thousands of square miles of undulating, almost empty veldt.

It was another nine weeks before Buller could follow up his success and seven before Roberts could do the same. In Roberts's case the delay was due to the need to bring the single railway line back into operation, accumulate thirty days' supplies for over 40,000 troops and 20,000 horses, and rest and refit his weary units. His horses were worn out: many thousand remounts had to make the laborious journey by way of his single-track line. Moreover, the forced march in searing heat and on half rations, combined with the foul water drunk at Paardeberg and after, was exacting its price. Sick lists lengthened. Typhoid took its hold: thousands were sick and hundreds died. So appalling were conditions in the Bloemfontein hospitals that a Royal Commission was later set up to investigate shortcomings described by a prominent civilian surgeon as similar to those reported by Russell from the Crimea.

No more interested in the details of his medical set-up than he was in his supply system – perhaps because he had never served with the British Army – Roberts's inadequate preparations were matched by his failure to cope with the subsequent disaster. All this was in marked contrast to Buller's arrangements, based as they were upon his understanding of the need to conserve his numbers and his very human concern for the welfare of his soldiers. Ensuring that supplies, ammunition and medical stores came safely up and casualties were moved quickly back often caused delay, but neither in Natal nor later in the Transvaal did Buller lose wagons through his supply-line being ambushed. On the other hand, Roberts's swift thrust, inevitably by-passing many of the enemy, resulted in a number of so-called 'unfortunate incidents' and two major defeats. At Sannah's Post in the eastern Free State on 31 March, a column of 1,800 Boers under Christiaan de Wet captured 117 wagons and 428 prisoners, together with seven guns of the Royal Horse Artillery, the latter a gunner disaster comparable to Colenso, but one for which Roberts largely escaped the calumny earned by Buller; then, only four days later, de Wet's use of his three artillery pieces caused the surrender of a further complete infantry battalion. Roberts had assumed that the capture of their capitals would crush his enemies' will to resist;[1] he was already being proved wrong.

But Buller also needed time to make his preparations. Every railway bridge and culvert north of the Tugela had to be rebuilt, his near bootless troops refitted, White's weak and half-starved garrison fed, and the sick and wounded evacuated. The inevitable delay stemming from all this was aggravated by a failure of understanding between Roberts and himself, two men who barely knew one another and who could exchange ideas only by easily misunderstood coded telegrams or much delayed letters, fifty of which passed between them during that enforced wait.

Either or both of two courses of action were open to Buller. He could advance northwards to clear Natal, using the railway to keep supplies flowing, or he could drive west through the Drakensberg passes into the Orange Free State. Three days after Ladysmith's relief, Buller proposed that he should do both, clearing Natal with three of his brigades and passing a division across the Drakensberg to reinforce Roberts.[2] This brought him a dampening reply, despatched the self-same day:

> I do not think it would be wise now to embark on extensive operations in Natal, which is evidently extremely suitable for the enemy's tactics and very difficult for our troops. To force the passes of the Drakensberg would undoubtedly be a very hazardous operation, and would probably enable the Boers, with a small force, to hold up a very much larger number of men for some considerable time.[3]

Instead, Roberts ordered him to send a division across to him by way of East London.

That same day, however, Buller formed a more accurate picture of the weakness of the attenuated Ladysmith garrison and the size of the problem of evacuating its 3,500 sick and wounded south. Estimating accurately that it would take six weeks to three months to get White's units back into fighting shape, he suggested to Roberts that the 'best defensive measures' he could take would be to reoccupy Dundee and possibly Newcastle as soon as he had got boots for his men . . .[4]. But the arrival of strong Boer reinforcements on both the Biggarsberg and Van Reenen's Pass leading into the eastern Orange Free State, allied to the difficulties Roberts was about to meet, compelled both commanders to rethink what action might be taken.

One consequence of this was that Roberts repeatedly changed his instructions to Buller, until at last, on 2 May, he informed him that he was advancing from Bloemfontein and that his subordinate's role would be to occupy the enemy's attention to the Biggarsberg.[5]

Roberts and his associates both then and later blamed Buller for what Amery described as 'vacillation and nervousness' and Rawlinson, now installed on Roberts's staff, as his seeing 'all sorts of difficulties' and 'sulking'.[6] As against this, even Lyttelton thought that Roberts overrated the difficulties and 'wished Buller to remain more or less quiescent while his own army was making progress northwards'.[7] The Boers thought the same: so inexplicable was Buller's inactivity that they ascribed it to mutual jealousy which resulted in Buller being artificially delayed 'in order to give his rival a chance of first entry into the Transvaal'.[8]

How intensely Buller was frustrated is clear from his successive letters to his wife. In one he complains:

> I am very vexed with Roberts; he has condemned me to inactivity here, when I could have done a great deal to help him. . . . I fear it will delay the end of the war a good bit, which is a horrid nuisance – besides I have no wish to take root in Ladysmith.[9]

Another letter to a close friend admits:

> I know this is wicked, but I have been here for 9 whole weeks, stopped from pursuing a flying enemy and ordered a policy of strict defensive, and why I cannot conceive: and I am tired of waiting every day I see the Boers digging a new trench [sic]. It seems to me a funny way of making war.[10]

Not surprisingly, this forced inactivity increased Buller's tetchiness, so much so that Dundonald, finding his general one day impatient and irritable, had the temerity to caution him, 'You are a changed Buller, you are not the Buller I knew in the Soudan,' an accusation Buller did not deny and attributed to his years of 'indoor life at that cursed War Office'. The manner in which Dundonald relates the tale suggests that Buller refrained from revealing to a subordinate – friend and confidant though he was – the principal cause for his ill-disposition.[11]

Buller's patience had also been stretched by the publication in April of the official despatches on Spion Kop. His own report, not written with a view to publication and forwarded to London under cover of Roberts's, had contained harsh but well-justified criticisms of Warren; it had also admitted that he was wrong not to have relieved him, set out the reasons why he had not done so, and added that he left it to superior authority to judge whether they were sufficient.[12] Because of the widespread press coverage of the battle, however, Lansdowne had felt bound to publish something; the result was that he instructed Roberts to approach Buller with a view to editing his despatch. Buller's reaction was:

> I do not at all like the idea of re-writing a despatch for publication. I much prefer to leave it in the hands of the Commander-in-Chief, and let him select for publication whatever he thinks proper.[13]

This Roberts did, but in his covering despatch he censured Buller on the grounds that 'the failure must also be ascribed to the disinclination of the officer in supreme command to assert his authority, and see what he thought best was done.'[14] He also excised Buller's self-criticism for failing to do just that.

In publishing such carefully edited despatches, Lansdowne consulted neither the Prime Minister nor Wolseley, who had both promised the Queen that they would not be made public. It was, then, hardly surprising that he managed to arouse the indignation of all three.[15] Buller's rage, to which he gave vent time and again in his letters home, was not because Roberts's criticism had been made public, but because his own admission of error had been omitted. It was 'hitting behind [sic] the belt'.[16]

In his correspondence with Lansdowne, Roberts's criticisms of Buller had been unrestrained.[17] His desire to be rid of him matched Lansdowne's, but the latter's was cautious:

> In spite of all, it would be most unwise to recall and supersede him at this moment. I do not know who you would put in his place, nor have we yet been told that his troops have lost confidence in him. With a large section of the army he is very popular, and in the eyes of the public he represents the dogged soldier who in the face of very great difficulties has persevered and succeeded. His supersession would, I believe, be received in many quarters, some of them very exalted, with indignation. Nor again, do I like the idea of washing all our dirty linen in public and before the eyes of a foreigner.

Nevertheless, wrote the Secretary-of-State, the Cabinet would share the responsibility for any action Roberts might take, although they had 'little doubt that you will leave Buller where he is'.[18]

When the waiting at last ended, Buller's problems were incomparably more difficult than those facing Roberts. The latter's advance into the Transvaal was largely unopposed and again mostly over flat and often featureless veldt; Buller was tackling country even more rugged than the hills he had fought across to reach Ladysmith. First there were the Biggarsberg Mountains, a spur of the Drakensberg running due east from that formidable range down to the Buffalo River, an immensely strong position, described as 'standing up like a wall'. Beyond the Biggarsberg lay Laing's Nek and Majuba – names that evoked bitter memories.

After being forced back from Ladysmith, the Boers had quickly reinforced the Biggarsberg with some 16,000 men and thirty guns; although the fighting in the Free State had in mid-April drawn off many of them, 8,000 still remained, all mounted. Two gaps pierced the range, both heavily fortified. One carried the road and railway north to Glencoe and Newcastle, the other that road to Dundee by which Yule had struggled back to Ladysmith in October. Along the Glencoe railway Buller now directed the 5th Division, its new commander Hildyard, his task to repair the line as he advanced; by way of the Dundee road Buller himself took Clery's 2nd Division, together with Dundonald's brigade and some additional horsemen. In Ladysmith he left its original garrison, now formed into the 4th Division under Lyttelton.

Buller's own force, which started out from Ladysmith on 7 May, approached the Biggarsberg in a wide turning movement. Although the Boers could watch the column's progress for most of the way, they were deceived into thinking that the movement was a feint and were surprised by its speed. Relying mainly on his few mounted men and some artillery, by 13 May Buller had penetrated well into the range, and the Boers, their rear suddenly threatened, abandoned their positions along its full length. The next day Dundonald's brigade, closely followed by Buller himself and with the infantry sweating along behind, covered twenty-five miles to reach Dundee, brushing aside the Boer rear-guards as it went. By 16 May Dundonald had reached Glencoe. In a smooth and fast-moving operation Buller had outwitted the Boers and expelled them from a massively strong position.[19] Even Amery had to describe his success as 'highly admirable', while criticizing him for not making full use of his cavalry and omitting to mention that the 1st Brigade, left behind in Ladysmith, was still short of two-thirds of its horses.[20] Buller's letters home betray his uninhibited satisfaction at his success. 'I have surprised and out-manoeuvred the Boers,' he wrote, 'and have got a considerable force out of an enormously strong position, with very small, and indeed infinitesimally small loss.'[21] The total was twenty-five.

Although instructed merely to occupy the enemy's attention, on 17 May Buller pushed on to Newcastle. Two days later his forward troops reached Laing's Nek where they could examine the far more forbidding task now confronting them. Parties of Boers and their conscripted black labourers were further strengthening the defences of that naturally strong position, digging yet more rows of entrenchments and hewing gun positions out of the solid rock. Buller, who had hoped to rush the pass, had to admit to Roberts on 20 May that it was now 'unassailable'.[22] For the time being he could only call a halt so that the railway could be repaired, supplies stocked up and Lyttelton's now rehabilitated division brought forward.

Inevitably the speed of Buller's advance had bypassed several large bodies of Boers; these now began to make a nuisance of themselves on his right, so threatening the railway, upon which his advance depended. A myth was to arise that the Boers lived and fought on a few strips of biltong hung from their saddles and a bandolier or two of ammunition slung around their shoulders, while the British either encumbered themselves with vast wagon-trains loaded with unnecessary supplies or clung to the railways. The Boers' superiority in mounted men did indeed give them the tactical mobility to switch troops rapidly from place to place. But during the first year of the war, for ammunition supply, especially for their artillery, for the evacuation of their wounded, for the carriage of supplies and stores for bodies of troops numbered in tens of thousands, and sometimes for the movement of the troops themselves, the Boers depended as much upon wagons and railway-trucks as did the British. Reinforcements for Laing's Nek had to be brought by rail from the Transvaal; Cronje had been annihilated at Paardeberg because he would not abandon his wagons; a 6,000-strong column of Boers, retreating from the Cape after Roberts reached Bloemfontein, succeeded in bypassing him despite being encumbered by a twenty-four-mile-long wagon-train. Later, when the Boers took wholeheartedly to guerrilla warfare, everything changed, but the British mounted units which chased their raiding columns could by then move almost as lightly as their opponents. However, we are getting too far ahead.

Before Buller rushed the Biggarsberg, Roberts had been urging him to push on fast towards the Transvaal; then, a little later, he was telling him instead to pass a division west across the Drakensberg to seize Vrede, so as to strengthen his own offensive. With his railway still threatened, Buller saw little merit in losing a third of his small force on such an errand. Moreover, there was the problem of finding the wagons to supply the division once it was over the Drakensberg, especially as Roberts failed to clarify whether he or Buller would support it when it reach Vrede, which lay equidistant between the two armies. The discussion continued as before by means of a flow of often delayed telegrams,[23] hardly a satisfactory way for two now antagonistic commanders to communicate, the senior of whom was reluctant to give the other a direct order.[24] On one hand Roberts thought Buller was too slow and cautious, on the other Buller was, with much justification, convinced that Roberts lacked understanding of both the rugged Natal terrain and the problems it posed.

In the meantime, while Buller was concentrating his force and bringing forward the railway, he approached Christiaan Botha, the Boer commander at Laing's Nek and Louis' brother, one among several Boer leaders who were concluding that their struggle was fruitless. Buller's suggestion to Botha was that they should discuss surrender terms so as to halt the needless loss of life, both Boer and British; in so doing, he banked upon his influence among the older Boers, many of whom had fought with him in Zululand. On 2 June the two enemies shook hands at the foot of Laing's Nek with Majuba's threatening slopes towering above them, a meeting arranged and witnessed by Henry Wilson. Warning Botha that Roberts's forces were now behind him, Buller suggested that the Boers should return to their farms, taking their rifles for self-protection, but leaving their guns behind. The outcome was a three-day armistice while Botha referred the offer to his superiors. Buller, however, had taken no counsel with him, either military or political: 'I fear that Buller may get into trouble over this,' Wilson noted in his diary.[25]

As Buller had already concluded, Botha had been largely playing for time so as further to improve his defences. Instructed to carry on the struggle, he did so, but it hardly mattered, as Roberts, when told of the truce, insisted upon unconditional surrender, with the Boers, but not their officers, being permitted to go home but without their indispensable rifles. The reasons for his tough stance are not altogether clear. As long ago as March both he and Milner had offered the Boers generous terms. He had, however, since then been disillusioned by surrendered Boers again taking up arms; furthermore the Rand gold-mines were now in his grasp and the war appeared to be nearing its end.

Buller lost nothing by giving Botha those three extra days: they allowed him to finish concentrating his force. In any case he had no intention of directly assaulting Laing's Nek, as formidable as Colenso, an operation which his concerned officers calculated would cost two to three thousand men.[26] Roberts's warning on 26 May that it was 'quite unnecessary that you should risk any undue loss with your force either in the Laing's Nek or Drakensberg direction'[27] was superfluous. Instead Buller planned to slip a division across the Drakensberg, so bypassing Laing's Nek and cutting Botha's communications.

Botha's Pass, rising 1,500 feet above the plain and guarded by rugged peaks on either side, was Buller's first objective. While one of his divisions distracted the Boers in front of Laing's Nek, on 6 June a brigade from Hildyard's division seized two large outlying hills east of Botha's Pass at small loss, repelling a sharp counter-attack in the process. To its summit were dragged both field and medium guns to support the attack on the pass itself. Two days later it was taken at a small loss in a finely tuned operation, the men clambering up precipitous slopes, closely covered by artillery fire, to seize the Boer entrenchments. For only fifteen casualties the back door to Laing's Nek had been pushed ajar.

That bitter freezing night Buller bivouacked with his soldiers on Botha's Pass without either food or blankets. The next morning a brigade began to follow up the retreating enemy, but for the rest a day's halt was needed while supply wagons and guns were dragged up from below. This done, Buller turned north-west to strike against the railway behind Laing's Nek. Fifteen miles ahead, another and more strongly held position at Alleman's Nek blocked his way. Here the Boers fought back hard from ridge to ridge, but in the end they fled. Again, as at Botha's Pass, the battle-winning factor had been superb co-ordination between Buller's infantry and artillery.[28] The cost was 150 killed and wounded. Eleven miles further on the railway was reached on 12 June, too late, however, to trap the main Boer force on Laing's Nek. Fast as Buller had moved during the previous seven days, Botha's commandos had gone. But Natal had finally been cleared of its invaders.

Even Amery granted that Buller had fought Alleman's Nek with 'skill and vigour'.[29] Lyttelton, however, later damned with condescending praise his advance as 'a well-planned and well-executed little campaign . . . he must have learnt something of strategy and tactics, for he acted with commendable promptitude and judgement in a pretty difficult country'.[30]

As for Buller, he admitted he 'was really rather pleased'. It was not just his neat removal of the Boers from Laing's Nek without serious loss: four hours after learning that they had evacuated their stronghold, he had received a telegram from Roberts telling him that 'the Boers were at least 4500 strong on Laing's Nek with 14 guns and were determined to fight and that I was not to try and turn them out as it was too great a risk of heavy loss – and I had already turned them out. That was rather pleasant.'[31] His previous letter to his wife, written from the top of Botha's Pass, was largely about his soldiers, how they had scrambled up the Berg 'like monkeys' and how 'nice' and how uncomplaining they were after that bitterly cold night at 6,000 feet without blankets or coats. That he had shared their misery, he does not mention.[32] How mistaken Hamilton had been when he wrote in his diary after Colenso:

> I doubt if a man who has been filling his belly with all manner of good things for over ten years in the neighbourhood of Pall Mall can ever quite rise to the rough and tumble of a big command with a formidable enemy.[33]

Buller's victory at Alleman's Nek coincided with a rather indecisive action at Diamond Hill, just north of Pretoria, but one in which Roberts cleared the Boers from his western flank. Reaching Johannesburg on 31 May, after capturing the Rand mines intact, he had entered the Transvaal capital five days later. The war seemed surely over. Kruger, with most of his Government, had fled east down the Delagoa Bay railway – the Boer's last link with the outside world – towards the Portugese frontier. Demoralization was widespread, not just among the rank and file but most of their leaders also. Numbers were drifting back to their farms. Overtures to surrender were being made, even by Louis Botha, now in charge of the Transvaal commandos; but he, like his brother, was merely playing for time.

To the south-east, however, commandos from the Orange Free State (now the Orange River Colony – renamed after its formal annexation) were still active, among them Christiaan de Wet's of 1,000 men. De Wet now struck at the British rear areas, capturing a large convoy and its escort on 3 June; two days later he destroyed a mountainous supply dump accumulated at Roodewall Railway Station, killing, wounding or taking prisoner a complete militia battalion in the process. Already, on 31 May, his brother, Piet, had surrounded and destroyed a battalion of Imperial Yeomanry, one of the new Volunteer units raised on the surge of popular enthusiasm after 'Black Week' and manned by young British farmers, yeomen and suchlike.

Roberts's reaction to Alleman's Nek had been to press Buller to push on to Standerton, fifty miles further up the railway towards Johannesburg; at the same time he was told to hurry through supplies from Natal[34] along this now vital line, the one through Bloemfontein now being unsafe. Buller required no urging, but it was taking double teams of his near worn-out oxen to drag wagons up Laing's Nek, and he was to need five days to clear the blocked railway tunnel. And in addition the railway had to be protected, menaced as it was not just by the few scattered parties of Boers left behind in his advance, but by some 5,000 Orange Free Staters as well, concentrated in the Brandwater Basin, only fifty miles west of Van Reenen's Pass.

Nevertheless, Buller reached Standerton on 23 June. Eleven days later his advanced troops made contact with Roberts's units. After ten months of battle the two forces had met, 1,000 and 500 miles respectively from the Cape and from Durban. All that now remained was to push Botha's men out of the eastern Transvaal into the sea and round up the aggravating guerrillas in the eastern Orange Free State. How this would be done was discussed between Roberts and Buller, when the latter took the now reopened railway to Pretoria on 7 July for their first meeting in South Africa. Recrimination was apparently avoided, and afterwards Buller was to reassure his understandably too partisan wife that 'Roberts has not done badly really, you must not let people think that I think he has, for he really has not'. Asked, in a 'long and interesting' talk with Kitchener, when he thought the war would be over, he had replied, 'Nine weeks from the 1st of July I said. Oh! he said, I hope to do it in less than that. I hope you will I said – I doubt it though – still matters are going fairly well.'[35]

After the meeting Roberts was aggravated to learn that Buller had told his staff that he was looking worn out, an accusation he heatedly denied to Milner.[36] Nor was Buller impressed by the luxury in which Roberts was living or his habit of taking a large cavalry escort out with him when he went for a ride.[37] Still less did he approve of Roberts's wife and daughter joining him in Pretoria; as he had earlier put it in a letter to young Algy Trotter's mother, 'I tell Audrey that wives are not part of a soldier's campaign kit'.[38]

Delay in re-equipping and supplying Roberts's force over such great distances, and in dealing with the Boers in the Brandwater Basin, was now being aggravated by their sabotage of the railways. To counter this Roberts resorted to destroying nearby Boer homesteads, a measure previously taken only when surrendered Boers were found to have helped their fellow countrymen. The consequence was that Boer families were being turned out on to the veldt to fend for themselves. Although locally raised troops who had seen their compatriots suffer in a similar way from the Boers were happy to comply with such orders, many British soldiers were revolted by the practice and some, among them Dundonald, realized how counter-productive it could be. Not surprisingly, Buller much objected to it, as he did to looters. The latter, if caught, could expect severe punishment.[39]

At the end of July the surrender of 4,000 Boers in the Brandwater Basin so lessened the threat to his communications that Roberts was ready to move against Botha. The latter, from a position on the Delagoa Bay railway west of Machadodorp where Kruger and his government had taken refuge, was facing the British at Middelburg, further to the west. Seized by French's cavalry on 25 July, Middelburg had since been developed as a supply base, and, to assist in the destruction of Botha's force, Roberts ordered Buller to move there with an infantry division and two brigades of horsemen. It was a hundred-mile march directly across the high veldt by way of Carolina. Buller chose Lyttelton's division for the task – its men now again fit and well – on the grounds that it was only fair to give them their chance.[40] His other two divisions were still fully occupied in protecting that other railway, the lifeline to Durban.

First Buller had to concentrate his widely scattered units which had been kept busy keeping marauding groups of Boers at arm's length and mounting forays to trap them; in May's words, 'every day almost we had an action of some sort'.[41] His preparations complete, Buller started on 7 August with 12,000 men, over 3,000 horses and twenty-six guns. Without the railway, 755 wagons were needed for his fourteen days of supplies, and his speed was limited to that of the oxen.

Throughout the march a fluctuating number of Boers, at first about 2,000, dogged the column, making a nuisance of themselves whenever possible, but a week after starting Buller reached Carolina and made contact with French. There Buller was near enough to Middelburg to replenish his wagons and near enough also to strike against Machadodorp. However, Roberts, who had previously been at such pains to hurry him on from Laing's Nek, now halted him for a week. To his wife he complained:

> I have twelve thousand men here, and I doubt his [Botha] having five thousand, and certainly half of those do not want to fight. It is an unfortunate delay, at an unfortunate moment, but the end of the war must come soon; we are now practically holding the high veldt, and all the Boer cattle are down in the low veldt, they will die if kept there beyond the middle of September.[42]

For once, however, Buller was perhaps being over-bold. Boer numbers had been underestimated and their morale for a time had improved. They were also occupying a heavily fortified and naturally strong position astride the railway; rugged hills and ravines protected their right flank, marshy streams and bogs their left. Although outnumbered by more than two to one, they were all mounted.

When, on 21 August, Roberts eventually allowed Buller to move, he twice cleared the Boers from strong delaying positions, actions which resulted in the award of three VCs. Following this a meeting – only his second – with Roberts on 25 August at Belfast resulted in the 11th Division under Lieutenant-General R. Pole-Carew (another member of the 'Indian Ring') being ordered to hold the Boers' attention around Belfast, while Buller swung around their position from the south. At the same time French was switched to protect the northern flank.

During 26 August Buller continued to fight forward towards the railway, his infantry skirmishing in extended order and harassed by Boer patrols and a 6-in gun firing from five miles away. That night they bivouacked close enough to the Boer main positions to give Buller a sight of them. Bergendal Farm, on a fortified kopje, so protruded from the centre of the Boer line as to deny it effective artillery or small-arms support from either flanks or rear. This, Buller decided, was the key to the enemy defences. The next morning, after forty guns had bombarded the kopje for three long hours, the infantry were unleashed against it. The surviving defenders, a body of gallant Zarps – the Transvaal regular policemen – stood firm until the end. At a cost of 120 killed and wounded Buller had smashed the apex of the Boer line. Mounting their horses, the rest of the burghers then fell back, too fast for the immediate pursuit Buller launched. That night they also abandoned their more northern positions and withdrew east of Machadodorp, reached by Buller later that day.

Sound coordination between Buller's infantry and artillery was the mark of this further success, just as it had been at Alleman's Nek: the gunners had now learned how to delay lifting their fire until the infantry were almost on their objective. This and their commander's appreciation of Bergendal as the key to the Boer position had produced victory in what was virtually the final major battle of the war. Dundonald, an enthusiastic but not uncritical admirer of Buller, whose battle-hardened mounted units had hardly missed a fight since Colenso, thought his commander 'in many ways a great man' but at times lacking in sufficient driving power. One of his several gifts, Dundonald emphasized, was his understanding of terrain[43] – of military geography – , that 'eye for country', so essential not just for junior officers but their seniors as well.

It is hard to gainsay Dundonald's judgement. Robustness, courage both physical and mental, together with common sense were what the shrewd Field-Marshal Lord Wavell sought in a general, the 'common sense' being an understanding of what is or is not practicable – a sound knowledge of the mechanism of war, its topography, movement and supply.[44] Add inspiration to these, and they covered Buller's qualities; lacking was the ruthlessness needed to accept heavy casualties.

Amery denigrated Buller's success, his criticisms as always repeated by others.[45] Buller's personal delight was uninhibited:

> I am as happy as a pig. We had a very pretty little fight, with the Field-Marshal and the whole Guards Brigade looking on. Certainly it went off very well and exactly as I could have wished. . . . Tomorrow I am off to Lydenberg having just missed catching Kruger. I hope to catch him next time. The end cannot be far off now I believe, but between you and me I do wish the Field-Marshal would move a bit quicker. He lets so many chances slip . . . it was not the least pleasure that I defeated the army and opened the road to Machadodorp, while Lord Roberts' army, which had got there before me, had missed the chance and had to sit looking on. What a beast I am! but I don't mean that, but the men liked it.[46]

Here again runs that same theme: Buller's firm belief, reiterated in his correspondence with Wolseley and his wife, that Roberts continually held him up.[47]

Roberts, with much success, switched the blame for the delays to Buller. Maurice, when compiling his Official History, cleared much of the material with Roberts among others, but not, so far as can be ascertained, with Buller. As will happen, Maurice's volumes were harshly censored: for fear of impeding reconciliation with the Boers, the Colonial Office cut the political chapters; inevitably the War Office ensured that those remaining were less than frank about the many military disasters.[48] Early drafts had been in no way anodyne, as is revealed by Roberts's angry reaction to what was to have been a critical chapter on the advance to Komati Poort; among Maurice's many strictures was that Roberts waited for seven months before he 'could venture to call for [Buller's] co-operation'.[49] All comments of this type were cut, so leaving unchallenged Roberts's disparagement of Buller. Such emasculation was to help ensure that Amery's work became the main source for the war's history, grossly ill-balanced though it was.

To return to the campaign. Buller's move to Lydenburg was part of a three-pronged advance ordered by Roberts when the Boers broke up into separate columns after Bergendal. One fled south-east towards Barberton, pursued by French's cavalry, one eastwards down the railway along which Pole-Carew continued to move and the third north in the direction Buller was to take.

As a crow might fly, Lydenburg lay some forty miles from the main railway. But for Buller and his men it was quite a different journey, one that passed over a region even more rugged than the Drakensberg, one pictured by Hamilton, who was about to join Buller, as 'more Himalayan than Alpine . . . extraordinary precipices, crags and ravines amongst & over which we have to manoeuvre armies – supply trains – big guns, etc, etc . . . enough to make anyone's hair grey with anxiety.'[50]

On only the second day out it had been brought home to Buller that he was to have no easy passage: from a horseshoe-shaped hill rapid and concentrated artillery fire – both 6-in and field – barred his advance. With his infantry now reduced to no more than half a dozen battalions – Roberts's complete force now numbered only 18,000 men – a frontal attack was out of the question.

Help was needed and, at Buller's suggestion, Roberts had provided this in the shape of a recently arrived 3,000-strong infantry column under Hamilton. Now temporarily a lieutenant-general, Hamilton had set the seal on his burgeoning reputation when in charge of a division of mounted infantry that protected Roberts's flank during the move to Pretoria; however, a gross failure to trap Christiaan de Wet, who in early August had slipped across into the Transvaal, had raised doubts among many about his ability. But he now handled his units ably and, with help from Buller's guns and infantry, he out-manoeuvred the Boers by way of a converging route towards their rear, compelling them to withdraw beyond Lydenburg.

However, the Boers now entrenched themselves in yet another immensely strong position, the 1,800-foot Paardeplaats mountain, its flanks so sheer as to be almost impassable even for infantry. But at the cost of only thirty-one men, on 8 September Hamilton's and Lyttelton's divisions carried it. And then, for a further two months, Buller's troops were to clamber around the precipices and ravines of the tangled mountains to the north, attempting to block possible escape routes, harassing and sometimes rounding up scattered parties of Boers.

When recounting the story of Paardeplaatz to his wife, Hamilton admitted:

> Buller was most generous in his expressions of thanks and had me to dine and all sorts of things. Really, if I had not *known* he was my deadly enemy I should have thought he was my very good friend. However, he certainly *was* generous in his acknowledgements and I am glad to say that I can no longer feel that strong dislike of him amounting to hatred which I had hitherto. . . . I am now in a more Christian state of mind regarding the great man . . . he handled his troops very well indeed.[51]

Even Lyttelton, who rarely had a good word for anyone, warmed slightly towards Buller at this juncture, observing to his wife that his commander 'had learned much and we have every confidence in him'. He had also come to appreciate that Buller's cautious step by step advances avoided the continual and expensive setbacks Roberts had undergone, and the unnecessary hardships which took toll of his troops when he pushed on too fast.[52]

French's operations towards Barberton had matched Buller's. Organized resistance seemed to be over. On 11 September Kruger had taken refuge in Portuguese East Africa en route to exile and death in Switzerland four years later. Across the border also went 3,000 Boers and foreign volunteers; a multitude of others had either surrendered or made off for their farms. When Pole-Carew's division, advancing steadily down the railway, entered Komati Poort on 24 September, they found nothing but vast and chaotic store-dumps and smashed rolling-stock and sidings.

But Botha, and others, including Jan Smuts, Kruger's brilliant young Attorney-General, had led the irreconcilable and stout-hearted off by little-known tracks. Well-mounted and unencumbered by artillery and large wagon-trains, some rode north to continue the struggle through what is now the Kruger National Park, some south along the Swazi border.

Like several officers on the spot, Buller had rightly feared that the guerrilla war, already being waged so successfully by de Wet, would drag on.[53] Roberts, on the other hand, while admitting to Milner that a troublesome guerrilla war had only just begun, informed the home government that the conflict was practically over and announced that some of his troops could be spared.[54] But Buller had had enough of the war.[55] His Natal Field Force had disappeared, and he was dissatisfied with what he saw as Roberts's poor generalship, just one facet of which was the delay he had been subjected to ever since Ladysmith. Tough though he was, almost a year's uninterrupted mental and physical strain in the harshest of conditions must have brought him to near exhaustion, although no record of his admitting so has surfaced. And, as ever, he yearned for Downes and his family.

So it was that a week after Paardeplaatz he asked Roberts to relieve him. As Rawlinson put it:

> Buller wired to say that he did not think he was doing any good by being at Spitz Kop and that he thought it was high time he went home. On this we persuaded the Chief to wire to Lansdowne that the war now having degenerated into a guerrilla warfare it seemed hardly necessary to keep a Field-Marshal in the field and that if the home government agreed he was prepared to hand over to Buller and return to England forthwith.[56]

Lansdowne's reply to Roberts that the Government lacked sufficient confidence in Buller ensured the latter's departure. On 24 October he sailed for England.

Commanding officers often order their troops to cheer generals during farewell visits, flattery that can leave a recipient with a false sense of his popularity. With Buller such orders were unnecessary. His round of visits to units whose hardships, successes and failures he had shared during the previous ten months was marked everywhere by spontaneous tributes to the affection he had inspired. For the first time during the campaign his usually impassive face was said to show signs of emotion.[57] A banquet and sword of honour awaited him in Durban; in Cape Town audiences went frantic when his figure appeared on the new cinematograph screens.[58]

Similar scenes of wild enthusiasm met him when he landed at Southampton in early November. A few days later an ailing monarch, whose long reign was nearing its end, received her old friend at Windsor Castle. After this, their last meeting, she recorded in her diary that 'When I urged that there should be no recriminations, Sir Redvers said there would be none from him'.[59] 'The dear old woman', as he had described her to his wife[60], had been regularly exchanging letters with him throughout his time in South Africa,[61] his last containing the uninhibited avowal, 'Yesterday was a joyful day for Sir Redvers as he received orders from Lord Roberts to go to Natal, close up the papers of the Natal Field Force and return to England'.[62] Her keen interest in the minutiae of the war, both military and political, comes out in the detail contained both in Buller's letters and her own diary. Although her regard for him is clear, she was by no means uncritical of his actions, giving due weight to the reports she received of him from Salisbury, Lansdowne and Roberts himself.[63]

Roberts's return was delayed by his daughter's illness, but when he returned he received an earldom, a grant of £100,000 and Wolseley's place as Commander-in-Chief. For Buller there was nothing except the reversion of his appointment at Aldershot, a cantonment now devoid of anything but semi-trained recruits.

The war's second phase – eighteen months of guerrilla warfare that lasted until May, 1902 – was to be handled by Kitchener. Two weapons in the end drove the Boers to accept the not ungenerous British surrender terms. Starvation was the first, brought about by the destruction of the farms from which they drew their food. The second was the 8,000 blockhouses, connected by barbed-wire entanglements and each manned by eleven incredibly bored soldiers, with which Kitchener bisected the veldt, so hampering the enemy's mobility. And the skills of the British mounted infantry and irregulars by then almost matched those of the Boers they pursued.

Over 400,000 British soldiers, including volunteer units from every white dominion or colony, were to take part; a quarter of them became casualties, with more killed by enteric than by the enemy. Probably one in twelve of the 87,000 Boers and foreign volunteers who took the field died; with them an unknown number – possibly as high as 28,000 – of men, women and children perished of disease in the inefficiently administered and unfortunately named 'concentration camps' where they were sheltered after their farms were destroyed. No worthwhile estimate exists of the thousands of black Africans who died, some of them in the pay of the Boers, others of the British.

Despite the bitterness aroused by the concentration camps, the memory of which prevails today, Boer and Briton were to live together reasonably at ease in the self-governing Union of South Africa, set up in 1909, but with a franchise restricted to the white races. The Union's first two premiers were Botha and Smuts; both were to command British armies during the First World War and Smuts attain the rank of field-marshal and prominence as a respected world statesman. In both that war and the next, South African contingents, volunteers from all races, fought ruggedly and well, first against the Kaiser's Germany and then against Hitler's.

13

RECRIMINATION

The triumphal welcome received by Buller on his return to Aldershot matched in enthusiasm his farewell to South Africa. The visit of the Kaiser seven years before had – as the local paper put it – stirred 'even the apathy of an Aldershot crowd', innured as it was to military spectacles. The scenes on Buller's return were far to surpass anything that military town experienced before or since. A series of excursion trains had brought in thousands of Londoners to join in the public rejoicing. His own beflagged train drew into the bunting-clad station to the sound of the Wesleyan school-children singing 'Home Sweet Home'. Dignitaries watched his arrival from specially erected grandstands, and wounded soldiers from wagonettes. Brass-helmeted members of the Aldershot Fire Brigade replaced his carriage-horses to draw him, alongside his beaming wife and daughter, through streets lined by red-coated troops and densely packed, cheering throngs; throughout the route, evergreen and flag-draped masts, surmounted by gilded crowns, supported triumphant banners proclaiming 'He obeyed the Empire's Call', 'The Nation Thanks You' and similar exhortations. For many years 10 November, 1900, would be remembered in Aldershot as 'Buller Day'.[1]

That was the formal welcome. It matched the spontaneous tributes paid to him by countless individuals. Congratulatory letters flooded Downes; many were from humble people, often in doggerel verse, not unusual at the time, perhaps a tribute to Victorian elementary education. Patriotic songs were dedicated to him. Others, such as 'Bravo Buller, Hurrah! for Buller', recalled his exploits. Numerous testimonials and expensively produced illuminated addresses arrived from bodies as diverse as working men of Liverpool and of the Rhondda Valley to one from the upper crust of Melbourne inscribed on vellum and bearing a thousand signatures. From the kilns of the Potteries came a variety of celebratory but hardly flattering memorial plates. Despite the current Anglophobia across the Channel, postcards of Buller were on sale in the Paris streets. Buttons depicting his likeness – some forty varieties have survived – were worn everywhere, some by adult members of so-called 'Buller button-clubs'. Numerous baby boys were named after him, especially in Devon; very old men alive today answer to 'Redvers'. Pop and football stars have supplanted military heroes as popular idols, but the latter were longer-lasting. At least one such 'button-club' was still active after his death.[2]

In the middle of a war, Aldershot was an undemanding command, the duties limited to coping with the thousands of newly enlisted volunteers passing through its barracks. Reunited with his family and with Downes, and basking in the adulation of his fellow-countrymen – unsought but nonetheless satisfying – Buller was happy recuperating from a year's intense pressures. Nor at first was he given reason to doubt that the Government thought as well of his work in South Africa as did his soldiers. Wolseley had even hinted to him that he was likely to succeed him as Commander-in-Chief, but that was before Roberts's appointment had been made public; his private letters both to Buller himself and to Lady Audrey make clear beyond doubt his deep affection for and confidence in his old subordinate. Hamilton thought so too – if the Liberals won the coming election.[3] But nowhere in Buller's papers is there any indication that Roberts's eventual selection for the post irked him, or, in fact, that he had taken Wolseley's suggestion seriously. Meanwhile, letters from old friends in South Africa brought him news of the war; especially percipient were those from 'Bimbashi' Stewart, an officer who strongly deprecated and foresaw the long-term consequences of Kitchener's 'clearing the country of supplies and taking away the women'.[4]

But it was not long before Buller realized that all was not well. Pin-pricks from above proliferated so that he was soon admitting to his wife that he was 'very busy here writing letters abusing the War Office'.[5] His trenchant comments to the Under-Secretary of State that clumsy financial control and lack of system had produced an officer corps poor in initiative and independence of spirit – that old hobby-horse – would have done little to further his popularity.[6] And the War Office regime had changed. Roberts sat in Wolseley's chair. A 'Khaki' general election, neatly timed by the Government to coincide with the apparent end of the war, had returned Lord Salisbury to power with an increased majority and brought St John Brodrick to the War Office instead of Lansdowne. That this new Secretary-of-State's dislike of Buller matched his predecessor's is evident from his virulent letter to the gossipy Lady Edward Cecil, the future Lady Milner, two weeks after Colenso in which he slandered every aspect of Buller's work, ranging from his strategy to his use of his transport and heavy artillery.[7]

Brodrick was an unfortunate choice for the post, from which Balfour, who had then succeeded Salisbury as Prime Minister, removed him two years later. Campbell-Bannerman, in comparing Brodrick with Lansdowne, thought Lansdowne 'weak and pleasant, but exceedingly secretive and anxious to get the credit for everything: but B[rodrick] with the same faults is brusque, underhand and crooked: which L. is not'. The two matched one another in vanity and jealousy, so the future Liberal Prime Minister believed. Prejudiced Campbell-Bannerman was, but his vignette cannot have been wholly inaccurate.[8]

Since Buller's return, the campaign waged against him by sections of the press, and especially *The Times*, had not eased. The serious accusation that he had categorically instructed White to surrender remained undenied by the Government who refused to publish the original telegrams. An oblique reference to this continuing criticism was made by Campbell-Bannerman, still Leader of the Opposition, who remarked to his old friend that 'To my mind the most remarkable fact is that those who do best are those who are least advertised or puffed up'. This led Buller to ask 'C-B's advice on making a personal statement to refute his critics. Contemptuous though he usually was about press attacks, at last they were drawing blood. But the politician urged him instead to 'lie-low' and so occupy 'the higher ground', counsel that for the time Buller accepted.[9]

But the crunch came in September, 1901. The humiliation already suffered by the nation and its army was being compounded by Kitchener's inability to finish off the Boer resistance. Army reform was a live issue, and one of several planned by Brodrick was the organization of the home regular army into an expeditionary force of three army corps, these to be commanded and trained by the generals who would lead them in battle. But his announcement of the change was maladroit indeed, given that the three chosen commanders were Evelyn Wood, the Duke of Connaught and Buller. The first by then was almost stone deaf and the second, as a Royal Prince, was denied the privilege of exposing himself to the perils of active service. As for Buller, in charge of the First Army Corps at Aldershot, not only was he clearly too old, but his reputation had been steadily eroded.

In this much needed movement towards reform, it was hardly surprising that little credit was given to what had been accomplished during the war: the fresh tactics and organizations rapidly developed to cope with the problems posed by modern artillery, effective musketry, smokeless fuel and a mobile enemy; the success of the War Office in shipping some 400,000 men, a force three times larger than planned, 6,000 miles and then maintaining them in a wild and largely inhospitable country. But, as always when failures occur, military or otherwise, a scapegoat was needed, and with much justification it was sought among the generals. As Brodrick put it, 'really our Generals and not W.O. are to blame in this war',[10] ignoring the fact that the generals were the product of the outdated and cash-starved system.

Leo Amery's return to England was opportune. A passionate advocate of reform, he had concluded that Colenso and its sequels had revealed 'on the part of Sir Redvers Buller, what none of our other generals had shown, a sheer lack of determination and even a disastrous loss of morale'.[11] Here was the scapegoat the Government needed, chosen by the press and ripe for sacrifice to the public opinion. So it was that there appeared in *The Times* of 28 September an anonymous letter signed by *Reformer*, Amery's pseudonym, reproaching Buller for:

> The utter fatuity of Colenso, the unnecessary abandonment of the guns, the message to Sir G. White suggesting the surrender of Ladysmith, the want of decision at Spion Kop, the half-hearted attempt at Vaal Krantz, the costly blundering back into the Colenso death-trap after the capture of Monte Cristo might have shown the way to the blindest, the inexcusable failure to pursue a demoralised enemy – is this the record for which the Government and Lord Roberts, who know all, have chosen the Commander on whom the first shock of the next war may fall?[12]

Other organs, particularly *The Spectator*, cast similar aspersions without quite matching *The Times's* virulence.

In the end Buller's patience snapped. On 10 October he was due to speak at a luncheon given by the Queen's Westminster Volunteers. His intention had been to do no more than say something in defence of an outstandingly gallant officer, whom, he judged, had been unjustly faulted by the press; the war, as he saw it, was dragging on because officers avoided running risks for fear that any error would invoke public obloquy.[13] Alarmed that Amery, whom he saw among the assembled journalists, and others might assume he was protesting indirectly about his own treatment because he dare not tackle them openly, Buller launched into an impromptu defence of his own actions. The attacks had also, as he admitted to a friend two days before, made him 'combative and quarrelsome', and he was concerned that others might suffer from leaping to his defence.[14] His unrehearsed outburst, recorded by Amery,[15] revealed publicly for the first time the circumstances in which that fatal telegram to White had been compiled and its wording. Moreover, he set out the reasoning behind its despatch: if White were forced to surrender, he, Buller, would take his proper share of the responsibility and blame.

The speech was undoubtedly intemperate and mistaken, as Buller was afterwards to admit. Because it was unprepared and delivered under stress – the sight of Amery in the audience could only have aggravated his rage – it was also ill-delivered. His enemies said afterwards that he had drunk too much, but the family friends with whom he had been staying overnight in Berkeley Square vehemently denied the accusation, as did his step-son, who was with him and further confirmed that he 'well knew what he was saying'.[16] The speech also gave Amery the opportunity to make yet another and even more bitter attack upon him, one that the writer himself was to admit in later life might 'seem an unduly passionate, and even vindictive onslaught'.[17]

Disastrous were the consequences for Buller, as both Roberts and Brodrick ensured. It was the opportunity both sought. Immediately the Secretary of State wrote to Roberts, telling him that he would submit Buller's removal from his command to the King forthwith.[18] The letter crossed with one from its recipient:

> Buller's speech yesterday is really an extraordinary help to us, and I am strongly of the opinion that we should take advantage of his indiscretion and remove him from his command. . . and I am under the impression that the King would approve of our taking the action I now suggest. Buller has brought this on himself.[19]

By then Roberts had anticipated events by giving Kitchener advance warning that he would probably hear of Buller's relegation to half-pay before his letter reached him.[20]

A follow-up from Brodrick to Roberts confirmed:

> I am very glad we are at one over the Buller question. . . . . I think, as you say, this faux pas on Buller's part may relieve me of a great difficulty. But he will fight to the death.[21]

The day after the speech Roberts had, through his Adjutant-General, Lieutenant-General Kelly-Kenny, conveyed to Buller his 'displeasure' at the speech, not just the reference to the Ladysmith telegrams, which he ordered Buller to refrain from publishing, but to other issues, including some comments he had made about conscription. Twenty-four hours later the printing of Amery's article, with its report of the speech, evoked from the War Office a brusque demand in an open telegram for an explanation. With this Buller complied, defending his conduct in terms polite yet firm.[22]

A personal letter to Brodrick was couched very differently, so outspoken and intemperate as to suggest that Buller mistakenly assumed that he was writing to someone well disposed towards him, someone he could trust, if not to a close personal friend. He had, he complained, been 'goaded past endurance' by the 'constant stream of misrepresentation and falsehood' he had borne. As far back as 10 January, an unnamed War Office official had refused to publish the accurate versions of the telegrams, so denying him the protection due to him. A 'gang', was, 'I think basely and I know falsely, attacking me'. He had never asked to be given command of the First Army Corps which 'came to me unsought, and I may truly say undesired. It was offered to me by the War Office. I am attacked: and what do the War Office do? Defend me? No. They damn me with faint praise and publish an official communique! "Oh! we are getting rid of him, and have only put him in to finish his two years and then die decently." Was this fair? I call it hitting below the belt, and do not believe that you had anything to do with it.'[23]

At the interview Buller requested and which took place on 17 October Brodrick demanded Buller's immediate resignation, adding that he had taken advice from Balfour and Salisbury.[24] This met with Buller's flat refusal. The only other person present was Roberts, who joined the others after the first half hour. There followed a protracted correspondence which ended on 22 October with his dismissal from Aldershot and relegation to half-pay.

It was the opportunity both Roberts and Brodrick had sought, a 'coup' (the word is Roberts's[25]) against the object of their dislike. Despite Buller's full explanation and expressions of regret, Roberts still put it to Lord Esher that 'after calling on Buller to explain and the latter's refusal to do so either he or Buller must go'.[26] In disposing of him, Roberts also ignored the advice of Kelly-Kenny – a well-balanced officer, recently in command of a division in South Africa – who minuted him the day before the interview recommending strongly that Buller should be no more than censured and cautioned. The culprit, he argued, was not alone in being indiscreet, and his previous service had been noteworthy; the press had criticized his appointment to Aldershot and should not now be given the opportunity of saying 'that the War Office had again to look for a lead and instruction to the Public'. To remove him would 'do more harm than good, not only in the Army, but in the eyes of the Public'.[27]

Buller asked for a court-martial, but this Brodrick refused, as was his appeal to the King. It was a bitter end to a long and distinguished career, one with which Buller never came to terms. In this he was encouraged by the strength of the support given him. As even *The Times* admitted, three days after he had been sacked he had already received many hundreds of letters from all classes of society expressing their sympathy and unshaken confidence. Prominent among his supporters was Sir Edward Grey, Liberal Imperialist and later Viscount Grey of Fallodon, the Foreign Secretary who, on 3 August, 1914, was to utter that unforgettable phrase, 'The lamps are going out all over Europe; we shall not see them lit again in our lifetime'. One of the first to tender his sympathy to Buller, the following July Grey initiated a debate in the House of Commons in which he avowed that the speech discussed no question of policy, and that it reflected neither upon the Government nor upon any officer in the Army. Although Sir Redvers Buller had in that speech defended himself, Grey pleaded, he withheld everything that could have in any way have touched the conduct of any other man.[28] But it was all to no effect.

The Royal Commission on the South African War, also known as the Elgin Commission, after its chairman, Lord Elgin, lately Viceroy of India, provided another forum from which Buller would defend himself, not for his speech, which he admitted both publicly and privately had been ill-judged, but for his conduct of the war. For successive weeks the Commission cross-examined every major figure, military or political, not just upon what had gone wrong but on their proposals for removing the flaws from the system. It could well be said that the Boer War was the salvation of the British Army. Its humiliation was taken to heart, not just by the soldiers themselves but by politicians and taxpayers as well. Already much had been done on the battlefield to overhaul the Army's outdated tactics, but lessons learned in war are too often forgotten later. This was not allowed to happen during the subsequent decade prior to the First World War. Taken to heart were both Elgin's findings and those of the subsequent Esher Committee which created a General Staff and an Army Council, so abolishing the post of Commander-in-Chief and setting out clear lines for the reorganization of the War Office. Upon this groundwork Lord Haldane, Secretary-of-State for War to the Liberal administration of 1906, together with his advisers – men who had learned their trade upon the veldt – set about creating an Army with a sense of purpose, one that could field the British Expeditionary Force of 1914, a body in nearly every way superior in training and tactics to both its European enemies and its allies. Only in its size, its lack of plans for rapid expansion and in some of its equipment was the Army of 1914 found seriously lacking – an unfashionable view today perhaps, but one hard to gainsay.

To advise Buller on his submission, the Hon John Fortescue, the foremost military historian of his day and author, among other splendid works, of the eleven-volume *History of the British Army*, gave his services.[29] A fellow-Devonian, who had known him since boyhood, Fortescue had already sprung to Buller's defence in a lengthy and closely-argued article in *The Nineteenth Century* to which he gave the title 'A Chapter on Scapegoats'. In this he was at pains to stress that he defended Buller of his own volition. Later Fortescue was to publish a pamphlet setting out why 'The evidence produced before the War Commission appears to demand a reconsideration' of Buller's case.[30] Another of Buller's many advocates, 'An Average Observer' (thought to have been Miss Flora Shaw) had, when the war ended, brought out a second edition of her 123-page book, *The Burden of Proof: England's Debt to Sir Redvers Buller*[31] in which she analysed Buller's case in depth.

The spate of words continued. Buller's evidence before the Commission, running to some 80,000, was published as a separate book.[32] It was, as Lord Esher reported to King Edward, given 'temperately, and with that officer's well-known acumen and knowledge of war'.[33] Esher was a singular figure. Rejecting power in favour of back-stairs influence, over the years he declined a succession of high public offices, from Viceroy of India downwards. As the *Dictionary of National Biography* had it, 'Inheriting marked ability, great social gifts and influential connexions, Esher possessed all the gifts for success in public life except the conviction that it was worthwhile'. A close friend of both Queen Victoria and King Edward, in percipient and often scurrilous letters he was to act as the latter's confidential informant.

At the time Esher was no friend of Buller. In describing the meeting of the Cabinet Committee at which his resignation had been discussed, Esher had pictured Roberts as being a 'courageous, honourable and straightforward gentleman. I don't think Buller is any of these things'.[34] It was a calumny seized upon by subsequent detractors. Not present at the meeting, Esher was probably repeating either Lansdowne or Brodrick's words. Nevertheless, after many hours spent in Buller's cross-examination, Esher was to warm towards him. Although criticisms of Buller abounded in his letters to King Edward, in one Esher concluded that on the whole:

he did not cut a poor figure, but appeared what he is, a brave and capable soldier, admirably adapted to hold a high secondary command, but unfitted, by his temperament, to be placed in supreme command of an Army in the field. He gave excellent evidence upon military questions generally, and upon War Office questions. Lord Esher finally was enabled to understand why Sir Redvers had won the affection of officers who served under him, and of the rank and file.

In spite of his great failings, he is a very human figure. Unpleasing in appearance, with no command of temper, he is nevertheless a man of strong sympathies and generous impulses. . . .

After the somewhat disagreeable passages of arms with Lord Esher, he came up to him in a friendly manner, and upon Lord Esher asking him *why* he had (assuming the explanation of his telegrams to be the true one) put himself in a position to be hopelessly misunderstood, and never again trusted by his countrymen, he said, 'It is my beastly temper. All my life long I have suffered from this. Since old Eton days I have had a formula for myself. "Remember Dunmore". It happened in this way. At a football match, the ball came to me, and I had it in my power to "run down" and secure a goal; but I stopped to have a "shinning match" with Dunmore, and lost my chance. Although always present in my mind, I have always failed to remember Dunmore.'

Your Majesty's remarkable appreciation, and kindness of heart, will readily understand how disarming so candid a confession necessarily must be upon the mind of a critic; and how completely an apology, offered with a certain rough humour, must often have won back the regard of men upon whom General Buller has trampled. . . .

It is the misfortune of the State and of Your Majesty's Army that his services, under conditions when he might still be useful, are, it is to be feared, irretrievably lost.[35]

Whether Buller so 'trampled' upon men is unproven. Certainly soldiers, officials and politicians could suffer the rough edge of his tongue – quite another matter – but such outbreaks were short-lived and rarely aroused rancour.

With journalists and politicians it could be different. Of the former there were some who, after suffering from his prejudice against their calling and his reluctance to grant them the help they sought, took lasting offence. Some took their revenge, among them Amery and Spencer Wilkinson.

But war correspondents were but one of several separate threads which, spun into a complex web, helped to bring about Buller's downfall. Interwoven with hostile pressmen were offended politicians and the anachronistic absurdity of the rivalry between the two 'Rings' – Roberts's and Wolseley's.

There is no doubt that the individual who did the most severe and lasting damage to Buller's reputation was Leo Amery, whose detailed and readable, but essentially and admittedly propagandist *Times History* was to be the primary source of information for three generations of biographers and historians. To give just two examples. Mr David James, the foreword to whose excellent *Lord Roberts* was written by Amery; to him James pays tribute for his help with the book. Amery, who later became a close associate and friend of Roberts, helped also to write the Field-Marshal's memoranda, speeches, and the larger part of his pamphlet on conscription,[36] much as Spencer Wilkinson had helped Roberts with his autobiography. Likewise, Mr Julian Symons in his preface to *Buller's Campaigns* – in many respects a fine book – went so far as to conclude that 'Amery's general assessments of military actions seem to need little amendment'.[37]

The ill-feeling and rivalry between Roberts and Wolseley have been voluminously documented, as have the careers of the able individuals selected for their respective 'Rings'. Not, however, until 1899 did the members of the two serve alongside one another, and their quarrels thus affected the conduct of both the war and its history. The reputation of White, a recent Commander-in-Chief in India, needed protection – and at Buller's expense, whose main critics were Hamilton and Rawlinson, both protégés of Roberts, and both sources for Amery. And another of the latter's close collaborators was À Court Repington, the one member of Buller's own team, other than Lyttelton, known to have been actively disloyal. But while Hamilton admitted to hating Buller, there is no evidence that Buller disliked him. He did criticize him, but he was not alone in this. Nothing, in fact, has come to light to suggest that Buller was a party to the inter-Ring rivalries. Nor had he need to be. The 'Indians' in no way threatened Wolseley's officers, whose influence was Empire-wide and stemmed from their proximity to the London-based sources of power, both military and civilian. Buller's position, prior to 1899, was unassailable.

As for the ill-will that in the end developed between Roberts and Buller, this had its roots in Roberts's jealousy of Buller, first in his acquisition of the post of Adjutant-General and secondly in his preferment for the command in South Africa. But it was a jealousy eventually overlaid by his explicable bitterness against the man he thought responsible for his only son's death.

The press campaign against Buller, especially after his return, might have been countered if he had been backed by his Government. At no time, however, did he receive the support he had the right to expect, and not merely against the press. From the start, when he was first warned for South Africa, he had been denied adequate political backing. Moreover, Lansdowne's personal dislike was equalled elsewhere in the Government. That already quoted letter from Brodrick, then his Under-Secretary, written after Colenso to a young society woman, was almost unmatched in its indiscreet venom.[38]

Nor did it help that that Buller was an old-fashioned Whig. Much as he had always disliked Gladstone with his 'Little-Englander' outlook, his closeness to the Opposition had long been apparent. A Liberal Imperialist, he was nonetheless as sympathetic to the Boers as he had been to the Irish. But in no way did he merit the pro-Boer label given him by Milner, close though his relations were with Campbell-Bannerman and Edward Grey, both fierce opponents of the War, a subject upon which the Liberals were split down the middle. Milner's concern had been expressed to the Colonial Secretary early in the war. Hoping that when the time came to withdraw troops, one of the first to go would be Buller – with all appropriate honours and thanks – he observed:

His return to England immediately after the war would be consistent with his being another Marlborough. What I feel sure is that his political influence will be bad. I don't want another Butler incident . . . and so far he has, except in private conversation, not committed himself at all. But if he were to be here for any considerable time after the war, I feel it is inevitable he should begin to play up the pro-Boer gallery.[39]

Milner foresaw self-government for the Boers – once they were beaten – as being the ultimate aim, but before that he looked forward to a long period of 'autocratic' Crown Colony rule.[40]

Linked to Lansdowne by close ties was Roberts, who had served him as Commander-in-Chief during his Viceroyalty and had become a personal friend. But the former Viceroy's dislike – and that of many other prominent Unionists – for Buller had deeper roots still. The soldier's sympathy for the Irish peasantry, revealed so publicly during his service in their country, hardly commended itself to Anglo-Irish grandees such as Lansdowne, Brodrick or Devonshire, all members of great Whig families who, as Liberal Unionists, had defected to the Tories in opposition to Gladstone's determination to grant Ireland home rule. Lansdowne, whose family once owned nearly 120,000 Irish acres,[41] mainly in County Kerry, for which Buller had been responsible, had been especially loathed by the Land League, while Brodrick's father had depended upon his Cork estates for two-thirds of his income.[42] To complicate matters further, Buller, despite being a strong supporter of the Union, unlike many others, would not make common cause with the Tories.

Why Lord Salisbury, the sole individual other than Esher known to have attacked Buller's integrity, so disliked him remains unexplained. Remote, if not out of touch, as he so often was, he relied too closely upon his ministers for his views, not least his nephew Balfour and his two successive Secretaries-of-State for War, as Esher probably did as well.

Perhaps Buller would have survived if King Edward had given him the same support as he had received from the old Queen. But that early refusal to compromise his principles and curry favour had alienated his future monarch.[43] Closely interested as he was in the Army, the King might otherwise have upheld Buller's personal appeal against Brodrick's demand for his resignation, something the Government would have found difficult to contest.

For it was a weak and broken-backed Government, led, until he handed over to his nephew Balfour in July, 1902, by an old and exhausted Prime Minister, devastated by his wife's death and now little more than a figurehead. Unconsciously perhaps, its members sought someone to blame for the errors that had plunged the country into a humiliating and near-disastrous conflict. As had happened before, and would often again, a military scapegoat for their mistakes might deflect the wrath of the voters. Buller had made mistakes, plenty of them, but so had Roberts and every other well-tried general in any era. In defending him from his attackers, Fortescue aptly quoted William Napier's aphorism of Wellington: 'To say that he made mistakes is to say he made war'.[44] It was unfortunate for Buller that in their treatment of him the Government had willing allies in Roberts and his Indian 'Ring'. With these were linked the newspapermen, prominent among them Amery, who in drawing the country's attention to the often gross military errors they had witnessed, found in Buller a ready scapegoat upon whom they could centre their invective. And, to crown it all, he had forfeited his Sovereign's goodwill.

14

EPILOGUE

The injuries Buller had suffered did not prevent him living his few remaining years to the full. Still fit, both physically and mentally, he could at last give first place to the care of his much-loved estates, unhampered by the demands of his profession. It was said that there was not a blade of their grass that he had not watched grow, not a cottage he had not planned, not a labourer he had not known from a boy. The woodlands and workshops, which had occupied him as a youth, now became subjects of serious study. Abhorrent was the concept that landed property was valuable only as a source of revenue.[1] Even today, after almost a century, his memory lingers in Crediton: how he and his wife would walk back from church with the miller; his insistence that working people should live in decent houses and not hovels; how his portrait hung in nearly every cottage, alongside the old Queen.[2]

Public affairs filled much of his days. It was usual then for landowners to take part in local government, often as mere figureheads; but Buller was a working councillor, his special concern education, a subject which engrossed him. Even when serving, he always found time to visit the local schools, however short his leave. His fellow councillors and church and charity workers, men often much younger than himself, he always handled with grace and sympathy. Further afield, there were further time-consuming responsibilities, such as Colonel-Commandant of the 60th Rifles and Prime Warden of the Goldsmiths' Company, whose Court he was remembered for managing with the greatest tact.

His family was very dear to him, not just his wife and Georgiana, his only child, but his surviving step-children as well, whom he treated as his own. He was good with the young of all ages, even to the extent of allowing a five-year old niece to join the adults for lunch – most unusual at the time – and administering no more than a gentle and in no way frightening rebuke at her late arrival.[3] But Georgiana was naturally his favourite and also his close companion, treated in many respects like the son he lacked. It was to be a bitter disappointment to her to discover that Downes was entailed, and so pass not to her but to her uncle, Tremayne Buller. As with many other women of her generation, her fiancé died in the war and she never married. Inheriting many of her father's qualities, capable war-time work as a hospital administrator resulted in her appointment as one of the first Dame Commanders of the British Empire; afterwards she was active in working for the disabled. Like her mother, she was always a doughty protector of her father's reputation.[4]

Buller never exploited his popularity so as to harm those he felt had injured him. And this popularity continued almost unabated, if not enhanced after Grey had defended him in Parliament and Fortescue with his pen. Nor was it confined to his native Devon or those soldiers who had served under him. Wherever he went, both on public and private occasions, he suffered what was for him the aggravation of being spontaneously cheered and sometimes engulfed by over-enthusiastic crowds. After nearly a century it is hard to understand why a not too successful general, reviled by much of the press, in manner rather remote, should have so appealed to all classes of society. Some said that the only parallel was Gladstone at the height of his fame.[5] Was it reaction against what was seen as unfair treatment, by a now unpopular government, of a fundamentally decent man who had served his country well?

Monuments to famous men are rarely erected in their lifetime, but in September, 1905, Buller watched the unveiling of the superb bronze thirteen-foot-high equestrian statue of himself that stands at the end of Queen's Street in Exeter. (Crediton people were said to be have been upset because he rides away from and not towards their town.) He found the ordeal trying, but suppressed his feelings. Wolseley had promised to perform the ceremony, but failed to consult his doctor, who then had to write to Lady Audrey to explain he had forbidden the Field-Marshal's attendance for fear of a calamitous breakdown. The strength of 'The Organisation for the Reinstatement of General Sir Redvers Buller', a body headed by a number of prominent public men, is shown by the day excursion trains run from Paddington, Waterloo, Bath and Bristol to bring crowds of his supporters and admirers to the ceremony.[6]

In the run-up to the general election of 1906, won by Campbell-Bannerman's Liberals by a crushing majority, both sides sought without success to enlist this ageing general as a candidate. Offers of seats abounded but all were refused. In declining one – and with the utmost politeness – primarily on the grounds that he 'had no liking for Parliament', he went on to say that 'I am not in any sense a party man, but I am not a Conservative. I suppose I am really a Whig and should now be called a Liberal Unionist, and a Unionist I am most decidedly'.[7] Nearly two years later, the *Westminster*

Gazette mentioned 'the emphatic terms' in which he had denied accepting a Unionist offer, adding that he was in favour of 'enlightened and generous trust in the Irish people' and spelling out the manner in which he had shown trust in them two decades before.[8] Here was the rub. Old party loyalties had broken down, their often petty previous differences transcended by problems of nationhood that transcended all else. And not only did Buller find politics unappealing, but like other liberal minds he could not channel the diversity of his views within the confines of an existing political party.

Only during the last six months of his life did his health start to falter, but even then he carried on as best he could, supervising his estate and dealing with his business affairs, facing pain and weakness outwardly with equanimity, determined to avoid increasing the distress others were suffering.

But on 2 June, 1908, Redvers Buller died in his house at Downes, the cause of his death carcinoma of the gall bladder and liver.[9] Among the vast number of letters of condolence received by his wife was one from Louis Botha.

Three days later he was buried in Crediton. With a new régime at the War Office, the funeral was worthy of the man. From Tidworth were despatched a battalion from each of the 60th Rifles and the Devonshire Regiment, together with a field battery to fire the salute; from Exeter rode a squadron of the Devon Yeomanry.[10] In a train, travelling to the funeral, a Gunner recounted with composure the deaths of his two brothers on the Tugela, only to break into tears when he spoke of the man who commanded them. Impressive indeed were the crowds of humble people, in the best clothes they could muster, their small children with black crepe pinned to their dresses, who lined the two-mile way from Downes to the quiet country churchyard. One family had walked there from twenty miles away, and then slept in a barn before walking back again.[11]

ABBREVIATIONS USED IN NOTES

AB	Lady Audrey Buller
ABD	Lady Audrey Buller's Diary (in Downes Papers)
Amery	By itself refers to *Times History*
ASC	Army Service Corps
CB	Campbell-Bannerman
C-in-C	Commander-in-Chief
DAAG	Deputy Assistant Adjutant-General
DAA&QMG	Deputy Assistant Adjutant & Quartermaster-General
DAQMG	Deputy Assistant Quartermaster-General
Downes	Downes Papers
DRO	Devon Record Office
GB	Dame Georgiana Buller
GBN	Dame Georgiana Buller's Notebooks (in Downes Papers)
GCMG	Knight Grand Cross of the Bath
GOC	General Office Commanding
GOC-in-C	General Officer Commanding-in-Chief
GRO	Gloucestershire County Record Office
HB	Miss Henrietta Buller
HBN	Miss Henrietta Buller's Notebooks (in Downes Papers)
JSAHR	Journal Society Army Historical Research
KCB	Knight Commander of the Bath
KCMG	Knight Commander of St Michael & St George
LHL	Liddell Hart Library, King's College London
L of C	Lines of Communication
NAM	National Army Museum
OH	Official History South African War
PRO	Public Record Office
psc	Passed Staff College
QV	Queen Victoria
QVJ	Queen Victoria's Journal

RA	Royal Archives
RAOC	Royal Army Ordnance Corps
RASC	Royal Army Service Corps
RB	Redvers Buller
RCT	Royal Corps of Transport
RCTA	Royal Corps of Transport Archives
RCWSA	Royal Commission on War in South Africa
RIC	Royal Irish Constabulary
RUSIJ	Royal United Services Institute Journal
W	Wolseley

NOTES

Only the bibliographical details of those books referred to on a single occasion are given in the Notes. For the rest the reader is referred to the Bibliography.

Introduction (pp. vii–x)

1. Pakenham, xvii, 457–8
2. Beadon, Col R. H., *The Royal Army Service Corps*, vol 2, Cambridge University Press, 1931. Introduction by John Fortescue, xli, who was, of course, referring to Kitchener's raising of the 'New Armies'.
3. Higham, Robin, *A Guide to the Sources of British Military History*, Routledge, Keegan & Paul, 1972, 313.
4. Downes, Fortescue to Lady Audrey Buller, 16 Jul 08.
5. Devon Record Office, 2065M add 2 SS18, Lady Fortescue to Dame Georgiana Buller, 20 Nov 20; ibid SS 25, Mr Watling to Dame Georgiana, 10 Nov 23; information Pakenham.
6. Melville, Col C. H., Note to vol 1 of *Life of Gen the Rt Hon Sir Redvers Buller*, Edward Arnold, 1923.
7. ibid.

Chapter 1 An Awkward Youngster (pp. 1–10)

1. The sources for RB's early days are primarily three, the first two held at Downes: notebooks of his sister, Henrietta Buller (HBN); his daughter, Lady Georgiana Buller's notebooks (GBN); Butler, Lewis, *Redvers Buller*, written by a fellow officer, first published in *The Chronicle of the King's Own Rifle Corps*, and based largely on the recollections of those who knew him in his younger days.
2. *Western Times* 22 Dec 1855.

3. Downes. Obituary dated 17 Mar 1865. Newspaper unknown, probably *The Western Mail*.
4. GBN.
5. HBN.
6. Harries-Jenkins, 32, quoting J. Bateman, *The Great Landowners of Britain*, 1883.
7. HBN.
8. Downes. Copy letter recounting accident and cutting, neswpaper unknown.
9. HBN.
10. Downes.
11. GBN.
12. Butler, Lewis, 7.
13. ibid, 8–9.
14. Butler, Lewis, is almost the sole source for RB's part in the Third China War. In HBN is a mention that he was under fire.
15. HBN.
16. ibid.
17. Again Butler, Lewis, is the main source for RB's first tour in Canada.
18. HBN.
19. Butler, William, *Autobiography*.

Chapter 2 The Ring (pp. 11–28)

1. Huyse, 65.
2. Huyse; Butler, WF, *The Great Lone Land*; copy RB letter to his sister HB of 24 Aug 70; and Assistant Controller Irvine's *Report on the Red River Expedition*, C 391 of 1871, the last two respectively in DRO 2065M add 2 SS 2 and 3, are the main primary sources for the Red River Expedition.
3. RB to HB, 24 Aug 70.
4. Wolseley, *Story of a Soldier's Life*, vol 2, 177–8. According to Butler, Lewis, 17, Wolseley had previously met Buller, as was to be expected in the small world of the Army in Canada; Buller, during his earlier tour, had wanted an interview with his general, but Wolseley had stopped him; but somehow the strong-willed subaltern had his way. The incident, which may have remained in Buller's mind, could easily have been forgotten by his senior, as could any possible meeting between the two in China.
5. Wolseley, *Letters*, W to Lady W, 5 Nov 84, 128.
6. Butler, WF, *The Great Lone Land*, 6.

7. ibid, 8.
8. ibid, *Autobiography*, 113.
9. ibid, *The Great Lone Land*, 168.
10. See Note 3.
11. ibid.
12. ibid.
13. After finding refuge in the United States, some years later Riel was elected to the Dominion Parliament. After taking the oath, he was later ejected, only to lead another and equally unsuccessful rebellion that led to his capture and hanging.
14. See Note 3.
15. Huyse, 214–8. Huyse himself read the captured papers.
16. See Note 3.
17. Butler, Lewis, 26.
18. ibid, 26–7.
19. ibid, 29.
20. Melville, vol 1, 54, after studying RB's untraced Staff College notebooks.
21. ibid, 55.
22. Buller and Huyshe were Wolseley's two junior staff officers. As was then customary, their duties were ill-defined and they have been described by different authorities as DAAGs, DAQMGs and DAA&QMGs.
23. Primary sources for Ashanti are RB's family correspondence, Brackenbury, *Ashanti War*, Stanley and Reade. Brackenbury's two-volume work, written in just six weeks at Wolseley's instigation, and with his help and support, was, in effect, a sanitized official history.
24. Downes, RB to LB, 14 Nov 73.
25. Brackenbury, *Ashanti War*, vol 1, 171.
26. DRO 2065M add 2/SS5.
27. Brackenbury, *Ashanti War*, vol 1, 170.
28. RA F7/24.
29. Downes, RB to LB, 31 Oct 73.
30. Wood, *From Midshipman . . .* , vol 1, 267.
31. Downes, RB to LB, 9 Dec 73.
32. Forbes, Archibald, *Souvenirs of Six Continents*, Macmillan, 1885, 158.
33. Downes, RB to LB, 14 Nov 73.
34. Stanley, 17.
35. Downes, RB to Tremayne Buller.
36. Brackenbury, *Ashanti War*, Vol 2, 356.

37. Stanley, 120.
38. Reade, 425.

Chapter 3   South African Accolade (pp. 29–44)

1. HBN.
2. ibid.
3. ibid.
4. ibid.
5. ibid; as well as his sister Henrietta; Lewis Butler and especially Sir Edmund Gosse all dwell on Buller's wide literary interests.
6. Butler, Lewis, 102.
7. Harries-Jenkins, 32.
8. Butler, William, *Autobiography*, 186.
9. DRO 2065M add 2/SS 4/9
10. Butler, Lewis, 31–32.
11. HBN.
12. Maxwell, Leigh, 187.
13. Downes, Wolseley to RB, 29 Jan 78.
14. ibid, RB to HB, 22 Apr 78. RB's correspondence at Downes, in PRO WO 132/1, and as reproduced in Melville (most of his letters from this period are untraceable), together with the autobiographies of other participants, are the primary sources for the Kaffir and Zulu Wars.
15. Mossop, 34.
16. ibid, 38–9.
17. Melville, vol 1, 92, quoting Wood.
18. Downes, RB to HB, 13 Aug 78.
19. ibid, RB to LB, 18 Feb 79.
20. ibid.
21. ibid, RB to HB, 9 Mar 79.
22. Mossop, 41.
23. Melville, vol 1, 109–10, quoting Wood's orders.
24. PRO WO 132/1, RB to aunt Miss Georgina Buller, 30 May 79.
25. Mossop, 51.
26. See Note 24.
27. PRO WO 132/1, RB to LB, 5 Apr 79.
28. Downes, RB to LB, 10 Jul 79.
29. Melville, vol 1, 127, op cit.
30. ibid, 126, op cit.
31. See note 17.
32. Melville, vol 1, 128, quoting Colley.

33. ibid, 129.
34. ibid, 133, quoting op cit 18 Jul 79.
35. Preston, *South African Journal* 1879–80, 55, 13 Jul 79.
36. ibid, 56, 14 July 79.
37. DRO 2065M add 2/SS 28(2), Stamfordham to GB, 2 Dec 23.
38. Tylden, 221.
39. Wood, *Winnowed Memories*, 186.
40. Melville, vol 1, 133.
41. Preston, *South African Journal, 1879–80*, 319, quoting Ponsonby to wife.

Chapter 4   Responsibility (pp. 45–61)

1. PRO WO 132/2.
2. DRO 2065 M/add 2/SS4/9 for the invitation.
3. HBN.
4. RA Queen Victoria's Journal: 2 Sep 1879.
5. ibid 9 Sep 1879.
6. HBN; Downes, op cit, 12 Sep 79.
7. Downes, QV to RB, 19 Sep 79.
8. HBN.
9. Preston, *South African Journal 1979–80*, 319.
10. HBN.
11. Wolseley, *Letters*, Lady W to W, 13 Nov 79.
12. Downes, Beaconsfield to RB, 16 Sep 79.
13. Butler, Lewis, 42.
14. The introductions to Preston's two volumes of Wolseley's *SA Diary* and SA Journal provide a fresh and thorough analysis of his tours in South Africa.
15. Forbes, 170–1.
16. ibid, 176.
17. Downes, newspaper cutting 6 Oct 79.
18. RA Add E1/9672
19. Downes, RB to LB, 7 Jun 81.
20. ibid, RB to HB, 15 Mar 81.
21. Wood, *From Midshipman . . .*, vol 2, 118.
22. Butler, Lewis, 46.
23. Downes, RB to LB, 20 Mar 81.
24. ibid, RB to HB, 16 May 81.
25. ibid, RB to LB, 7 Apr 81.
26. Melville, vol 1, 179, quoting a Natal newspaper.

27. ibid, 153, quoting RB letter of 18 Oct 81.
28. GBN and HBN continually dwell on this.
29. Downes, RB to LB, 25 Jan 81.
30. HBN.
31. ibid.
32. ibid.
33. Wolseley, *Letters*, passim.
34. Dixon, 283.
35. HBN.
36. GBN.
37. Wolseley, *Letters*, Lady W to W, 10 Aug 82.
38. PRO WO 132/2, Wolseley to RB, 15 Aug 82.
39. Melville, vol 1, 158, quoting RB to sister.
40. Bond, *Victorian Military Campaigns*, 262, quoting Childers, Spenser, *Life of Rt Hon Hugh C. E. Childers*, vol 2, John Murray, 1901, 88–9.
41. Melville, vol 1, 158, quoting RB to AB, 2 Sep 82. RB's letters to AB of this period cannot be traced.
42. Lehmann, 322–3.
43. Melville, vol 1, 166, quoting RB to AB, 12 Sep 82.
44. Butler, W, *Autobiography*, 237.
45. Melville, vol 1, 163, quoting RB to AB, 12 Sep 82.
46. ibid, 166, quoting RB to AB, 17 Sep 82.
47. ibid, 168, quoting RB to AB, 24 Sep 82.
48. Walters, 142.
49. Dixon, 316.
50. ibid, 317.
51. Butler, W, *Autobiography*, 289–9.
52. Melville, vol 1, 167, quoting RB to AB, 18 Sep 82.
53. ibid, 166, quoting RB to AB, 27 Sep 82.

Chapter 5 Distinction (pp. 62–80)

1. Melville, vol 1, 169.
2. ibid, 173–4, quoting RB to AB, 8 Feb 84. All RB's letters to his wife from Egypt and the Sudan are missing.
3. ibid, 179, quoting RB to AB, 2 Mar 84.
4. Private papers. Letter of 15 Mar 84.
5. Melville, vol 1, 186–7, op cit.
6. *Sheffield Daily Telegraph*, 18 Mar 84.
7. WO 132/2, RB to W, 4 Mar 84.
8. RA Add. E1/10663/5, 2 Mar. 1884

9. RA Add. E1/10692/5, 18 Mar. 1884
10. Royle, 307.
11. Melville, vol 1, 188.
12. ibid, 189.
13. Symons, *England's Pride*, 89–90. quoting War office records.
14. RA Queen Victoria's Journal, 21 Aug. 1884.
15. Preston, *In Relief of Gordon*, 75–6, quoting 30 Nov 84. W wrote his campaign journal up daily and sent it to his wife.
16. ibid, 75, quoting 30 Nov 84.
17. Wolseley, *Letters*, W to Lady W, 5 Nov 84, 25 Dec 84 and 2 Jan 85, also refer to his troubles with Butler.
18. Preston, *In Relief . . .*, 49, quoting 27 Oct 84.
19. ibid, 126, quoting 26 Jan 85. With Wood, the quarrel rankled. The following year, when giving evidence before a committee appointed to consider the respective duties of a Chief of Staff and the GOC L of C, he wrote that Buller had 'unduly and to the disadvantage of the Public Service' interfered with him. (Wood, *Winnowed Memories*, 153). He waited until long after Buller's death to publish the book.
20. Melville, vol 1, 193, quoting W to Cambridge, 11 Oct 84.
21. Preston, *In Relief . . .*, 112–3, quoting 9 Jan 85.
22. ibid, 166, quoting 13 Mar 85.
23. Melville, vol 1, 204, quoting RB to AB, 3 Oct 84.
24. Downes, RB to LB, 20 Mar 81.
25. Melville, vol 1, 201–2.
26. Melville, Note 1, 5; Buchan, John, *Gordon at Khartoum*, Peter Davies, 1934, 120.
27. ibid, vol 1, 205, quoting RB letter 9 Oct 85.
28. ibid, 202–4, quoting RB to AB, 29 Sep 84.
29. ibid, 208, quoting RB letter 18 Dec 84.
30. Parker, *In Relief . . .*, 67, quoting 17 Nov 84. Lehmann, 360, goes so far as to use this to accuse Buller of 'dereliction of duty'.
31. Fortescue, *RASC*, 200–202.
32. Melville, vol 1, 207, quoting RB letter of 8 Nov 84.
33. ibid, 208–9 quoting RB letter.
34. Fortescue, *RASC* 205–7.
35. Lehmann, 365, for one instance.
36. Melville, vol 1, quoting RB to AB, 22 Jan 85.
37. Marling, 135.
38. PRO WO 132/2, W to RB, 29 Jan 85.
39. ibid, dated 4 Jan 85 clearly an error for 4 Feb 85.
40. ibid, 12 Feb 85.

41. ibid, 16 Feb 85.
42. Preston, *In Relief* . . ., 112–3, 158 & 166 quoting 9 Jan, 1 & 13 Mar 85.
43. Marling, 135.
44. Melville, vol 1, 237–8, quoting RB to AB, 20 Feb 85.
45. Dundonald, 61.
46. PRO WO 132/2, W to RB, 21 Feb 85; Preston, *In Relief* . . ., 151, 157.
47. Wolseley, *Letters*, W to Lady W, 173, 22 Feb 85; PRO WO 132/2, ibid . . .
48. Lehmann, 349, provides the figure of 40 camels, but source not given. Symons, *England's Pride*, quotes Col C. P. Stacey, *Records of the Nile Voyageurs*, 1959, for Wood's baggage.
49. Marling, 130.
50. Wood, *Winnowed Memories*, 176.
51. PRO WO 132/2, W to RB, 12 Feb 85.
52. DRO 2065M add 2/SS 29.
53. eg Arthur, Sir George, *Life of Lord Kitchener*, vol 1, Macmillan, 1920.
54. Hamilton, *Listening for the Drums*, 172–3.
55. Hamilton Papers, 25/12/3/76, letter to father, 29 Nov 84.
56. Melville, vol 1, 251–2, quoting RB to AB.
57. *Letters Lord and Lady W*, 213, W to Lady W, 28 Apr 85.
58. Melville, vol 1, 252.
59. Downes, op cit.

Chapter 6   Irish Interlude (pp. 81–96)

1. PRO WO 132/4A, Smith to RB, 16 Aug 86.
2. Verner, vol 2, 328.
3. RA Add E1/11568, RB to Duke, 18 Aug. 1866.
4. RA L15/96, Home Secretary to Private Secretary, 4 Mar 1886.
5. PRO WO 132/4B. Pamphlet XVIII 'Irish Royal & Patriotic Union'.
6. GRO PCC 45, op cit, 4 Sep 86. A number of RB's letters, together with Hicks Beach's replies, are held in the Hicks Beach Papers, GRO PCC series. These, and further correspondence in PRO WO 132/4A and at Downes, together with two large albums of newspaper cuttings at Downes provide the bulk of the primary source material for this chapter. There are also several untraced letters between RB and Hicks Beach quoted in Melville, vol 1.
7. GRO PCC 45, op cit, 30 Aug 86.
8. Various letters in PRO WO 132/4A and at Downes.
9. GRO PCC 17, Hicks Beach to RB, 8 Sep 86.

10. *The Cork Examiner*, 26 Nov 86, contains a long and seemingly well informed piece on the subject.
11. GRO PCC 17, op cit, 18 Sep 86.
12. Melville, vol 1, 307 quoting letter to Hicks-Beach.
13. Butler, Lewis, 53.
14. GRO PCC 17, op cit.
15. Downes. Quotations are from ABD.
16. Melville, vol 1, 308, quoting op cit.
17. ibid, 311–2, quoting RB to Hicks Beach, 4 Sep 86.
18. GRO PCC 17, Hicks Beach to RB, 14 Oct 86.
19. ibid, 5 Nov 86.
20. *Daily News*, 25 Oct 86.
21. GRO PCC 17, op cit, 1 Oct 86.
22. GRO PCC, 45, op cit, 15 Nov 86.
23. *QV, Letters*, Third Series, vol 1, 291.
24. Morley, John, *Life of Gladstone*, vol 3, Macmillan, 1903, 372–3.
25. GRO PCC 45, op cit, 20 Oct 86.
26. Downes, op cit, 30 Nov 86.
27. RA Add E1/11649, op cit, 28 Nov 1986.
28. GRO PCC 17, Hicks Beach to RB, 26 Nov 86.
29. GRO PCC 45, op cit, 27 Nov 86.
30. DNB.
31. GRO PCC 17, op cit.
32. Midleton, 49.
33. See note 27.
34. GRO PCC 31, op cit, 20 Oct 86.
35. Downes, copy undated letter.
36. GRO PCC 17, op cit, 22 Sep 86.
37. GRO PCC 45, op cit, 15 Jan 87.
38. GBN.
39. ibid; ABD.
40. Downes, RB to LB, 26 Mar 87.
41. PRO WO 132/4A correspondence RB – Balfour.
42. Dugdale, vol 1, 128–9 & 137, quoting Balfour to Buller, 12 Mar 87 and undated.
43. Melville, vol 1, 326, quoting letter Feb 87, presumably to Hicks Beach.
44. ibid, 327, quoting letter probably to Balfour.
45. *QV, Letters*, Third Series, vol 1, 279, diary, op cit.
46. Melville, vol 1, 328, op cit.
47. 'Periscope', 'Last Days of Dublin Castle', *Blackwoods*, Aug 1922, 143.
48. Butler, Lewis, 55.

Chapter 7   Desk-bound (pp. 97–112)

1. DRO 2065M add 2/SS28(2). Stamfordham to GB, 2 Dec 23.
2. RCWSA RB Q 15501.
3. PRO WO 132/2, Wolseley to RB, 15 Sep 86.
4. Wavell, Gen Sir Archibald, *Generals and Generalship*, The Lees Knowles Lectures, CUP, 1939, 2.
5. Melville, vol 1, 285. It was to be close on a century before this occurred. In 1982, Lt-Gen Sir Paul Travers, late RCT, became QMG.
6. HBN.
7. Melville, vol 1, 288, quoting from an undated draft of RB written some 12 years later.
8. RCTA, RB to Robinson, 23 Oct 89.
9. Wolseley, DNB.
10. *QV Letters*, 3rd Series, vol 2, 623, Lansdowne to QV 5 Jul 90; Roberts, Field Marshal Lord, *Forty-One Years in India*, vol 2, Bentley, 1897, 437–8.
11. Wheeler, 250.
12. Downes, LB to AB, 15 Sep 05, quoting from letter.
13. Lyttleton, 167.
14. Bond, *Victorian Army & Staff College*, 147.
15. *QV Letters*, 3rd Series, vol 1, 583, QV to Ponsonby, 20 Mar 90.
16. RA E39/9, RB to Bigge, 10 Dec. 1895.
17. RA E39/2, Abstract of a letter from Lieut. Genl. Sir Redvers Buller to Sir H. Ponsonby 4 Apr. 1891.
18. RCWSA, RB Q 15502; Spiers 40. The memo was submitted eleven years after he first broached the proposal but reflects his earlier views.
19. Spiers, 40, 52.
20. Atlay, 119.
21. Melville, vol 1, 256.
22. RCSWA, RB Q 15633–5.
23. ibid, RB Q 15502.
24. Melville, vol 1, 267, quoting evidence before Sandhurst Committee.
25. Spiers, 137–8.
26. Melville, vol 1, 269.
27. ibid, 256–8; Spiers 73.
28. Butler, Lewis, 57–8.
29. ibid, 58.
30. DRO 2065M add 2 554/27 contains a bundle of letters between RB and Brackenbury covering 1892–4.

31. Spender, vol 1, 130.
32. Wilson, John, 214.
33. Melville, vol 1, 273; Butler, Lewis, 58–9.
34. Downes, op cit, 9 Dec 94.
35. Gosse; DNB suggests that in his youth Gosse 'had not allowed his reverence for celebrities to interfere with his powers of critical observation'.
36. Melville, vol 2, 306. Writing only a decade after King Edward's death, Melville's reference to the incident was guarded. His Note 2, 15–16, is more outspoken.
37. Melville, Note 2, 15.
38. ibid.
39. St Aubyn, 287–90.
40. ibid, quoting letter of 13 Feb 91 in Fitzgeorge Papers.
41. Melville, Note 2, 15.
42. ibid.
43. *QV Letters*, Third Series, vol 2, 503, QVJ, 9 May 95.
44. PRO WO 132/5, Bigge to RB 16 May 95.
45. *QV Letters*, Third Series, vol 2, 516–7, QV to Bigge, 11 Jun 95; Bigge to QV, 11 Jun 95.
46. ibid, 519, QV to Bigge, 16 Jun 95.
47. ibid, 518, Bigge to QV, 15 Jun 95.
48. RA E41/21, letter 9 May 1895.
49. Churchill, *Great Contemporaries*, 52.
50. *QV Letters*, Third Series, vol 2, 549, QV to Salisbury, 11 Aug 95.
51. ibid, 550, Salisbury to QV, 11 Aug 95.
52. ibid, 551, QV to Salisbury, 22 Aug 95.
53. ibid, 551, Connaught to Bigge, 13 Aug 95.
54. See Note 1.
55. RA B48/10, op cit, 16 Aug 95.
56. Lehmann, 382, quoting W to Lady W, 22 Jul 95.
57. ibid, 383, 3 Jul 95.
58. Newton, *Lord Lansdowne*, 131.
59. *Wolseley Letters*, Lady W to W, 346, 15 Jul 95; Melville Notes, vol 1, 3, makes the same suggestion.
60. Lehmann, 384.
61. PRO WO 132/5 Campbell-Bannerman to RB, 29 Jun 99.
62. Downes, Spender to Melville, 18 Sep 22.
63. Melville, vol 1, 275. He describes the writer as 'An old friend, a member of the Court'. It is clearly Bigge.

Chapter 8   The Reluctant Commander (pp. 113–130)

1. Melville, Note 2, 5.
2. May, 186–7.
3. Melville, vol 1, 277; Lady Milner, 110; RUSIJ, Mar 1899, contains the 'Official Report on the Salisbury Plain Manoeuvres in 1898'.
4. Midleton, 132–3.
5. Walters, 147.
6. Interview Pakenham.
7. Jerrold, 227–32.
8. RCWSA, Q 14964.
9. Downes, RB to AB, 24 Apr 00.
10. Headlam, vol 1, 222, Milner to Chamberlain, 23 Feb 98.
11. Butler, William, *Autobiography*, 407–8.
12. ibid, 415.
13. ibid, 427.
14. Headlam, vol 1, 353, Milner to Chamberlain, 4 May 99.
15. PRO WO 132/6. RB to Tremayne Buller, 3 Nov 99.
16. Melville, vol 2, 4.
17. See note 15.
18. Wilson, 217, quoting C–B to friend, 3 Sep 03.
19. ibid, op cit.
20. Melville, vol 2, 1–3, quoting memorandum on which RB's evidence to RCSWA was based. This was considerably pruned when submitted.
21. Wood, *Winnowed Memories*, 291–3.
22. ibid, 291.
23. ibid.
24. Lyttelton, 200–1.
25. ibid, 170. Lyttelton wrote that this failure was visible to him and remarked upon by RB two years before.
26. RCWSA, W, Q 9080–3, 9035.
27. RCWSA, RB, Q 14970; DRO 2065M add 2 SS4/14, RB to W 6 Jul 99.
28. Pakenham 41–2, 69; Amery, vol 2, 84.
29. RCWSA, W, Q 9085.
30. ibid, Lansdowne Q 21170
31. Pakenham 79, quoting Milner to Chamberlain, 23 Jun 99.
32. See Note 15.
33. RCWSA, Lansdowne 21247–9.
34. Pakenham, 97.
35. Melville, vol 2, 16–17. Chamberlain had, however, been urging Lans-

downe to do so; Pakenham 96, quoting letters from Chamberlain to Lansdowne of 14 Jun and 10 Sep.

36. DRO 2065M add 2 SS4/14, RB to Stopford 3 Sep 99.
37. ibid, McDonnell to RB, 4, 5, 6 Sep 99. Buller's close friendship with McDonnell is evident from his use of his first name, unusual at the time. Known as 'Pam', McDonnell was to resign to join the Volunteers for active service in South Africa. Volunteering again in the Great War, he was killed serving with the Gordon Highlanders in 1915 at the age of 54.
38. ibid, RB to Lord Salisbury, 5 Sep 99. Printed for use by the Cabinet 7 Sep 99.
39. ibid, Mcdonnell to RB 6 Sep 99.
40. Pakenham, 96–7.
41. DRO 2065M add 2 SS4/14, W to RB, 7 Sep 99.
42. ibid, RB to Lansdowne, 9 Sep 99.
43. Midleton, 133.
44. DRO 2065M add 2 SS4/14, RB to Lansdowne, 9 Sep 99.
45. ibid, RB to Lansdowne, 30 Sep 99.
46. Pakenham, 97, quoting RB to Bigge, 4 Jan 00.
47. RCWSA, W, Q 262.
48. Melville, vol 2, 20.
49. RCWSA, RB, Q 14964.
50. ibid, Q 14963, 15005, 15006, 15012 and Appendix.
51. Fortescue, 'Scapegoats', 353.
52. Pakenham, 98.
53. Hamilton, Ian BM, 145; Hamilton, *Listening for the Drums*, 172, 214–5.
54. Pakenham 98.
55. NAM 5201/331, Rawlinson diary, 7–11 Oct 89.
56. See note 45.

Chapter 9   The Tightest Place (pp. 131–144)

1. Melville, vol 2, 37.
2. RCWSA, RB, Q 14693, 15007.
3. ibid.
4. RA QVJ, 5 Oct. 1899.
5. Downes, unidentified cutting 9 Nov 99.
6. *Times*, 16 Oct 99.
7. Repington, 201.
8. Churchill, *Great Contemporaries*, 230.
9. Butler, Lewis, 63.

10. Hamilton, Ian BM, 128.
11. Milner Papers 69, op cit.
12. Downes, Stopford to AB, 8 Jan 00.
13. PRO WO 132/6, RB to Tremayne Buller, 3 Nov 99.
14. Pakenham, 158, quoting RB to Lansdowne, 7 Nov 99.
15. *QV Letters*, 3rd, vol 3, 415–6, RB to Queen, 7 Nov 99.
16. Maurice, *Boer War*, vol 1, 199–200, quoting RB to Lansdowne, 2, 3, 4 Nov 99.
17. See note 15, QVJ, 4 Nov 99.
18. RCWSA, RB, Q 14693, 15104.
19. ibid, Q 14693, 15105–11.
20. Fortescue, *Buller*, 3.
21. RCWSA, RB, Q 14693, 15164.
22. ibid; Melville, vol 2, 45–6.
23. The author's father, at school there for a time, was one.
24. RCWSA, RB, Q 14693, 15161.
25. Milner Papers 170/72, Milner to Chamberlain, 2 Feb 00.
26. Headlam, vol. 2, 25, Milner to Chamberlain, 9 Nov 99.
27. Pakenham, 160, quoting Milner to RB, 5 Nov 99.
28. RCWSA, RB, Q 14963.
29. ibid.
30. Amery, vol 2, 186.
31. Milner 212/586, Chamberlain to Milner, 31 Oct 99.
32. RCWSA, RB, Q 14963.
33. Amery, vol 2, 288.
34. Repington, 199.
35. For example Amery, vol 2, 116–7; Newton, 158.
36. RCWSA, RB, Q 15277 and Lansdowne, Q 21138–47, in which the latter admits that the telegram was 'unfortunately worded' but suggests that the matter was again discussed between RB and his Under-Secretary before the reply was sent.
37. Maurice, *Boer War*, vol 1, 200, quoting RB to Lansdowne.
38. Melville, vol 2, 67; RCWSA, RB, Q 14693.
39. Milner 212/457, Hely-Hutchinson to Milner, 31 Oct 99.
40. Melville, vol 2; Pakenham 161 quoting RB to Lansdowne 11 Nov 99.
41. Maurice, *Boer War*, vol 1, 209–10, quoting RB to Walker, 20 Nov 99.
42. Repington, 201.
43. RCWSA, RB, Q 14693.
44. Milner Papers 69, diary 7 Dec 99, 4 Jan 00.
45. Viscountess Milner, 79.

46. ibid, 146–7.
47. ibid, 146–8.
48. Headlam, vol 2, 27; 54–5.
49. Milner Papers 212/627, Hely-Hutchinson to Milner, 23 Nov 99.
50. ibid, 69, 23 Nov 99.
51. ibid, 170/121, Milner to Chamberlain, 3 Jan 00; Headlam, vol 2, 27 Dec 99.
52. Milner Papers, 212/370, Fleetwood-Wilson to Milner, 14 Oct 99.
53. ibid, 170/68, Milner to Chamberlain, 31 Jan 00.
54. ibid, 212/490, Hely-Hutchinson to Milner, 2 Dec 99.
55. RCWSA, RB, Q 14963.
56. ibid.

Chapter 10   Black Week (pp. 145–161)

1. Maurice, *Rawlinson*, 40.
2. RCWSA, RB Q 14693, Q 15115–9
3. Melville, vol 2, 78–9.
4. ibid, 194, 302; Pakenham, 209–10; at Downes are several letters from his ex-soldiers.
5. Downes, RB to AB, 2 Dec 99.
6. Headlam, vol 2, 32.
7. Melville, vol 2, 85.
8. See Note 5.
9. Melville, vol 2, 92–4, quoting RB to Lansdowne, 13 & 14 Dec 99.
10. RCWSA, Lansdowne, Q 21360–3.
11. Maurice, *Boer War*, vol 1, 336–7.
12. Dundonald, 100–1.
13. Spiers, 135.
14. RCWSA, Long, Appx 51.
15. Atkins, 163.
16. Downes, Ogilvy to father, 20 Dec 99.
17. ibid, RB to AB, 18 Dec 99.
18. Dundonald, 109–11.
19. Symons, *Buller's Campaign*, 86.
20. Wood, *Winnowed Memories*, 198.
21. Dundonald, 107.
22. May, 194.
23. Lyttelton, 208.
24. Pakenham, 236, quoting RB to Lansdowne, 16 Dec 99.

25. Dundonald, 107–8.
26. RCWSA, RB, Q 15305–10
27. Atkins, 174
28. Melville, Note 2, 6–7.
29. RCWSA, RB Q14693, Q 15314.
30. Esher, 380.
31. RCWSA, RB Q14693, Q 15320–8.
32. ibid, Q 15328.
33. *QV Letters*, 3rd, vol 3, 434, QV to RB 17 Dec 99; Journal 17 Dec 99.
34. RCWSA, RB Q 15315–9; Melville, vol 2, 124.
35. Robertson, 101–2.
36. RCSWA, RB Q 14693; Melville, vol 2, 129, quotes in slightly different words.
37. Melville vol 2, 130.
38. ibid, 127–8.
39. ibid, 128.
40. ibid.
41. Downes, W to AB, 17 & 18 Dec 99.
42. ibid, RB to AB, 18 Dec 99.
43. ibid, RB to Skinners Company, 20 Dec 99.
44. NAM, 71001–23–10, RB to Roberts, 30 Apr 90, 20 Jan 93. Roberts, when writing to the Military Services in 1891 confirms that 'the only communications I have had with him [Buller] since he became Adjutant-General . . . have been of a most friendly character'. Quoted by Robson, Brian, *Roberts in India: The Military Papers of Field Marshal Lord Roberts, 1876–93*, p. 410 from Roberts Papers 100–3/CLXXXII, Alan Sutton, 1993.
45. Hamilton, Ian BM, 100, part letter quoted.
46. ibid, quoting Hamilton to wife, 2 Sep 00.
47. Newton, 161–2, quoting letter 10 Dec 99.
48. James, 284.
49. Wood, *Winnowed Memories*, 293.
50. Newton, 163, quoting letter 10 Dec 99.
51. James, 490, quoting Lansdowne to friend.
52. NAM, 7101–23–10.
53. RCWSA, RB Q 14693.
54. ibid, Q 15343–75; Melville vol 2, 130–9.
55. ibid, Q 15348, Q 15356.
56. Melville, vol 2, 137.
57. Repington, 208, accuses Buller of a lack of understanding of the

mechanisms of modern staff work. This was general among his generation.

58. Wilson, Jeremy, *Lawrence of Arabia*, Heinemann, 1989, 37.
59. Wilson, John, 171, quoting Balfour's memo written in 1928.
60. Walters, 152.
61. Symons, *Buller's Campaign*, 149.
62. Repington, 55.
63. Amery, *My Political Life*, 192.
64. Spiers, 316.
65. Amery, vol 3, 301.
66. ibid, 551.
67. ibid, vol 2, 459.
68. Downes, part letter from RB's sister and Melville, note 2, 6, recount the anecdote but in different words.
69. Marling, 254.
70. Walters, 143.
71. Churchill, *My Early Life*, 241.

Chapter 11 Ladysmith (pp. 162–177)

1. Melville, vol 2, 143, quoting signal; RCWSA RB Q 14963.
2. Melville, vol 2, 148–50, quoting op cit, 28 Dec 99.
3. Downes, RB to AB, 18 Jan 00.
4. Melville, vol 2, 151, quoting White signal, 6 Jan 00.
5. May, 234.
6. NAM 5201–33–7, Rawlinson diary 17–18 Dec 99.
7. Marling, 264.
8. RCWSA, RB Q 14963, Q 15416; Lansdowne Q 21253–59.
9. Atkins, 207.
10. Dundonald, 127.
11. RCWSA, RB Q 14963; Dundonald 133. RB confided in the latter, blaming himself for not sacking Warren and explaining why.
12. Pakenham 282–3, quoting letter Lewis Butler-Fortescue; RCWSA, RB Q 14963.
13. NAM MFN 8505.22, Trotter to mother, 21 Apr 00.
14. Atkins, 237.
15. Repington, 217.
16. RCSWA, RB Q 14963.
17. Churchill, *Ladysmith*, 340.
18. RCWSA, RB Q 14963.
19. ibid.

20. ibid, quoting Roberts to RB, 28 Jan 00.
21. ibid, quoting RB to Roberts, 4 Feb 00.
22. ibid, quoting Roberts to RB, 6 Feb 00.
23. Melville, vol 2, 179; Amery, vol 3, 323.
24. Lyttelton, 217–21; Pakenham, 344, quoting Herbert to father, 29 Jan 00.
25. Powell, Geoffrey, *Plumer: The Solders' General*, Leo Cooper, 1991, 95, quoting Arnold-Forster Papers, BL Add Ms 50343, diary 16 Dec 05.
26. Bond, *Victorian Army*, 223, 242.
27. Calwell, 33–4.
28. Melville, Note 1, quoting Roberts's Director of Supplies & Transport; Fortescue, *RASC*, vol 1, 234–6.
29. Pakenham, 341, quoting Lt-Gen Kelly-Kenny diary 19–23 Feb 00.
30. RCWSA, RB Q 14963.
31. Maurice, *Boer War*, vol 2, 155.
32. Repington, 234–5; Atkins, 267; Maurice, *Boer War*, vol 2, 459; Churchill, *My Early Life*, 337–8.
33. RCWSA, RB Q 14963.
34. Melville, vol 2, 206, quoting RB to AB, 3 Mar 00.
35. Maurice, *Boer War*, vol 2, 466–7.
36. Atkins, 313.
37. Lyttelton, 229–30; Maurice, *Boer War*, vol 2, Appx 13.
38. Amery, vol 3, 343.
39. ibid, 544–5.
40. See note 34.
41. Atkins, 314–5; Churchill, *Ladysmith*, 472.
42. NAM 5201–33–7, Rawlinson diary, 3 Mar 00.
43. ibid, 9 Feb 00.
44. Repington, 24.
45. See note 42, 3 & 5 Mar 00.
46. ibid, 12 Mar 00.
47. Spencer-Wilkinson, 248–9, quoting letter 8 Mar 00.
48. Hamilton Papers, 25/12/2/ op cit, 9 Mar 00.
49. ibid, 21 Mar 00.
50. Pakenham, 369, quoting Hamilton to Roberts, 10 Mar 00.
51. Hamilton, Ian, IBM, 145.
52. See note 49.
53. See note 51.
54. Pakenham, 161, quotes RB to Lansdowne, 8 Nov 99 accusing Hamilton of being 'a dangerous adviser' to White and 178, Methuen to wife, 12 Nov 99, relaying RB's description of White as 'frightened' and Hamilton as 'mad'.

Chapter 12   Final Success (pp. 178–193)

1. James, 315.
2. Maurice, *Boer War*, vol 3, 255; RCWSA RB Q 14963, Q 15439–15464.
3. Maurice, ibid, 256.
4. ibid, 257. Providing boots for infantrymen was a frequent limiting factor in war. Marlborough, the winter prior to his march across Europe to Blenheim, set up dumps from which they could be drawn.
5. ibid, 257–8; RCWSA RB Q14963, Q15439–15463.
6. Amery, vol 4, 167; Maurice, *Rawlinson*, 63.
7. Lyttelton, 234–5.
8. Smuts, 62–3.
9. Downes, RB to AB, 10 Apr 00. Every surviving letter between 1 Apr and 3 May 00 contains a similar complaint.
10. ibid, RB to Col Lonsdale Hale, 3 May 00.
11. Dundonald, 156–7.
12. Comd 968 of Apr 02, *Spion Kop Despatches*.
13. Comd 155 of May 00, *Telegrams Relating to Publication of Despatches*.
14. QV, Third Series, vol. 3, 533, reprints Roberts's despatch.
15. ibid, 533, Queen to Lansdowne, 18 Apr 00; 533–4, 535, Queen to Salisbury, 19 & 20 Apr 00; Downes, Wolseley to AB, 19 Apr 00; Wolseley to RB, 10 Apr 00; Lansdowne to Queen, 19 Apr 00, quoted Newton 183.
16. See Note 9.
17. Newton, 170, quoting Roberts to Lansdowne, 29 Jan 00.
18. ibid, 181–2, quoting Lansdowne to Roberts, 1 Apr 00.
19. Maurice, *Boer War*, vol 3, 263–5.
20. Amery, vol 4, 177–8; Maurice, OH, vol 3, Appx 2, 539.
21. Downes, RB to AB, 15 May 00.
22. Maurice, *Boer War*, vol 3, 218.
23. NAM 7101.23.117 and 179 contain samples of these telegrams which RB also summarizes and discusses in RCWSA RB Q 14963.
24. ibid 183.5, Roberts to Maurice 16 Aug 07, explains his reasons in detail.
25. ibid 118, RB to Roberts, 3 Jun 00, and Roberts to RB 4 Jun 00; Downes, RB to AB 11 Jun 00; Calwell, vol 1, 40–1.
26. May, 246.
27. NAM 7101.23.118.
28. May, 250–1.
29. Amery, vol 4, 192.
30. Lyttelton, 234–5.
31. Downes, RB to AB, 13 Jun 00.

32. ibid, 9 Jun 00.
33. Hamilton, Ian B, 145.
34. NAM 7101. 23, 179, Roberts to RB, 13, 15, 16, 17 Jun 00; RCWSA RB Q 15470.
35. Downes, RB to AB, 11 Jul 00. His letters immediately before and after this date have not been traced.
36. Milner Papers, 175/55 Roberts to Milner, 10 Aug 00.
37. NAM MFN 8502.22, Trotter to mother, 11 Jul 00.
38. ibid, RB op cit, 5 Apr 00.
39. Dundonald, 167–8.
40. Downes, RB to AB, 18 Aug 00.
41. May, 255.
42. See Note 40.
43. Dundonald, 175.
44. Wavell, Gen Sir Archibald, *Generals & Generalship: Lees Knowles Lectures*, Cambridge, 1939.
45. Amery, vol 4, 458–9. eg Kruger, 360.
46. Downes, RB to AB, 20 Aug 00.
47. Downes. Especially RB to W, 16 Apr 00.
48. Pakenham, xvi.
49. See Note 24.
50. Hamilton Papers, 25/12/2/25, Hamilton to wife, 12 Sep 00.
51. ibid.
52. Pakenham, 452, quoting Lyttelton to wife, 8 Aug & 6 Jul 00.
53. Downes, RB to AB, 16 Sep 00.
54. Headlam, vol 2, 88, quoting Roberts to Milner, 3 Sep 00; Amery, vol 4, 484.
55. See Note 53.
56. NAM 5201.33.7.3, diary 17 Sep 00.
57. Amery, vol 4, 485.
58. Melville, vol 2, 264.
59. RA QVJ: 17 Nov. 1900.
60. Downes, RB to AB, 1 Apr 00.
61. ibid, for RB's letters; the Queen's are in RA P7 to P 14.
62. RA P14/14, RB to Queen: 5 Oct. 1900.
63. See especially RA QVJ: 12 Feb. 1900.

Chapter 13 Recrimination (pp. 194–205)

1. Cole, Lt-Col HN, *The Story of Aldershot*, Southern Books, 1990, 114–6.
2. At Downes there is a museum of RB memorabilia.

3. Downes, W to RB, 17 Sep 00; Hamilton Papers, 25/12/2/27/, to wife, 30 Sept 00.
4. WO 132/2 includes several letters Stewart to RB; others are at Downes.
5. Downes, RB to AB, 10 Feb 01.
6. DRO 2065M add 2 SS4/11. Report by RB to US of S, 27 Nov 00.
7. Viscountess Milner, 159.
8. C–B to Earl Spencer, 6 Sep 03; C–B to Viscount Bryce, Jan 03. Both quoted Wilson, 216–7.
9. Downes, C–B to RB, 18 & 24 Feb 01.
10. Brodrick to Curzon, 3 Jan 00, quoted Spiers, 327.
11. Amery, *My Political Life*, 152.
12. op cit.
13. Butler, Lewis, 96.
14. Downes, part letter RB to unknown friend, 8 Oct 91.
15. Amery, *My Political Life*, 153–4.
16. DRO, 2065M add 2 SS12/63, note by member of family. Symons, *Buller*, 288, repeats the accusation that he had drunk too much.
17. Amery, *My Political Life*, 155–6.
18. NAM 7101–23–13–112, Brodrick to Roberts, 11 Oct 01.
19. ibid, 7101–23–122–2–146, Roberts to Brodrick, 11 Oct 01.
20. ibid, 145, Roberts to Kitchener, 11 Oct 01.
21. ibid, 7101–23–13–113, Brodrick to Roberts, 13 Oct 01.
22. Downes. Proof copy of a 'Strictly Private and Confidential' 56-page booklet 'published for private circulation only' of *correspondence between Sir Redvers Buller and the War Office*, apparently prepared by RB for use in his defence. PRO 138/16 contains many of the original War Office papers.
23. ibid.
24. Various accounts of the interview have been published, apparently based upon hearsay. For Buller's see Note 22. Brodrick's, which largely tallies, is in RA W22/64, Brodrick to King Edward VII, 17 Oct. 1901.
25. Pakenham, 457.
26. Esher, 308–9, to MVB, 22 Oct 01.
27. PRO 138/16, Kelly-Kenny to Roberts, 16 Oct 01.
28. Hansard, 17 Jul 02.
29. John Hussey, 'John Fortescue, James Edmonds, and the History of the Great War', JSAHR, Summer, 1992, 102. Downes, RB writes Tremayne Buller, 2 Feb 03, that John Fortescue had helped in the preparation of his 'clear and truthful' evidence to the Commission, and in so doing had he thought given it 'some literary merit'.
30. Downes. A copy of the pamphlet has been initialled 'JWF'.

31. op cit.
32. *Evidence of Gen the Rt Hon Sir Redvers Buller taken before the Royal Commission on the War in South Africa*, Longmans, Green, 1903.
33. Esher, 378–9, to King, 18 Feb 03.
34. See Note 26.
35. Esher, 379–1, to King, 19 Feb 03.
36. James, xi, xv; Amery, *My Political Life*, 219–30.
37. op cit, xi.
38. See note 7.
39. Milner, Milner to Chamberlain, 3 Jan 00.
40. ibid, Milner to Roberts, 25 May 00.
41. Cannadine, 206.
42. Midleton, 49.
43. Melville, Note 2, 16, recounts Lord Grenfell telling him how he hesitated to accept his field-marshal's baton because Buller had the stronger claim but was told that, so long as King Edward lived, there was not the slightest chance of Buller being so honoured.
44. Fortescue, 'Scapegoats', 16.

Chapter 14 Epilogue (pp. 206–208)

1. Butler, Lewis, 101.
2. Information family; Mr Hubert Vigor.
3. ibid, family.
4. ibid.
5. Melville, vol 2, 279.
6. Downes. Current railway posters; letter Dr Batty-Shaw to AB 13 Aug 05; circulars from 'Organisation for the Reinstatement' of RB.
7. Downes, RB to Mr Ley, 28 Feb 04.
8. op cit, 7 Dec 05.
9. WO 138/16 for death certificate.
10. ibid.
11. Information Mr Hubert Vigor.

SOURCES AND BIBLIOGRAPHY

Unpublished

Public Record Office	WO 132 & 138 series.
	WO 1883 Narrative Zulu Wars.
Downes	Buller Papers
Devon Record Office	Buller Papers
Gloucestershire Record Office	Hicks Beach Papers
Liddell Hart Library	Hamilton Papers
Bodleian Library	Milner Papers
National Army Museum	Rawlinson Papers
	Roberts Papers
	Trotter Papers
Royal Corps of Transport	Buller Papers
Royal Archives	Queen Victoria Papers
	King Edward VII Papers
	Duke of Cambridge Papers.

Published books and articles

Anon, An Average Observer, *The Burden of Proof: England's Debt to Sir Redvers Buller*, Grant Richards, 1902.

Amery, LS, *The Times History of the War in South Africa*, vols 2, 3, 4, Sampson, Low, Marston, 1902, 1905, 1906.

—— *My Political Life*, vol 1, Hutchinson, 1953.

Ashe, Major Waller & Edgell, Capt the Hon EV, *The Story of the Zulu Campaign*, Sampson Low, Marston, Searle & Rivington, 1880.

Atkins, J. B., *The Relief of Ladysmith*, Methuen, 1900.

Atlay, J. B., *Lord Haliburton*, Smith Elder, 1909.

Beeching, Jack *The Chinese Opium Wars*, Hutchinson, 1976.

Bond, Brian (ed), *Victorian Military Campaigns*, Hutchinson, 1967.

—— *The Victorian Army & The Staff College 1854–1914*, Metheun, 1972.

Brackenbury, Henry, *The Ashanti War: A Narrative*, 2 vols, Blackwood, 1874.

—— *Some Memories of My Spare Time*, Blackwood, 1909.

Buller, General the Right Hon, *Evidence taken before the Royal Commission on the War in South Africa*, Longmans Green, 1903.

Butler, Lewis, *Sir Redvers Buller*, Smith & Elder, 1909.

Butler, Lt-Gen the Rt Hon Sir William, *An Autobiography*, Constable, 1911.

—— *The Great Lone Land: A Narrative of Travel & Adventure in the North-West of America*, Sampson Low, Marston, Low, & Searle, 1972.

Calwell, Maj-Gen CE, *Field-Marshal Sir Henry Wilson*, vol 1, Cassell, 1929.

Cannadine, David, *Decline & Fall of the British Aristocracy*, Yale, 1990.

Churchill, Winston S, *London to Ladysmith*, Longmans, Green, 1900.

—— *Lord Randolph Churchill*, vol 2, Methuen, 1906.

—— *Great Contemporaries*, Macmillan, 1942 ed.

—— *My Early Life: A Roving Commission*, Reprint Society, 1944 ed.

Colville, HE, *The Sudan Campaign*, vols 1 & 2, HMSO, 1889.

Curtis, Edmund, *A History of Ireland*, Methuen, 1945.

Dixon, Norman, *On the Psychology of Military Incompetence*, Cape, 1976.

Dugdale, Blanche EC, *Arthur James Balfour*, Hutchinson, 1936.

Dundonald, Lt Gen The Earl of, *My Army Life*, Edward Arnold, 1934 ed.

Dunlop, Col John K, *The Development of the British Army 1899–1914*, Methuen, 1938.

Edgerton, Robert B, *Like Lions they Fought: The Zulu War and the Last Black Empire in Africa*, Weidenfeld & Nicholson, 1988.

Emden, Paul H, *Behind the Throne*, Hodder & Stoughton, 1934.

Esher, Viscount, *Journals & Letters*, vol 1, 1870–1903, Ivor Nicholson & Watson, 1934.

Farwell, Byron, *The Great Boer War*, Allen Lane, 1977.

Forbes, Archibald, *Services in Six Continents*, Methuen, 1885.

Fortescue, John, 'A Chapter on Scapegoats', Nineteenth Century, Aug 02, 2.

—— *General The Right Hon Sir Redvers Buller* (published anon), n.d.

—— *The Royal Army Service Corps: A History of Transport & Supply in the British Army*, Vol 1, Cambridge University Press, 1930.

Foster, RF, *Modern Ireland: 1600–1972*, Allen Lane, 1988.

French, David, *The British Way in Warfare 1688–2000*, Unwin Hyman, 1990.

Gosse, Edmund, 'Sir Redvers Buller: A Character Study', North American Review, Jan 1900, 108–120.

Hamilton, General Sir Ian, *Listening for the Drums*, Faber, 1944.

Hamilton, Ian BM, *The Happy Warrior: A Life of General Sir Ian Hamilton*, Cassell, 1966.

Harries-Jenkins, Gwyn, *The Army in Victorian Society*, Routledge & Kegan Paul, 1977.

Headlam, Cecil, *The Milner Papers*, vol 1, Cassell, 1931.

Hicks Beach, Lady Victoria, *The Life of Sir Michael Hicks Beach*, vols 1 & 2, 1932.

Holt, Edgar, *The Opium Wars of China*, Putnam, 1964.

Huyshe, Capt GL, *The Red River Expedition*, Macmillan, 1871.

James, David, *Lord Roberts*, Hollis & Carter, 1954.

Jeal, Tim, *Baden-Powell*, Hutchinson, 1989.

Jerrold, Walter, *Sir Redvers H Buller, VC*, Partridge, 1900.

Kennedy, AL, *Salisbury 1830–1903*, Murray, 1953.

Knight, Ian, *Brave Men's Blood: The Epic of the Zulu War 1879*, Greenhill, 1990.

Knox, E. Blake, *Buller's Campaign: With the Natal Field Force of 1900*, R. Brimley Johnson, 1902.

Lehmann, Joseph H, *All Sir Garnet: A Life of Field-Marshal Lord Wolseley*, Cape, 1964.

Lyttelton, General Sir Neville, *Eighty Years*, Hodder & Stoughton, n.d.

McCalmont, Major-General Sir Hugh, *Memoirs*, ed Sir CE Calwell, Hutchinson, 1924.

Marling, Colonel Sir Percival, *Rifleman & Hussar*, John Murray, 1931.

Maurice, Sir J Frederick, *The Military History of the Campaign of 1882 in Egypt*, 1888.

—— *History of the War in South Africa*, vol 1, 2, Hurst Blackett, 1906, 1907.

—— *The Life of Gen Lord Rawlinson of Trent*, Cassell, 1928.

Maxwell, Leigh, *The Ashanti Ring*, Leo Cooper, 1985.

May, Major-General Sir Edward, *Chances & Changes of a Soldier's Life*, Philip Allan, 1925.

Melville, Col CH, *Life of Gen the Rt Hon Sir Redvers Buller*, 2 vols, Arnold, 1923.

Midleton, The Earl of, *Records & Reactions 1856–1939*, John Murray, 1939.

Milner, Viscountess, *My Picture Gallery*, John Murray, 1951.

Mossop, George, *Running the Gauntlet*, Nelson, 1937.

Morley, John, *The Life of William Ewart Gladstone*, Macmillan, 1903.

Morris, Donald R, *The Washing of the Spears: The Rise & Fall of the Great Zulu Empire*, Cape, 1966.

Newton, Lord, *Lord Lansdowne*, Macmillan, 1929.

Pakenham, Thomas, *The Boer War*, Weidenfeld & Nicholson, 1979.

—— *Scramble for Africa 1876–1912*, Weidenfeld & Nicholson, 1991.

Preston, Adrian (ed), *In Relief of Gordon: Lord Wolseley's Campaign Journal 1884–1885*, Hutchinson, 1967.

—— *The South African Diaries of Sir Garnet Wolseley, 1975*, Balkema, 1971.

—— *The South African Journal of Sir Garnet Wolseley, 1879–1880*, Balkema, 1973.

Reade, Winwood, *The Story of the Ashantee Campaign*, Smith, Elder, 1874.

Repington, à Court, Charles, *Vestigia*, Constable, 1919.

Robertson, Field-Marshal Sir William, *From Private to Field-Marshal*, Constable, 1921.

St Aubyn, Giles, *The Royal George: The Life of HRH Prince George, Duke of Cambridge* Constable, 1962.

Sheppard, Edgar, *George, Duke of Cambridge*, vol 3, Longmans, Green, 1907.

Smuts, JC, *Jan Christian Smuts*, Cassell, 1952.

Spender, JA, *Life of Sir Henry Campbell-Bannerman*, vol 1, Hodder & Stoughton, 1923.

Spiers, Edward M, *The Late Victorian Army 1868–1902*, Manchester University Press, 1992.

Stanley, Henry M, *Coomassie*, Sampson, Low, Marston, 1896 ed.

Symons, Julian, *Buller's Campaign*, Cresset Press, 1963.

—— *England's Pride: The Story of the Gordon Relief Expedition*, Hamish Hamilton, 1965.

Terraine, John, 'Remember Dunmore: A Cautionary Tale', RUSIJ, Dec 1979.

Tylden, Major G, 'The Frontier Light Horse', JSAHR, vol 18, 1939, 224.

—— 'The British Army & The Transvaal, 1875 to 1885', JSAHR, vol 30, 1952, 159.

Verner, Coke Willoughby, *The Military Life of HRH George, Duke of Cambridge*, vol 3, John Murray, 1905.

The Letters of Queen Victoria, ed George Earle Buckle, Second Series, vol 2, 1870–78; vol 3, 1879–85, John Murray, 1926 & 1928.

—— Third Series, vol 1, 1886–90; vol 2, 1891–95; vol 3, 1896–1901, John Murray 1929, 1930 & 1932.

Walters, John, *Aldershot Review*, Jarrolds, 1970.

Wheeler, Captain Owen, *The War Office Past & Present*, Methuen, 1914.

Wilkinson, Henry Spencer, *Thirty-Five Years 1974–1909*, Constable, 1933.

Williams, Charles, *Life of Lieutenant-General Sir Evelyn Wood*, Sampson, Low, Marston, 1892.

Wilson, John, *A Life of Sir Henry Campbell-Bannerman*, Constable, 1973.

Wolseley, Field-Marshal Viscount, *The Story of a Soldier's Life*, Archibald Constable, 1903.

——, *Letters of Lord and Lady*, ed. Sir George Arthur, Heinemann, 1922.

Wood, Field-Marshal Sir Evelyn, *From Midshipman to Field-Marshal*, vols 1 and 2, Methuen, 1906.

—— *Winnowed Memories*, Cassell, 1918.

INDEX

(Final ranks and titles, where known, are given in brackets)

Rawlinson, Lt-Gen Henry (Gen Lord), 113, 128–9, 145, 155, 163, 171, 175–6, 180, 192, 202
Reade, Winwood, 26, 28
Red River, 11, 16, 18
Red River Expedition, 11–19, 21, 25, 69, 98
Repington, Lt-Col à Court, 133, 139, 140, 168, 173–4, 176, 203
Rhodes, Cecil, 115, 116, 135, 136, 141, 146–7, 171, 177
Rhodesia, 115, 116
Riel, Louis, 11, 16–19 (passim), 213
Roberts, Field-Marshal Lord, 47, 51–2, 79, 101, 105, 125, 151, 155, 156, 157, 158, 197, 202, 204; India, 79, 101, 106, 111, 128, 155; War Office, 101, 111; 2nd Boer War 133–193 (passim); C-in-C, 192–5; and Buller, 113, 156–7, 169–70, 179, 180, 181, 183, 186–7, 190, 192, 198–9; and Hamilton, 79, 128, 155
Roberts, Lt F., 151, 157
Roberts (India) Ring, 119, 125, 163, 188, 202, 203, 204–5
Robertson, Capt W. (Field-Marshal Lord), 153–4
Robinson, Commissary-General W. G. W., 100
Roodeval Station, 186
Rorke's Drift, 34
Rosebery, Lord, 109
Royal Irish Constabulary, 83, 84, 85
Royal Commission on War in South Africa (Elgin Commission), 121, 122, 139, 153, 158, 200–1
Royal Marines, 21, 24, 26, 64, 67, 68
Royal Navy, 24, 57, 64, 136, 153
Royal Naval Brigade, 149, 150–1
Russell, Maj-Gen Baker (Gen Sir), 48, 56
Russell, Lt-Col John, 36–7
Russell, Sir William, 42, 178

Sandbach, Lt-Col A. E. (Maj-Gen), 174

Sandhurst, (see Royal Military College)
Sandhurst Committee, 105
Sannah's Post, 178
Salisbury, Lord, 82, 92, 95, 109, 127, 141, 157, 195, 204; Ireland, 87, 92, 96; 2nd Boer War, 115, 116, 122–5, 127, 134, 153, 157, 181; and Buller, 96, 103, 110, 125, 199, 204
Salisbury Plain, 113
Savage Club, 107
Scott, Thomas, 12
Sekukini, Chief, 42
Shaw, Miss Flora (Lady Lugard), 122, 200
Shebandowan Lake, 13, 15
Shepstone, Sir T., 31
Skinners' Company, 155
Smith, Rt Hon W. H., 81–2, 90, 91, 97, 102
Smuts, Jan, (Field Marshal), 191
Souls, The, 107–8
Spender, J. A., 112
Spion Kop, Battle of, 166–9, 174, 180–1, 197
Spitz Kop, 192
Springfield, 165
Stamfordham, Lord (see Bigge)
Standerton, 186
Stanhope, Sir Edward, 97, 100
Stanley, H. M. (Sir Henry), 26, 28
Stephenson, Lt-Gen Sir F., 70
Stewart, Maj-Gen Sir Herbert, 66, 70, 74, 75–9 (passim)
Steyn, President, 127
Stopford, Col (Gen Sir Frederick), 134, 142, 150, 152, 176
Stormberg, 135, 147, 153
Suakin, 63, 64, 69, 77, 163
Sudan, 62–80, 100, 126, 148, 180
Suez, 57
Suez Canal, 55–8
Suffolk, Lady, 46, 54
Sweetwater Canal, 56–7
Symons, Julian, 202
Symons, Maj-Gen Penn, 121, 127, 128–9, 131, 133, 158